"This book is conversationally encyclopedic, comfortably competent, and warmly professional... just like Rich and Jim. It's what you would hope for from friends who are wonderfully gifted to help us minister to teens in crisis."

- *Dr. Dave Rahn, Huntington University Professor & Vice President of Ministry, YFC/USA*

"This book presents the dark side of youth ministry. It is the under-belly of our youth groups. It is the messy, complicated and uncomfortable side of life. Rich and Jim are tackling some difficult subjects in this book. This book will be a valuable tool that will not remain on the shelf but will draw you back to it year after year. You'll gain insights and practical advice on how to minister to hurting students. You will learn how to build relationships, how to reach out, how to lend a caring hand and a listening ear. These situations presented in the book offer opportunities to come along side students in crisis. The book is filled with real life stories that you will identify with. I highly recommend it."

- *Les Christie, Chair, Youth Ministry Department, William Jessup University*

"A must-have resource for every church and parachurch ministry. Rich and Jim have done a great job of describing and defining every possible crisis situation a youth worker will face."

- *Chap Clark, Ph.D., Associate Professor of Youth, Family, and Culture, Fuller Theological Seminary*

"What we hear in these pages are the voices of two tested and trusted youth workers who know what it's like to be in the trenches of real life ministry and to come alongside hurting kids (One wonders sometimes if there are any other kinds of kids; sometimes they all seem to be hurting!). The landscape of their combined youth ministry experience is a vast expanse of all kinds of terrain: local church parish ministry, parachurch ministry, ministry with institutionalized kids, counseling ministry - all the peaks and valleys of everyday youth work, deep canyons, steep cliffs, dark caves, scary places. And yet they remind us that all of these trails can lead us to a place of 'dangerous opportunity'."

"What makes this book so valuable to youth workers is that these two guides lead us, with steady hands, capable minds and compassionate hearts to explore these places, to meet kids in these places, and to help bring them back to a place of sanctuary. There's enough meat to be effective and enough step-by-step advice ("action plans" throughout) to be practical. This book will be a user-friendly guide for youth workers, counselors, parents, pastors and teachers who have a desire 'to seek and to save the lost'."

- *Duffy Robbins, Professor of Youth Ministry, Eastern University, St. Davids, PA*

"Every person who works with students should have this book... including parents. We live in a time where it is vital to know how to help kids deal with life and all the messed up stuff that happens in it. Rich and Jim speak out of much wisdom and years of experience. They communicate brilliantly and succinctly. Read this. It's important!"

- Lanny Donoho, author of God's Blogs and Producer of Big Stuf Camps and Catalyst Conferences.

"Kids are in crisis and many times youth workers are in the middle of the crisis – ill-prepared to handle what faces them. Jim and Rich have drawn on years of experience with kids in crisis to offer practical and usable resources for youth workers dealing with troubled students. In my 30 years of youth ministry, I have wished for a resource like The Youth Worker's Guide to Helping Teenagers in Crisis."

- Dr. Charles N. Neder, National Director, PFR Youth Ministry

THE YOUTH WORKER'S GUIDE TO

HELPING TEENAGERS IN CRISIS

Rich Van Pelt and Jim Hancock

ZONDERVAN®

ZONDERVAN.com/
AUTHORTRACKER
follow your favorite authors

youth
specialties

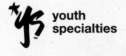

youth specialties

The Youth Worker's Guide to Helping Teenagers in Crisis
Copyright 2005 by Rich Van Pelt and Jim Hancock

Youth Specialties resources, 300 S. Pierce St., El Cajon, CA 92020 are published by Zondervan, 5300 Patterson Ave. SE, Grand Rapids, MI 49530.

Library of Congress Cataloging-in-Publication Data

Van Pelt, Rich.
  The youth worker's guide to helping teenagers in crisis / by Rich Van Pelt and
        Jim Hancock.
     p. cm.
  Includes bibliographical references.
  ISBN 978-0-310-28249-5
1. Church work with young adults. 2. Church work with youth. 3. Pastoral
counseling.   4. Crisis intervention (Mental health services) I. Hancock, Jim,
1952- II. Title.
  BV4446.V365 2005
  259'.23—dc22   2005011502

Web site addresses listed in this book were current at the time of publication. Please contact Youth Specialties via e-mail (YS@YouthSpecialties.com) to report URLs that are no longer operational and replacement URLs if available.

Cover and interior design by SharpSeven Design
Printed in the United States of America

10 11 12 13 14 15 • 15 14 13 12 11 10 9 8 7 6 5 4

Remembering Ken West who taught us so much about loving God and loving kids toward wholeness.

TABLE OF **CONTENTS**

1.0 LIFE BEYOND **COLUMBINE**

Rich Van Pelt: *You probably don't live anywhere near Columbine; you may not even know where Columbine is—which is fine. It's in Littleton, Colorado—not exactly the center of the universe, or anything else for that matter—more the southwestern edge of the Denver metro area. But on April 20, 1999—and for about a month after—Columbine seemed like the center of the universe, judging by news coverage. On that day two students came to school armed to the teeth and started shooting people. They killed 12 students, one teacher, and themselves in a bloody rampage.*

Until the felling of the World Trade Center towers in September 2001 there was, I suspect, never a more photographed crime scene. Like the terror on 9/11, the Columbine coverage was all from the outside—a crisis covered from every angle except the one where people were caught struggling between life and death.

Jim Hancock: Ask a dozen youth workers about life beyond Columbine and you'll hear about tipping points, wake-up calls, and rumors of revival; about law enforcement cover-ups, gun control, and Michael Moore; about increased school security and purely cosmetic changes; about freaks, geeks, jocks, and bullies; about a terror notable mainly for its demographics (meaning the shooters and victims were mainly suburban and relatively affluent).

Ask a youth worker on the south side of Chicago who met with his group on the evening of the massacre. He'd tell you the adult leaders in his church followed the news from Littleton throughout the afternoon and arrived early to pray and prepare to deal with the trauma once students started showing up. What was truly shocking, he'd say, was how little emotion there was of any sort—not anger, not fear, not even compassion. Kids were fooling around like it was just another Tuesday. He could hardly believe it.

What emerged from the group as leaders tried to engage the students in talking about the shootings surprised him even more: *What's the big deal?* his students wondered. *We feel bad for those people and all, but we have shootings in our community all the time.*

"I got shot," a boy said, lifting his shirt to show the scar.

"My brother got killed," a girl said.

And one by one the adults learned that every kid in the room was acquainted with violence and brutal death to a degree none of the leaders knew before that night. That youth worker would say he felt terrible for the Columbine families and he felt terrible for the children and families in his own church whose loss went unrecorded all those years because it was—what? Less concentrated? Less affluent? Browner-skinned? (He wouldn't include that last question, but I certainly would.)

So that's one version of life beyond Columbine; one where it would be nice to grieve the loss of strangers if we just had the emotional reserves. But most of us live well beyond Columbine, and, due respect, we have our own crises.

Ask a youth worker who actually had kids at Columbine, and you may hear about outsiders swarming Littleton to profit from the misery; about cameras, microphones, and relentless scrutiny; about quick in-and-out visits from fear-mongering and fund-raising Christian carpetbaggers who came mainly to talk about themselves.

All these years later, the anger and sadness about those things are just under the surface for some folks, mixed with images and memories they can't quite believe another person would comprehend: Crouching behind a hardened police vehicle listening to gunfire inside the school. Six, seven, eight, nine ambulances screaming out of a cul-de-sac, every one bearing injured students—23 in all. A fireman hosing blood off the walkway of a house repurposed as a triage center. Walking about in a fog. Burying youth group kids. Working to exhaustion and sickness. Feeling guilty about an ordinary pleasure enjoyed for the first time since the killing.

RVP: Here's a story you maybe haven't heard: When all hell broke loose at the high school—and before, during, and after the outsiders came and went—there was a network of youth workers quietly looking after kids in Littleton and the communities that weave around it: Highlands Ranch. Southglenn. Greenwood Village. Cherry Hills. Englewood. Sheridan. Bow Mar. Ken Caryl. Columbine.

It's always been a relational thing—this network, formalized only to the extent that we gave it a name—The Southwest Connection—just so we'd have something to call it. No Web site. No agenda. Just relationships with people who understand each other in the ebb and flow of ministry with kids and families. Youth workers in the Southwest Connection come from all over the theological and ecclesiological map: Baptist, Presbyterian, Episcopal, Bible church, Catholic, independent, nondenominational. They come to know each other as colleagues in ministry to students at a dozen or so high schools and probably twice that many middle schools. That's what's always drawn us together: Our love for kids. And shared space: 80123, give or take.

With physical proximity, theological diversity, shared identity as youth workers, and the nurturing that blossoms when we come together, these remarkable people walked each other through the terror; finding each other here and there in the craziness and taking strength from the horrible, blessed realization this was really happening and we were not alone.

In the process, we learned that relationships are everything in a crisis. It wasn't the public extravaganzas that helped; it was one person listening to another. It was off-sites with a few students. "I suppose the big public meetings were helpful," one of my friends says, meaning most weren't very helpful at all. "I mean they were well-produced and all, but what really helped was contact with people."

His wife takes a softer tone toward the high profile gatherings: "Some of the big meetings gave groups of four and five students a place to focus their attention on each other and process their experiences together." Back to relationships.

We learned that no two kids (or youth workers) needed the same treatment. Some wanted attention, others anonymity. Some were afraid to leave Littleton; others couldn't wait to get out of town. Some concealed where they came from, whether they were going across town or across country; others basically bought the T-shirt.

We learned not to avoid the pain; to ask direct, specific questions about each person's experience during those awful hours. And we learned the value of having those conversations sooner rather than later.

We learned not to give kids answers they know are smoke-screens.

We learned the value of admitting honest confusion about God mingled with self-abandoned trust.

We learned about grace from co-workers, parents, and especially students at the other schools whose less concentrated, less noisy crises got bumped when the shooting started.

We learned we didn't need to know everything (as if anyone could); we needed to know people who could intervene for us and bring the right help at the right time.

We learned it isn't going to be over next week—or next year.

We learned to be wary of an outsider with a plan—not suspicious necessarily, but wary.

We learned that the revival we'd heard about didn't happen after all. What happened was depth.

We learned to trust God when we were afraid the Columbine kids wouldn't come back to youth group.

We learned we couldn't do everything (but not before we got tired and sick from trying). We learned to do something simple like meeting a couple of kids for a soft drink and a conversation, because God uses simple, frictionless connections to generate enough power to keep going.

And bit-by-bit we lived sort of unselfconsciously into the other story of life beyond Columbine, where most things *returned to normal even if some things may never be the same. And it's all right because God is present either way.*

JH: We wrote this book for people who are willing to be with teenagers when no one else wants to be—in the chaos and brokenness of life as we know it. We wrote for youth workers willing to bring *themselves* to a kid's crisis and stick with her until she finds her balance again.

This book is as smart and practical as we know how to make it at this point in our lives. Mostly we've written with one voice; but here and there, as we've done above, the text reflects Rich's tone or mine in different fonts.

Between us, we lived through almost everything in these pages and can vouch for what we say here from personal knowledge (except direct experience with a big honkin' natural disaster, which we hope to go on avoiding indefinitely). That said, we're the first to admit we don't know much compared to all there is to know about crisis. So we've included lots of citations from sources we believe are credible. You'll find the endnotes and appendixes occasionally updated on the Web site at www.youthspecialties.com/store/crisis.

RVP: *We're glad you're taking up the challenge of this book. We hope you find it not just stimulating but intensely useful in your work with adolescents and their families. Let us know how you use this book and how we might improve future editions.*

Rich Van Pelt & **Jim Hancock**

1.1 UNDERSTANDING **CRISIS**

It was a muggy night on the back side of a very tough week. Programming for a hundred middle schoolers was the last thing standing between the youth worker and his desperately needed day off.

As he watched—perhaps a bit detached by fatigue—the air filled with high-pitched voices, flapping sandals, sweaty hair, and that heady testosterone/progesterone mix that clings to a mob of middle school kids, he had to smile. Whatever else may have been true at that moment, he loved those kids, and he would rise to the occasion.

Moving outdoors, he directed a frenzied, mostly-safe game of Capture the Flag. Wind 'em up and wear 'em out. Herding them back inside for a Bible lesson proved challenging (no surprise there), but with a competent blend of persistence and sheer force of will, he restored order—mostly.

The wild card that night was a kid named Stevie, who was determined to capture attention. Eventually Stevie got what he wanted with a noisy distraction that derailed the youth worker's train of thought, along with what remained of his patience. "You!" shouted the youth worker, "Out!" An uneasy silence settled on the room. Stevie looked up to see everyone staring at him. "And don't bother coming back until you know how to behave," the man concluded.

Stevie stood and threaded his way past smirkers, gigglers, and eye-rollers to the back of the room and out of the building. The youth worker tried to pick up where he'd left off, but anyone could see the focus had shifted from what he was saying to what he just did.

RVP: *I was in the room that night. I was a college sophomore volunteering in the youth group at my home church. That pastor was my role model. He had, after all, gone to seminary where he studied Hebrew and Greek, hermeneutics, homiletics—a whole laundry list of subjects I could barely pronounce. And I was "just a volunteer." But sitting there, thinking about it, a knot grew in my stomach. Somehow the way things went down with Stevie didn't feel right.*

I didn't know whether to stay put or go talk to him. I tried to imagine what my mentor would do if he were me. I knew his heart. So I got up and slipped outside to look for Stevie. I found him huddled on the front steps of the church, sobbing. I sat down and tried to communicate my concern—without reinforcing his behavior.

He cried so hard it was difficult to understand him, but here's the story behind the story. The events of the previous week rolled over Stevie like a tsunami: His mom and dad announced their separation, which he was afraid would lead to divorce—in which case Stevie would live with his father who was taking a job in another state. The implications were staggering. He was potentially losing his family, his friends, his home, his neighborhood—everything familiar—and start all over from scratch.

Stevie's behavior at youth group was a not-very-subtle expression of pain too fresh and too deep for words. It would have been a clue to anyone who really knew him that Stevie was in *crisis*. Part of the problem was that the people who may have known him best—Stevie's parents—were also in crisis.

In therapeutic terms, crisis is a period of *disequilibrium* that overpowers a person's *homeostatic* mechanisms. In plain English, crisis throws people off balance—emotionally, spiritually, cognitively, and maybe even physically.

Gary Collins called crisis "any event or series of circumstances which threatens a person's well-being and interferes with his or her routine of daily living."[1] In other words, crisis is a *self-defined* experience. Think about it for a moment, and you'll see it can't be any other way. Like every painful experience, crisis can only be endured first-hand. One woman rates the pain of childbirth as a 10, another person rates it a six. Which is it? Well, for the first person it compares with the most painful events in her life: It's a 10. The second woman compares childbirth to much less intense pain in her experience. They're both right, because we each experience pain individually; there is no absolute, objective scale for pain.

That's why crisis is difficult to predict. It could be brought on by anything, where *anything* means: "Any event or series of circumstances that threatens a person's well being...." That said, circumstances that once overwhelmed a person might be endurable later because *she* has changed.

Nobody gets to vote on another person's crisis. We do a great disservice if we're dismissive about a crisis because it wouldn't rise to the same level for us. The heartaches of "puppy love" spring to mind. Think what you will, puppy love is *very* real to the puppy. Adults who don't take that experience seriously are not only rude, but they also may endanger the well-being of someone they love by taking his heartbreak too lightly.

Of course there's also no reason to borrow trouble. It's not our responsibility to predict, deny, define, or validate another person's crisis. It *is* our responsibility to pay attention and engage people who are, by their own definition, in crisis.

If that brings to mind someone whose life is defined by one crisis after another to the point you doubt he even knows what a true crisis is, that's fair enough. That's partly why we wrote this book: To help youth workers discern what's really at stake in kids' lives and act appropriately to help them survive and thrive as adults.

Not that it's easy. What youth worker hasn't lost patience (or courage) and wondered: *Why did I get involved in this mess? What was I thinking?* If you engage people in crisis, there's a good chance you'll experience wide-ranging emotions. With any luck they won't all land at once:

- Compassion. *This is terrible! What can I do to help?*
- Fear. *If I don't get involved, this person may die. But I'm not trained; what if I do more harm than good?*
- Resentment. *Does he think he's the only one who ever faced this? Does he really not see how much worse this could be?*
- Impatience. *How long is this going to drag on? Why doesn't she do something to change her situation? It's a simple decision! When is she going to choose?*
- Trapped. *What have I gotten myself into? Is this person going to be dependent on me forever?*
- Guilt. *I'm such a poser. If I really care about people, why am I so resentful?*
- Anger. *When are they gonna stop acting like babies and get this thing solved? How long does she think she can take advantage of me? Who does he think he's kidding?*

There's no sense in denying these feelings—better to be honest with ourselves and share them in confidence with people who support us. Some emotions say more about our inexperience in the psycho-dynamics of crisis than our enduring emotional condition. Hearing ourselves admit this can be a reality check that tells us whether we can buck up and keep going or whether we need to refer the crisis to someone who's in better shape to help at the moment.

If a weak emotional response from a crisis helper doesn't necessarily indicate a permanent condition, the same can be said for someone she's trying to help. Crisis does strange things to people, making them think, feel, and behave in ways that are out of character with who they truly are. All of us who've lived through a crisis know this. The rest will learn shortly.

You'll encounter three kinds of crises while working with adolescents:

- *Acute* crises are pointed, painful, and immediate.
- *Chronic* crises are enduring, recurring, and persistent.
- *Adjustment* crises are temporary, transitory, and situational.

The first two terms—*acute* and *chronic*—are borrowed directly from medical diagnosis and treatment.

An *acute* crisis is urgent and severe enough to demand immediate intervention. It presents the possibility of serious emotional or physical danger. Acute crises include suicidal episodes, drug overdoses, serious flight from home, crisis pregnancies, physical and sexual assaults, and losing a loved one or friend.

A *chronic* crisis results from persistent, ongoing, accumulated pain. Chronic crises surface in behavior patterns that demand attention and care. Long-term conditions like physical, emotional, and sexual abuse; parental neglect; and child endangerment often yield behaviors that may in turn become chronic themselves: obsessive or compulsive sexuality, abusing alcohol and other drugs, eating disorders, fighting, high-risk-taking, and cutting are chronic crises with dangerous consequences if left unchecked.

Some chronic crises appear to have biochemical roots: Attention Deficit Hyperactivity Disorder (ADHD) and clinical depression, for example. These are medical diagnoses, not youth worker hunches. It's unlikely a youth worker will be the first to see evidence of ADHD (that's usually a parent or school teacher spending hours every day with a child). But it's not so unusual for a youth worker to spot early signs of clinical depression (as distinct from merely feeling depressed).

Finally, some are *adjustment* crises that simply reflect difficulty adjusting to the demands of growing up or adapting to rapid change. Adjustment crises include lying, trust violations, communication breakdowns, defiance of reasonable standards and values, and impulsive behavior. Adjustment crises tend to be non-lethal, but they can stress relationships to the breaking point and may generate unhealthy alliances with other kids who are acting out.

HOW CRISIS AFFECTS PEOPLE

Countless personal, relational, and environmental factors influence how individuals experience crisis, so it's only a tiny exaggeration to claim no two people have the same experience. That said, some psycho-dynamics are common to most crisis situations—this will definitely be on the test:

- Crisis takes people by surprise.
- Crisis overwhelms.
- Crisis awakens other unresolved life issues.
- Crisis reduces people to inaction.
- Crisis distorts thinking, feeling, and acting.
- Crisis paints a gloomy picture of the future.

CRISIS TAKES PEOPLE BY SURPRISE

What could possibly prepare a teenage girl for date rape—prime time programming on the WB? How many families have even minimal emergency plans should a disaster destroy their homes? Show us the parents who are ready to hear their child has been arrested for possession and sale of narcotics. We're never quite ready for some things—this is why they're *crises*.

JH: I had 20 years' notice that my father would die from congestive heart failure. That did exactly nothing to prepare me for news of his "sudden" death: "Uncle Willard found your dad dead in his apartment today." How do you prepare for that phone call?

RVP: When my father was diagnosed with lung cancer, the prognosis wasn't good. The cancer progressed very quickly, and he died within months of the diagnosis without much of the suffering that often accompanies cancer. I'll never forget the last day of his life. His lungs filled with fluid, and ultimately he died from suffocation. Our family gathered around his bed and prayed that God would spare him any further suffering and mercifully take him to his eternal home. After about six grueling hours, Dad breathed his final breath, and it became obvious that our prayers were answered. Even so—even after praying that he would die and experience relief from his suffering—when he finally did, we still found ourselves in a state of disbelief. As much as we think we're prepared for crisis, it seems we never really are.

Adolescents are famous for believing bad things only happen to bad people—or at least *other* people. Teenagers forget—or maybe adults forget to tell them—what Jesus said about the good, the bad, and the ordinary. Making reference to people who died when a tower fell on them, Jesus demanded: "...do you think they were more guilty than all the others living in Jerusalem?"[2] They weren't. Jesus said his Father causes the "sun to rise on the evil and good, and sends rain on the righteous and the unrighteous."[3]

Truth be told, people are caught unaware, unprepared, and maybe unwilling to face life as it is and not as they would have it.

CRISIS OVERWHELMS

When a 15 year-old finds out she's pregnant, there's a good chance clear thinking may elude her for a while. Denial, fear, anger, wonder, regret, confusion, embarrassment, doubt, isolation—it's a lot to sort out.

If a parent loses the last scrap of trust in her son, the next thing she's likely to lose is perspective. Anger, fear, shame, regret, and resentment may conspire to declare a state of martial law in the household.

The onset of a crisis can short-circuit normal mental and emotional capabilities. A driven, highly motivated, self-starting, "type A" personality may find the most ordinary tasks slipping from his hyper-competent grasp.

RVP: I was shocked to find myself incapacitated by situational depression about a work crisis. Here I was, traveling for a living and barely able to pack for an overnight trip. Fortunately the crisis passed, and soon after so did the depression. But it was a sobering reminder of how human I am.

JH: For the record, I don't believe in *writer's block*. But through a cluster of family crises, I found it almost impossible to concentrate on writing this book. This early in the manuscript, it's too soon to tell if I've pulled out of it...

CRISIS AWAKENS OTHER UNRESOLVED ISSUES

When a crisis strikes, other issues come grumbling out from the back of the emotional cave—grumpy and demanding food. Suddenly half a dozen other voices join the howl of the immediate crisis. It's no wonder so many people in crisis mutter, "It's just more than I can handle."

Consider: A high school junior loses his part-time job three weeks before prom. While talking with him you learn that in addition to being worried about paying for prom, he's also concerned about completing an English essay on time and finding a store that sells the right *trucks* for the new skateboard he bought on the Internet with a credit card, which, by the way, he only "sort of" had permission to use.

After deciding it doesn't really matter whether or not you know what a skateboard truck is, your natural response to him might be, "Just a second: What does finding a new job, writing an essay, and locating those whatchamacallits for a skateboard you'll probably have to return anyway have to do with each other?"

If you're not careful (as in full-of-care), you may be inclined to dismiss his entire concern because you've forgotten what life can be like for a high school junior. If you project your own values, perceptions, perspectives, and experiences on him, you'll fail to respond to what he genuinely needs (which, of course, may have little to do with the details of his complaint). It's easy to miss that, in the grip of an immediate financial challenge, he's also trying to cope with three other, only marginally connected, issues. Of course he's thrown off. Given the often-delicate balance of adolescence, the question is not, "Why is this such a big deal?" The question is, "What can I do to help you sort this out?"

CRISIS REDUCES PEOPLE TO INACTION

Crisis stops people in their tracks, sometimes leaving them stuck there indefinitely. No one this side of Superman can reverse the clock, which is what it would take to alter the events leading to a crisis. So many people invest a lot of energy wishing things were different—so much energy there may not be enough left to take the next step (even when they're convinced that step could lead out of the dark hole they're in). Think Miss Havesham in Dickens' *Great Expectations*, stuck in a dark room, wishing for a different ending.

When feelings of hopelessness combine with a short-circuiting of normal operating capabilities—especially if you throw addictive substances and behaviors into the mix—it's enough to bring the most proactive person to a grinding emotional halt. Everybody knows someone who seems stuck at age 15 (or 11), their emotional growth frozen in time. It's remarkable how often that stagnation can be traced back to an unresolved crisis.

CRISIS DISTORTS OUR THINKING, FEELING, & ACTING

We must anticipate that the youth and families with whom we work in a crisis may not be "themselves."

Chemical dependencies are an excellent case in point. When young people begin to abuse alcohol or other drugs they're likely to undergo personality and/or behavioral changes. The drug of choice soon becomes life's primary occupation; they will do anything to repeat the experience that drug provides. In the grip of that craving, behavior that was once out of the question seems viable.

An adult stressed by a loved one's death is vulnerable to unwise financial decisions because her thinking is clouded by grief.

RVP: I've struggled with the American way of death, shaking my head at the craziness of dumping thousands of dollars into the ground with the body of a lost loved one. But then my father died, and my rationality went out the window too.

At times, youth workers must attempt to protect people from themselves—encouraging kids and families to delay major decisions for a while following loss, heartbreak, or tragedy. Healing takes time—but not just time. It's a crude analogy, but it might help to think about crisis as a broken bone. Proper healing requires immobilizing the breakpoint long enough for the wound to mend.

For adolescents in crisis, a rebound romance, the sudden move to another household, walking off the team, and the snap decision to drop out of school or join the military—all carry the potential for extending, rather than resolving, the crisis. This is not to say that fleeing a toxic environment may not be exactly the right thing to avert further crisis. It's only to note that sustained growth takes sustained time and careful attention to allow the emotional vulnerabilities of a crisis to subside, leading to more responsible and rational long-term decision-making.

CRISIS PAINTS A GLOOMY PICTURE OF THE FUTURE

People in crisis question whether things will ever get better. They doubt it. Emotional distress overwhelms judgment. They feel Helpless, Hopeless, and Hapless—The Three "H's."

- Helpless—*This is too much; I can't handle it.*
- Hopeless—*There's no way out; this pain will never end.*
- Hapless—*I'm unlucky, and that's that.*

In the grip of The Three "H's" it's difficult to embrace the wisdom that "this, too, will pass." Identifying options collapses under the weighty conviction that resolution is out of the question. The hopelessness shows up in a person's voice and countenance as a *flat affect*, an emotionlessness written on her face and posture and heard in the way she sighs and speaks.

Understanding crisis involves learning to spot the underlying causes and effects of experiences that knock people off balance. It means mastering the listening and talking skills that bring perspective; followed by hope; followed by concrete, forward motion to regain equilibrium. Understanding crisis involves paying attention to our own experiences in a way that enables us to express empathy for people who are not better or worse or really that much different from us.

1.2 DANGEROUS **OPPORTUNITY**

RVP: *Upon hearing a veteran youth worker say, "I love crisis!" I wondered if maybe he could use some counseling, or at least some comp time because clearly the guy had lost perspective.*

JH: But really, who doesn't enjoy a good crisis from time to time, huh? Well…me for one. I had an invitation to sit on the mix desk platform at a U2 show one time. It was youth group night, so I was going to get someone to cover for me, knowing no kid would begrudge me the chance to be at the show, right? But I decided not to tell anyone; I figured it would be a better story after the fact.

A couple of days before the concert one of the peer leaders gets caught in a lie that leads to a terrific blowup in the leadership team. We defuse the immediate crisis, and in a fit of remorse the guy says he wants to come clean with the rest of the group on Sunday night. "Okay," I say, swallowing hard. "I'll help you do that." So I call the friend who invited me to the show and say, "Thanks for the invite, but something's come up with my group and I think I'd better stay home. My loss."

Well *that* was an understatement. Sunday night rolls around, and the kid chickens out. Not only does he not come clean, he doesn't even come to the meeting. I could be sitting on the mix deck at a U2 show! And what can I say? I can't even bring it up.

> I've suffered this indignity alone all these years. It feels really good to finally share this pain with my peers.
>
> Okay, actually it feels really whiney, and I'm sorry I brought it up. All I'm saying is: I *don't* love a crisis.

We're all busy people. Juggling work and family and ministry and trying to serve multiple masters and figure out who's going to be disappointed when there's not enough of us to go around. There's just no good time for a crisis. We couldn't possibly fit one in this week or next. Get back to us early next month; we'll see what we can do. Sure, that'll work.

Nothing against balance and all, but it seems entirely possible that a preoccupation with time management and healthy boundaries in ministry could keep us from being there when people are in crisis. And if we don't show up, we can't help. So if we're convinced God is calling us to be helpers...you can probably take it from there. For what it's worth, we're pretty sure the Good Samaritan endured more than mild inconvenience. This is part of what made him a *Good* Samaritan.

In fairness, some of us avoid crisis situations because we're afraid we don't have the training and experience to be effective helpers. We're just youth workers, right? Sure, lots of us have youth ministry—and maybe even seminary—degrees (and there's nothing like a specialized diploma to give the impression we know what we're doing). But that doesn't necessarily translate into feeling anything but ill-equipped to respond to actual people in actual crisis until we've actually done it a few times.

Well, of course. Because *readin' ain't doin'*, is it? And *doing* is the only way to gain the kind of experience that makes a youth worker feel she can show up and actually do some good.

> **RVP:** And then there's that thing about God's calling and God's enabling that turns a marginally qualified helper into a genuine asset. Madeleine L'Engle put it nicely:
>
> > In a very real sense, not one of us is qualified but it seems that God continually chooses the most unqualified to do His work, to bear His glory. If we are qualified, we tend to

think that we have done the job ourselves. If we are forced to accept our evident lack of qualification, then there's no danger that we will confuse God's work with our own or God's glory with our own.[1]

One of our friends was recently tasked with helping his church and high school community respond to the awful loss of three students in a car accident. How do you prepare for that? If God doesn't show up in the middle of that kind of pain, it doesn't matter what kind of certificate is hanging on your wall. It can be daunting. Especially if a youth worker has unresolved issues of his own—and who doesn't?

RVP: I served as a chaplain with the Division of Youth Services for the Colorado Department of Corrections for more than a decade. My "youth group" consisted of young men and women locked up for every crime imaginable—and a few unimaginable acts. At one point I was asked to conduct a memorial service for a young man who died tragically after running away from the lockup. The day before the service I was saying goodnight to a staff member who was particularly close to the boy. "See you at the service tomorrow," I said.

His immediate response was, "Oh, no you won't!"

I was surprised by his response and asked what he meant. He said he couldn't handle the boy's death. He was very competent at his job, but his personal fears and inability to cope crippled his capacity to help when it really mattered to the other inmates.

Plenty of youth workers understand this dilemma. Death, sickness, depression, substance abuse, and sexual identity are *no go zones* for some people—especially sexual identity. Too many youth workers resist the very notion of helping young folks working through gender identity issues. It becomes clear in a thousand ways that they are unavailable for that particular duty.

Pity. They pass by on the other side, leaving people for dead because they haven't fully resolved their own sexual issues. In their heads, youth workers know people struggling with sexual identity are the subjects of God's grace as much as anyone else—

but it's not about what's in youth workers' heads, is it? Under such stringent rules of engagement, how will they respond when a young person turns up HIV positive (whether the infection was sexually borne or not)? Can pastoral care be so easily neutralized by immaturity and fear of vulnerability? It can.

Following Christ into the world of the young and vulnerable sometimes makes us vulnerable, too. Author Doug Stevens put his finger right on the bruise:

> Youth ministry cannot be long-distance. We must enter the world of the adolescent, just as Christ entered ours. We are sent onto their "turf." We must become accessible to them by intentionally placing ourselves in the midst of their subculture. In the same way that Jesus moved close enough to touch and be touched, so too, we are called to minister to youth at close range. It's sobering to remember that the person who's close enough to be touched is also close enough to be vulnerable, hurt, abused, even crucified.[2]

Youth work in general—and crisis care in particular—takes us places we never thought we'd go to help people we never expected to meet with problems we'd rather not know about.

RVP: *I've traveled the globe training youth workers, pastors, therapists, school administrators, counselors, teachers, peer counselors—and anyone else who will listen—in crisis prevention and intervention. I typically begin by asking workshop participants to say the first thing that comes to mind when they hear the word* crisis. *In my third decade on the road, I can almost predict the responses:* emergency, help, disaster, fear, police, danger, predicament, *and* terrorism.

Everyone agrees that crisis *evokes images of physical, spiritual, emotional, and relational harm. Few, if any, immediately associate crisis with the word* opportunity. *But they could. I haven't had the chance to teach in China yet, but I've learned that the simplified Chinese characters for* crisis *combine characters that signify "danger" and "opportunity" (危机).*

Do the Chinese see something the rest of the world needs to learn? Do opportunity and danger come wrapped together in the form of crisis?

Consider 2 Corinthians 1:3-7:

> Praise be to the God and Father of our Lord Jesus Christ, the Father of compassion and the God of all comfort, who comforts us in all our troubles, so that we can comfort those in any trouble with the comfort we ourselves have received from God. For just as the sufferings of Christ flow over into our lives, so also through Christ our comfort overflows. If we are distressed, it is for your comfort and salvation; if we are comforted, it is for your comfort, which produces in you patient endurance of the same sufferings we suffer. And our hope for you is firm, because we know that just as you share in our sufferings, so also you share in our comfort.

The prolific Earl Palmer claims the Greek word typically translated "comfort" is better translated "coming alongside." In other words, the practice of ministry—and crisis care—modeled by God himself is "coming alongside." Here are verses three and four again with Palmer's translation:

> Praise be to the God and Father of our Lord Jesus Christ, the Father of compassion and the God of all coming alongside, who comes alongside us in our troubles, so that we can come alongside those in any trouble with the coming alongside we ourselves have received from God.

If we can apply Paul's charge to the Corinthians to our situation, we're looking at a pretty clear instruction to "come alongside" people in trouble. That's where the opportunity lies! To channel God's "coming alongside" through our "coming alongside." Paul saw the opportunity inherent in crisis. Somehow, in a miracle of presence, God shows up when we show up with what we learned when God showed up for us (whew!). And where God shows up, new hope and life rise from the ashes.

After decades of walking with kids and families through life's most difficult terrain, we believe crisis intervention is so much more than a duty or an interruption in our busy schedules. Crisis is certainly permeated with danger, but it is just as surely infused with opportunity for growth.

So, truly, like the crisis-loving (or at least crisis-*welcoming*) youth worker whose stability Van Pelt once questioned, we've also learned to embrace crisis as a means through which God's grace operates on this broken planet. Please don't misunderstand. It's not that we take morbid delight in watching people suffer. To the contrary, Paul reminded us that to really come alongside requires a willingness to suffer *with* those who suffer. We can come alongside hurting people only because Jesus has come alongside us in our pain. We're doing for others what we would have them do for us if the situation required it. *We're only giving as good as we already got from the God of all coming alongside.*

EXAMINING OUR MOTIVES

There's no end to the opportunities youth workers have to come alongside hurting people. What's up for grabs is motivation. On the other side of the coin from the fear we have about engaging people in crisis lies the self-referential, everybody-calm-down-I'm-here-now, pseudo-heroic rush of being needed. Shocking as it may be to the naïve and innocent, there's more than one reason to respond to a crisis.

MORBID CURIOSITY

Have you ever slowed down to rubberneck at the scene of an automobile accident or found yourself in hot pursuit of a fire truck? Did you intend to help, or did you just want to find out what was going on? Sometimes youth workers get involved with people in crisis mainly out of morbid curiosity.

PERSONAL GAIN

Some people capitalize on the crises of others to achieve recognition or some other benefit. Jessica Mitford's classic *The American Way of Death* exposed funeral directors who prey on the guilt and grief of surviving family members to sell expensive funeral packages.

JH: The youth worker who followed me at one church was accused (credibly, I thought) of molesting two girls in the group. Three other staff members at that church were involved in a sexual triangle. My own father confessed with great shame to using his position as pastor and counselor to seduce women in crises.

You think it can't happen that close to home, but it can: People wreaking havoc by doing the right things for the wrong reasons.

GOSSIP

The author of James paints the tongue as a small body part capable of doing big damage (James 3:5). Sometimes youth workers use crisis as a source of fresh gossip. That's not what they started out to do, but the power that comes with gossip can be very tempting.

RVP: Listening to a young man's story between sessions at a retreat, I became convinced he would really benefit from professional counseling. So I suggested we both talk to his youth worker about follow-up help back home. The boy's reaction was immediate and disturbing. "You will not tell him anything!" When I asked why, he said, "Because about a year ago my friend told him that he struggled with compulsive masturbation, which he then told the core group so they could 'pray about it.' It didn't take long before most of the kids in the youth group knew about it. So, no; I don't want him to know."

Whatever that youth worker thought he was gaining by carrying tales, he lost the trust of who-knows-how-many students.

The adolescent years have always been troubled waters, and navigation is certainly not getting easier. That's why it's so important for caring youth workers to come alongside kids and their families. Each time you sort through your motives for engaging students in crisis, answer these six questions thoroughly and fearlessly:

1. What do I expect to gain as a result of my involvement in this crisis?
2. Are there obvious reasons why I should choose not to be involved?
3. Is there any reason I can't be trusted to honor this confidence?
4. Will this person's success raise my feeling of self-worth?

5. Will this person's failure cause me to think less of myself?
6. Am I willing to step aside if someone with better skills is available?

2.0 INTERVENTION

If you're the one on the ground when the sky falls, that makes you the one who must respond and keep responding until someone more qualified shows up. You don't have to do it perfectly. You don't even have to do it well. You only have to do the best you can do.

Experience tells us that if you learn what's in this section, the-best-you-can-do will be pretty good.

2.1 TRIAGE

Thanks to syndication, *M•A•S•H* is guaranteed an audience more or less forever, at least in the form of school kids stuck at home with the flu and no video games or online access. (Okay, so it will be a shrinking audience, but with more than 250 episodes, there's plenty to see before it disappears into the vaults.)

Back in the day, *M•A•S•H* broke new ground on television by mixing hilarity and human tragedy in a potent cocktail that drew 100 million viewers to its final network broadcast.

The show was based on a novel and movie about real-world Mobile Army Surgical Hospitals (MASH units) deployed during the Korean military campaign in the early 1950s. MASH units were primary-care providers for seriously wounded combatants.

Week after week on the TV show, Radar O'Reilly's clear, high voice cut through whatever hijinks were underway with the dreaded "incoming wounded" alert. Doctors and nurses scrambled to the landing zone as helicopters arrived with casualties. Each wounded person received an initial assessment to determine the appropriate level of medical intervention: Some went immediately to surgery in hopes of repairing life-threatening wounds; others, less seriously wounded, were delivered to a surgical staging area to wait their turn; the rest were declared dead or beyond help. That grim process is known as *triage* (tree-ahj), from a French word that means "to sort." Triage, in one form or another, is the first step in crisis intervention.

Psychiatrist Karl Menninger, founder of the famous Menninger Clinic, asked students to identify the most important element in the treatment process. He received many responses, none of which satisfied him. The answer he was looking for was *diagnosis*. Henri Nouwen concurred: "The first and most important task of a healer," he wrote, "is making the right diagnosis. Better stated, diagnosis is the beginning."[1]

If you work with young folks for any period of time, you'll become acquainted with the "incoming wounded" alert. At which point, no matter what hilarity you're up to with your group, you'll have to scramble out to the landing zone to assess the damage and try to figure out your next step.

We say *try*, because triage may not be as simple as recognizing a gunshot wound or a compound fracture. There's a good chance the kid, her parents, or her friends already did their own seat-of-the-pants triage, delaying the moment of your involvement until the problem reached unmanageable proportions.

RVP: I spend a lot of time on airplanes. I have to admit I've always admired those travelers who maximize the opportunity of being seated next to a stranger for evangelistic purposes. But if I'm honest, I also have to admit I'm the kind of traveler who prays the seat next to me will be empty. By the time I get on a plane, I'm generally so exhausted I'm just looking forward to a nap. The last thing I want to do is start a conversation with someone I'll probably never see again.

That's what makes it notable that I even noticed the woman seated next to me giving every indication that things were not well with her soul—or any other part of her. So I was going against type when I asked, "Are you okay?"

Skipping any pretense of small talk, the woman told me her daughter had just made a serious suicide attempt at school and she was traveling to be with her in the hospital. Part of what made the ordeal so painful was that the dear woman had been totally unaware of how unbearable life was for her daughter.

• The Youth Worker's Guide To Helping Teenagers In Crisis

She said it was different when the children were younger and easier to read. There wasn't much the kids got away with, and when they demanded to know how she'd caught them, she always answered, "A little birdie told me!"

Once, after a day making Christmas candy and cookies, she sent the kids to get ready for bed while she finished cleaning up the dishes. The kids didn't know that a mirror in the kitchen provided an unobstructed view into the dining room where the homemade goodies were stored—and the family parakeet lived.

She watched with amusement as the seven year-old tiptoed into the dining room, draped his blanket over the parakeet's cage, and summoned his little sisters to join him for the score. The children filled their pockets until they were satisfied they had enough loot to get through the night. The girls headed for the bedroom while their brother lingered just long enough to take the blanket off the bird's cage.

Picture their shock when, moments later, their Mom called them out and demanded they turn over the loot. When the sisters turned to give their brother the stink-eye, he threw his hands in the air and shouted, "I swear, I covered the bird!"

Now my seatmate was heading into perhaps the toughest conversation of her life. And this time they both knew there was no little bird to let her in on her daughter's secrets.

Someone estimated that most parents of drug-abusing children have a *hunch* two years before acting on it. Two years! And it's not just parents. We've both experienced situations when we sensed something was wrong with a student or family but for one reason or another we didn't follow through to check it out. The older we get, the more we're learning to trust our gut feelings and intuition and at least explore to see if there's a viable reason for concern.

Triage is different. It's the first step a youth worker takes when she *knows* there's reason for concern. The daughter of a board member admits to binge-and-purge eating. A sophomore mistakenly pulls up his sleeve and exposes what appear to be self-inflicted cuts on his wrist. A parent calls to talk about her daughter's best friend who has hinted to peers she may be thinking about ending her life. The pastor's son is arrested for mutilating a cat while the pastor is out of town and you are "child sitting."

These are not gee-I-wonder-if-there's-a-problem situations. There *is* a problem. Job *one* is finding out how great the risk is so you can determine the best course of action.

CREATE A SAFE PLACE

Jon calls from school. He wants to stop by and talk. He sounds pretty fragile, so you ask if everything is okay. "No," he says, "but I don't want to talk about it on the phone."

Your preference would be to get with him immediately. "Are you sure this will wait?" you ask.

"Yeah," he says. "I'll see you after school." That will have to do. It doesn't sound like life is in the balance. Meanwhile, you clear a block of time and pray for Jon's well-being.

He arrives at a quarter after three with his girlfriend, Sarah, whom you don't know well. You welcome them, offer seats, and ask the obvious question, "So...what's goin' on?"

Jon is barely audible when he responds, "She's gonna have a baby." Sarah begins to cry.

Your immediate reaction is anger, but you conceal it. You've warned Jon about his "evangelistic dating." His mother is one of your volunteers; this will break her heart. *Calm down*, you think. *Ask a question. You can kill Jon later.* "Tell me about it," you say calmly.

What you hear banishes the anger in a heartbeat—or at least shifts it away from Jon. Sarah's pregnancy resulted from incestuous abuse by her stepfather. Rather than bringing shame on her family, Sarah believes she should end the pregnancy. Jon brought her to you for help. You breathe a wordless prayer of thanks that you chose to listen before speaking.

Helping people like Jon and Sarah requires the creation of safe places by:

- Getting the facts
- Taking time to listen to their stories

- Building trust
- Allowing for the expression of feelings
- Assessing the level of immediate risk
- Questioning the appropriateness of your involvement

GET THE FACTS

You can respond in a vacuum, but it will probably just suck. Triage begins with gathering basic information to make initial decisions about how to proceed. That means asking for the facts, of course. It also means seeking to understand each person's *perceptions* about the facts.

People have difficulty presenting facts with complete objectivity, because no one experiences life objectively—and all the more when emotions and thought patterns are distorted by crisis. An experience filtered through the perceptions of two individuals can make you wonder if they're even talking about the same event.

JH: My wife and I once agreed to meet in the lobby of a hotel in downtown Denver. I showed up in a timely manner and waited. Then I waited some more. This was back when cell phone calls cost 25 cents a minute or any part thereof, and there was no text messaging—period. We weren't yet in the habit of calling each other 10 times a day. But after half an hour, I started to worry and called her cell. "Where are you?" I asked.

"I'm in the lobby," she said. "Waiting. Where are you?"

"I'm in the lobby," I said, looking around. "Right beside the statue of the horse."

"I'm in the lobby, and there's no horse," she said. "What hotel are you in?"

"The Adam's Mark," I replied, chilly now. I knew which hotel we agreed to meet at. "What hotel are *you* in?"

"I'm standing right next to the check-in desk at the Adam's Mark and you're not here," she said. This is when it occurred to me that, though I could think of no reason for such a thing, I'd better check to see if there were two lobbies at the Adam's Mark. There were, an employee told me, as if anyone should know this. Two lobbies on opposite sides of the street. We were both waiting as promised with no hope of ever actually meeting.

Sometimes you just have to keep asking until you hit on the right question.

> **RVP:** *Sometimes I tell a student, "I think I understand what you believe happened. If I were to ask your mom and dad about this, what do you think they would say?" More than once I've been surprised to hear the same student give an entirely different account of the event as he imagined it might look through the eyes of his parents.*

"What do you think they would say?" is an important triage question, but it remains at the level of speculation. The student may have a distorted notion of what her parents think and feel. She might, for example, base her assessment on a tone of voice she perceived from her mother. *A tone of voice*—that's a bit like mind reading, isn't it? This is why it's important to acquire more than one perspective if you can. That usually can't happen in the initial stages of an intervention, and confidentiality can make it difficult to accomplish at all. But it's worth pursuing if circumstances allow.

When conflicts revolve around parental expectations or other complications at home, there's not much you can do to provide assistance without involving other family members. There may be times when you simply can't gain access to the family—but don't give up too quickly. When a kid in crisis says, "My dad would never talk to you; he *hates* Christians," don't take his word for it. He's in crisis. His thinking and emotions may be distorted. If he resists your attempts to gather as many facts and perspectives as possible, it may indicate a deeper problem, or at least a different problem than the one you think you're working on. Get the facts. Facts are the raw material for solving the problem.

TAKE TIME TO LISTEN TO THEIR STORIES

Jumping to conclusions is not just unfair; it's also dangerous if it drives an already-at-risk student out your door without getting help. There is no shortcut to listening to the story—the whole story. And listening takes time.

It's not a bad idea to use a note pad to record the details. Assuming you're as busy as most youth workers, it'll be easy to forget particulars or worse, confuse one student's situation with another's. (For more tips about record keeping, see the "Documentation" part of section 3.2.) Some students may be put off by procedures that seem too "shrinkish." You can lessen uneasiness about what you're writing with a simple explanation: "If you don't mind, I'd like to jot down some things while we talk. For your benefit, I want to remember as many details as possible."

Here's a list of prompts to get the ball rolling:

- Tell me what you'd like to talk about.
- Tell me where your story begins.
- Who else is involved in this story? How are they involved?
- How have you managed to cope until now?
- Who is supporting you through this?
- If you were your friends, would you be worried about you?
  - Say more about that.
- Have you considered hurting yourself or someone else?
- Are you under the care of a doctor or counselor?
  - When was your last visit?
  - How helpful is that? (Put it on a scale of 1 to 10.)
  - Tell me more about that.
- Are you on medication?
- Are you self-medicating?
  - Talk more about that.

A student may test the waters to see if you're really interested and able to help. This test could come in the form of a *presenting problem* that has little to do with the core issue—though, in fairness, the student may not have identified the core issue yet. So, without dismissing what *seems* to be the matter, move the conversation deeper, one layer at a time, until the student feels safe enough (or aware enough) to tell the story behind the story.

One way to get beyond what's obvious in the presenting problem is by asking the follow-up question: "And how's everything else going?" It's remarkable how often that can lead to a description of the "real" issue behind the presenting issue.

In situations where the presenting problem is something like *I'm depressed, I feel alone, I'm confused, I'm tired all the time, I can't concentrate, I just feel sad, I'm always losing my temper, I can't sleep, I just don't care anymore, I can't eat, I can't stop eating*, ask, "When was the last time this *wasn't* a problem? Tell me about that."

BUILD TRUST

Perhaps you've heard the story about the soldier who, before returning home from combat, called his family to see if he could bring a friend home for an extended visit. Their initial reaction was positive until he provided more detail.

"My friend was hit by a grenade that blew off one of his arms." Although hesitant, the soldier's mom still encouraged him to bring his buddy home. "You should also know that he lost one of his legs in the attack." There was a long pause on the line but they still encouraged him to bring his friend home. "I think you should also know he's pretty disfigured because shrapnel tore up the left side of his face."

"Well you know," his mom replied, "maybe it really would be better if you just came alone for a while, and then when things stabilize, we can talk about your friend coming to visit for a bit." His mom heard a *click* on the other end of the line.

A few weeks later the soldier's family received notification that their son's body had been found, the victim of an apparent suicide. Confused and wanting to be certain it was really their son, the soldier's father asked how positive identification was determined. The officer said, since the boy had no ID, they used dental records. "Why," replied the father, "couldn't you have just used a photo from his file?"

The officer's response was devastating. "Unfortunately sir, your son sustained severe injuries in combat—he lost his right arm, took shrapnel in the face, and lost his left leg. His face was so disfigured that a photo would have been very little help."

The soldier wasn't asking if he could bring a friend home. He wanted to know how he would be received when *he* came home.

Teenagers and families sometimes fear that if we *really* knew the truth about them, we'd want nothing to do with them—which is too often how it turns out.

Ask the parents who are alienated from the Christian community because their son heads the gay caucus at his college. Ask the boy who confessed his difficulty resisting marijuana and was made into an example of worldliness in his Christian school. Ask the abusive father who is afraid to ask for help because he fears rejection from his pastor.

What a contrast to the model of Jesus during his encounter with the woman at the well.[2] She had two strikes against her:

1. As a Samaritan she was an *untouchable*, as far as the Jews were concerned.
2. She had a reputation for being a loose woman.

She tried to present herself with an air of respectability, but Jesus knew better. He knew her past. He loved her as she was. Jesus learned that from his Father. David sang the praises of a God who is near to the brokenhearted, who saves those who are crushed in spirit.[3]

That's how high the bar is set for us as we draw out the stories of the brokenhearted and crushed in spirit where we are. God help us provide a safe place where they too can find hope and healing.

ALLOW FOR THE EXPRESSION OF FEELINGS

Younger teenagers, especially boys, have difficulty articulating their feelings. It's not unusual to hear wide ranging, even conflicting emotions—especially in matters of family and sexuality—encompassing intense love and hate for the same person. These emotions are clearly at odds (*Am I crazy? How can I feel these things about him?*) and they are just as clearly *real*. They must be faced, expressed, and unpacked for healing to take place.

A crisis helper can complicate the process by agreeing too quickly, or prematurely assessing an emotional expression. Imagine being the helper who hears Sarah talk about being victimized by her stepfather. After disclosing some of the details of the abuses, she exclaims in tears, "I hate him so much—I wish I could kill him!"

In an attempt to be empathetic and sensitive to her deep hurt, a naïve helper might respond, "And I'd like to help." That response might be an honest reaction. Unfortunately, it could stifle the airing of other emotions like, "But I love him too much to hurt him, and I'm afraid he's going to get in trouble."

Conflicted emotions are difficult to feel, let alone admit and express—and they can't be explored until they're identified. Part of our job as helpers is to invite the open expression of complicated emotions—then stay out of the way while the complications emerge, uncolored by our assessment. (Remember: Deep listening takes time.) The emotional and spiritual release that may accompany an honest verbalization of such deeply felt conflict could be therapeutic in and of itself.

Open-ended, guiding questions can facilitate a more thorough process. To help the person go deeper, say things like:

• And what did you feel then?
• Talk about your other feelings.
• What did you think he or she was trying to do?
• What did that make you want to do?
• What else would you like me to know?

Of course, finding the words to express feelings isn't easy for people who don't have a reliable emotional map. You can use the emotional map in section 6.3 to help people zero in on unfamiliar territory. Use it like you'd use a street map to locate someone: *Are you closer to City Hall or Washington Park, First or 57th?* Only here you're mapping an emotional experience: *Did you feel more disappointed or let down? Closer to fear or panic?* The clearer the emotional description, the nearer you are to finding an appropriate next step.

ASSESS THE LEVEL OF IMMEDIATE RISK

Creating a safe place includes:

1. Not blowing things out of proportion by assigning too high a risk factor for the circumstances, and
2. Demonstrating that you take the individual seriously by testing the level of risk.

You've just spent an hour listening to Jeff's confession. He was caught cheating on a midterm in the last semester of his senior year. He is mortified. He's already been accepted at a major university, but failure to pass this subject would mean not walking with his class at graduation. Once the news of his cheating spreads, he also faces the loss of a scholarship from his grandfather's fraternal organization. Embarrassment turns to shame, followed by tears. Jeff murmurs that he might be better off dead—at least then he wouldn't dishonor his family. You've never seen him so despondent, and you fear he might actually be suicidal. Bypassing the incongruity in his suicidal proposition, you say, "You know Jeff, if I were in your situation and felt as badly as you feel right now, I think I might at least consider killing myself. Is that something you've been toying with?"

By initiating the question, you communicate two important things to Jeff:

1. You acknowledge how bad he feels, and
2. You're not afraid to talk about it with him.

If Jeff admits he's considering suicide, you'll need more information to determine whether to take immediate steps to protect his life. Here's a simple acrostic to help you determine when someone is a suicide risk.

SLAP

S - SPECIFIC DETAILS
- Is there a plan?
- How well has he thought through the plan?
- Has he determined a time? A place? A method?

- On a scale of 1 to 10 (where 1 = I would never kill myself, and 10 = As soon as I have an opportunity, I will do it) where would he place himself? You may not think a person who's thinking about killing himself would tell you the truth; but if he's starting to believe he has nothing to lose, there's a high likelihood he will.

L - LETHALITY OF METHOD
- Does the method indicate a clear desire to die? (Guns and jumping are more frequently lethal than pills, for example.)
- Could this be a cry for help?

A - AVAILABILITY OF METHOD
- If the method includes a gun, poisons, or other lethal measures, are those means readily available?

P - PROXIMITY TO HELPING RESOURCES
- Does the plan involve a location where he might be difficult to reach?
- Does the plan indicate that he might *want* to be interrupted?
- Can he name someone who'd want to stop him if he tried to kill himself? A person who has difficulty naming such a person is at high risk. He may be wrong in his assessment—but if he believes it's true, he may *act* as if it were true. If he identifies someone he believes would intervene, that tells you whom to involve in a suicide watch.

Use the SLAP outline to form a series of questions that are both direct and relationally warm. His responses will help you assess the apparent seriousness of intent, which in turn will help you narrow your options and take appropriate action. (See section 5.20 for more information about suicide prevention.)

If Jeff's responses to your questions about suicidal thoughts and intentions convince you he's not suicidal, you've still communicated that you take his pain seriously and you're not afraid to enter that pain with him and look for healing.

- Don't fail to seize the moment as an opportunity for prevention.
- Set up a conversation the next day—it never hurts to have a warm conversation to look forward to.

- Consider whether you need to help him talk with his parents or refer him to a mental health specialist—maybe you don't, but consider the benefits.
- You've come this far, so just say it: "Will you promise me, Jeff, that if things ever get so bad that you want to die, you'll come find me?" Now Jeff knows at least one person who doesn't want him to die. Sometimes that's all it takes.

QUESTION THE APPROPRIATENESS OF YOUR INVOLVEMENT

Right now you may be saying, "Whoa! I didn't sign on for this when I agreed to serve spaghetti at the fundraiser." That's not all bad. In fact, "Why me, God?" is a good question, because it reminds us of who we are and who we aren't when it comes to helping people. Honestly, sometimes we get involved because no one else is available—because God put us in the right place at the right time with the promise to make us the right people for the job, at least this once. Whoever said, "God doesn't use us because we're qualified; God qualifies us when he uses us," had a finger on the pulse of reality. That's a good reminder for those of us who don't have the clinical preparation to make us at least *feel* prepared for crisis intervention. There are times when we're invited into crisis situations with people we care about simply because they believe we care—in a pinch, that can mean more to their survival than clinical expertise.

That said, part of the triage process involves determining who is best qualified to extend care. (Think Major Winchester—the thoracic surgery specialist on *M•A•S•H*. He may have been a pain in the neck, but for treating some patients he was a much better choice than Hawkeye.) Just because our involvement is invited, that doesn't necessarily mean we should be on point for the long haul. Once basic equilibrium is restored, effective helpers always ask, *Am I the right person to move this intervention forward? Can I take them where they need to go? Do I have the skills necessary to help in the long term?*

Not to flog this to death, but if someone with better skills or experience is available, we need to entertain the possibility of bringing them into the conversation. Helping people get what they need is more important than being the one who delivers the goods; if we doubt that, we have another problem to deal with.

2.2   MAKING **CONNECTIONS**

Robert Veninga knew something about people in crisis—he was, after all, a counselor. But it wasn't until Veninga faced a crisis of his own that he began to observe the differences between those whose lives are laid waste by crisis and those who not only survive, but also go on to thrive in the aftermath of trauma. In *A Gift of Hope: How We Survive Our Tragedies*, Veninga identifies characteristics shared by survivors. Perhaps his most instructive observation, for our context at least, is: "Almost without exception, those who survive a tragedy give credit to one person who stood by them, supported them, and gave them a sense of hope."[1]

Think about it: *One person...*

WHO WE ARE IS MORE IMPORTANT THAN WHAT WE KNOW

RVP: *My friend Todd was ordered to see a court-appointed psychologist. He was an innocent party in his parents' bitter divorce, and the court was poised to decide who would be the custodial parent—hence the psychological evaluation. Todd was incredibly apprehensive. He asked his accountability group to pray about his fear of counseling and stereotypical shrinks. I was the adult facilitator for Todd's small group and felt comfortable asking how things went after the initial meeting.*

> *"A disaster," Todd said. His worst nightmare had come true, including the doctor's opening question, So, Todd, tell me how you're* really *feeling? "I wanted to tell the guy, 'You give me the creeps and I want out of here as soon as possible!'" Todd said. He refused to go back for a follow-up session.*
>
> *The doctor was a licensed psychologist. No question about his professional preparation; no reason to believe he didn't know his stuff—it just wasn't the right stuff. If we're going to be helpful, especially to young people, we have to become adept at making person-to-person connections.*

Psychotherapists talk about the importance of the *therapeutic alliance*. Michael Craig Miller, editor in chief of the *Harvard Mental Health Letter*, writes:

> The therapeutic alliance, also called the working alliance, is essential for successful psychotherapy. Of course, common sense dictates that any consulting relationship should involve a strong partnership that enables two people to do serious work. But there is more to it than that. Many professionals believe that in psychotherapy, the quality of the alliance is more important than any other aspect of the treatment.[2]

Unless we find a personal connection, there may not be much we can do to help a person in crisis. Conversely, making a genuine connection goes a long way toward overcoming deficits in formal training. On any given day, "who we are" as helpers in crisis may be more important than "what we know."

THE ANATOMY OF A HELPER

Young people in crisis rarely approach adults whom they only *hope* will care about their problems. They're drawn to men and women who have already *demonstrated* they are approachable and willing to help no matter what. Here's what that kind of person looks like...

HUMOR

The staging area was prepared for the graveside service of a young marine killed in combat training exercises. An open-sided tent covered the area with a dozen or so folding chairs for the immediate family. The family arrived, and Grandma (an unfortunately large woman) was seated front and center.

Toward the end of the service, the chaplain signaled the honor guard to begin the customary 21-gun salute. Grandma was so startled by the sound of the first volley of gunshots that she literally lifted off her seat. The chair, it should be noted, was not engineered for her particular combination of mass and velocity. So when Grandma came crashing back down, it collapsed beneath her, pitching her onto the ground. Horrified, her six-year-old grandson screamed, "My God, they've shot Grandma!" There wasn't a dry eye in the place, and for the first time in days it wasn't from tears of sorrow. Even Grandma laughed uncontrollably!

There's obviously nothing funny about the loss of a loved one, nothing comical about terminal disease, sexual abuse, or crisis pregnancy. Laughing at people or the source of their pain is, and will remain, in bad taste. But sometimes, in the middle of life's most difficult moments, funny things happen—and there's something very therapeutic about a good, hearty laugh at the right time. In fact, when we really laugh (the kind of laughter that results in watering eyes and runny noses), our brains release endorphins that attach to the same receptors as morphine. Holy laughter is a painkiller. Proverbs 17:22 says, "A cheerful heart is good medicine, but a crushed spirit dries up the bones."

JH: At their request, Rich and I hosted a closed gathering for Littleton area youth workers five days after the massacre at Columbine High School. The meeting was closed (no media, no out-of-towners), because the local youth workers were exhausted from nonstop crisis intervention. Littleton was crawling with reporters, and presumably well-meaning outsiders were beginning to come into the community to do ministry on the population—whether they wanted it or not.

My job was to help create a safe place for youth workers to share stories about how God was showing up in the middle of fear and pain. Rich's job was delivering the message in this chapter. When he started with humor as a characteristic of people-helpers, there was the briefest catch, the slightest pause, before it seemed to me like a wave of grace washed gently across the gathering. It felt like the whole room relaxed a little—hunched shoulders loosened a bit, and people took their first unrestricted breath in days.

Rich didn't try to be funny; he only opened the door to the possibility that these dear people might smile again soon. And we laughed together, not hilariously maybe, but naturally and generously, as people living in the mercy of God.

EMPATHY

A sign on a camp nurse's office wall reads: "Empathy is feeling your pain in my heart." Not bad. Young people in crisis are drawn to people they sense *understand* or are willing to *work at understanding* what they're going through. It wouldn't hurt for us to remember our own experiences in adolescence (well, maybe it would hurt a little, but that's the point). Remembering helps us identify with the struggles of the kids we serve.

That said, there's a vast difference between empathy and the arrogant conceit that says, "I know exactly what you're feeling. When *I* was your age..." The empathetic adult shuts her mouth and takes time to listen while a young person tells his story. Empathy is the heart of coming alongside. In *Living through Personal Crisis*, Ann Kaiser Stearns observes that the empathetic person:

- Does not shock easily, but accepts human feelings as human feelings
- Is not embarrassed by tears
- Does not often give unwanted advice
- Is warm and appropriately affectionate
- Reminds you of your strengths when you forget you have these strengths within yourself
- Recognizes that growth is a process
- Trusts that you are able to come through your difficult time
- Treats you like an adult, capable of making good decisions
- Acknowledges that he is human, too, and shares this humanness
- May sometimes become impatient or angry, but never attacks your character when telling you so
- Is not afraid to question you directly about your feelings of loss
- Respects your courage and sense of determination

- Understands that grief is not a disease
- Has been through troubled times and can tell you this without making everything seem to be about her
- May not be comfortable with a feeling you are expressing, such as hatred or a particular sexual yearning, but tries to understand what the feeling means to you
- Tells you honestly when he is unable to be with you because of problems or needs of his own
- Remains faithful to commitments and promises[3]

AVAILABILITY

RVP: My sister Ruthann was in labor in Pittsburgh, and I was waiting in Denver for the phone to ring with news of her delivery. I imagined over and over what my brother-in-law would say when he called: "Hey Rich, it's Dan! You're an uncle, man!"

Dan's call was nowhere near that much fun. "Ruthie's okay," he said, "but the baby died in delivery."

Everyone was in shock. My first inclination was to call the travel agency and get on the next flight to Pittsburgh. Looking back, I wish I'd gone with my gut. Years later my sister would confess that as much as she appreciated my calls, cards, and flowers, she really wanted her big brother with her at that incredibly difficult time. It's one thing to say we care—but our presence shouts it so loud it can hardly be missed.

Get in your car and go see the kid in the hospital. Take the train to visit with the kid who's laid up at home. Invite the pregnant girl to come hang out with you for a while when you sense she feels awkward hanging out with the teeny boppers at the food court, or—even worse—when she feels uncomfortable in her own home. Sometimes just being there makes all the difference.

EMOTIONAL FOCUS

Physical presence demonstrates our care, but it's not enough by itself. We must be *emotionally* present as well. We all know it's entirely possible to be physically present but lack emotional focus. After her father responded to a challenge to become a better listener, a high school girl reported arriving home one day to find her dad in the living room, reading the newspaper and watching television. As she passed behind his mega-lounger, he murmured, "So, how was your day, honey?" Not that she didn't appreciate the gesture, but she said, "If my dad really wanted to know how my day was, why didn't he shut off the TV, put down the paper, look me in the eyes, and then ask the question?"

Okay, so maybe she didn't appreciate the gesture. She went on to speculate that maybe he wasn't capable of doing two things at one time—watching TV and reading the newspaper—let alone really listening to her, too. She had very little (meaning *no*) interest in being the object in a workshop assignment designed to make her father feel better about his parenting skills—not unless he actually got personally engaged. She wanted to know by his posture that he was genuinely interested in her day.

Mike Yaconelli was fond of saying the spiritual gift of teenagers is "crap detection." As much as they long for authentic connections, kids resent (and reject) manipulative techniques. You can't get away with feigning interest just so you can check it off the list—not for long.

APPROACHABILITY

Accessibility is not the same as approachability. We know plenty of youth workers who pride themselves on being accessible to teenagers. They might even claim they're *available*, but they're not. They spend lots of time at school and hanging out socially without learning much about the deep hurts, fears, and tough times kids endure. These folks are physically accessible but emotionally unapproachable. Youth workers who are approachable:

- Value the importance of each person and communicate those feelings through their words and actions
- Never willingly embarrass anyone in front of others
- Avoid telling or even listening to ethnic, racial, or gender jokes
- Never challenge a young person's sexual identity, and always challenge those who do
- Avoid competitive activities that exclude people who lack physical prowess
- Can be trusted to keep a confidence

RESOURCEFULNESS

People in crisis can feel like passengers on a runaway train careen-ing through a moonless night. They hold on for dear life as the train picks up speed in the terrifying dark. Every bump and curve reminds them how utterly and totally out of control they feel—up to a point. Past that point, the passengers expect to die; so they ride grimly on, wishing it could be over sooner rather than later.

In a good action/adventure movie, this is where the hero shows up—godlike—from the outside bringing new hope. "Hold on," he says, "I'll help you get off this thing alive!" This is what people want us to be, and since we're not in the grip of the crisis, we bring clearer perspective and greater capacity to identify solutions than those caught in the middle of it.

RVP: A youth worker I was helping through a rough spot said, "Gosh, having done this for as long as you have, there's prob-ably nothing you haven't dealt with." I chuckled and responded that just when I think I've heard everything, something new surfaces. But my friend wasn't far off. My experience helping students and families in crisis makes me unusually resourceful. I'm not bragging; I'm just saying I haven't become less effective with time (despite the wags who remind me the first word in youth worker is—well, you can read it yourself).

The moral is: *Don't stop now—you're really starting to get somewhere!*

TRAINING

Just because who you *are* may be more important than what you *know,* that doesn't mean what you know is unimportant. Imagine you've just been rushed to the hospital. A donor organ has become available and your long-awaited liver transplant is about to take place. You lie in the surgical prep room pondering the operation, your anxiety level elevated by the news that your personal physi-cian is on a fishing trip and completely unreachable somewhere in Alaska. The hospital's chief of staff has arranged for another surgeon to perform the procedure.

Attempting to set you at ease, a nurse makes small talk about the replacement doc. He tells you what a nice—in fact, *funny*—

person she is. "No kidding," the nurse says, "of all the surgeons I've worked with, this one has such a good manner. People just feel so comfortable. And funny! Did I mention that? You'll be unconscious, of course, but the rest of us will be howling throughout your procedure. Hmm, I see your blood pressure is spiking; are you not hearing what I'm saying here?"

This is when you interrupt: "Look! All I want to hear you say is how fortunate I am to have this surgeon because she's the best cutter in the business. Funny is good; we'll have dinner if I survive. But what I need is to hear you say I'm going to come through this with flying colors and a new liver! Is that too much to ask?"

Parents have a right to expect that their children are safe in our care. If we're genuinely committed to coming alongside parents to raise competent young adults, we simply must do everything we can to prepare for the task.

Opportunities for professional development are readily available to the career-oriented youth worker. And for those of us who work with students after we finish our day jobs, the number and quality of learning experiences improves every year. Christian colleges and seminaries offer undergrad and graduate degrees in youth ministry, family ministry, counseling, and related fields. Youth ministry organizations like our friends at Youth Specialties host national conventions and area training events for veteran and novice youth workers. Colleges, universities, civic organizations, hospitals, and non-profits sponsor useful workshops and certificate programs.

If you want to be trusted and rewarded in ways that exceed the stereotypical "youth guy" who's "so good with the kids," become a diligent student of students, sharpen your skills, and deepen your understanding of what helps kids and their families succeed.

SERVANT SPIRIT

RVP: I took a group of students to work at Centre Siloe, *an orphanage founded by Tony Campolo in Haiti—the poorest country in the Western Hemisphere; regarded by many as a fourth world nation because it lacks the resources to sustain itself.*

The orphanage staff determined that our group could be most helpful if we spent the week cleaning and disinfecting the facility. Not a pleasant job, but we went there to be helpful. Living standards in Haiti are worlds away from what American teenagers are accustomed to. The cement walls and floors of the orphanage were caked with what seemed like years of filth. The temperature hovered in the high 80s and the humidity must have been 90 percent or worse. But our group asked to be useful, not comfortable.

When the orphanage overhaul was complete, one of the high school guys admitted he was relieved they weren't asked to clean the toilets. The receptacles in question were as crude as your typical national forest latrine, but just having an indoor bathroom was relatively uptown in that part of Haiti. The 40 children living at the orphanage plus 400 more attending the day school gratefully used the facility early and often. No one had to stick his head in the door to know what was in there.

So, when Chris expressed his relief, my immediate reaction was to assure him I never would've asked the group to do something that nasty. He was quiet for a moment and then responded, "But you know, I'll bet if Jesus were here, that's where he would have started." Perhaps for the first time, Chris and some of the rest of us understood what it really means to be a servant. The American teenagers did a wonderful thing that week, but I sometimes wonder if I robbed them of an even greater opportunity for service.

ONE IS ENOUGH

Crisis intervention is seldom glamorous. People in crisis may need help dealing with everyday tasks that have become overwhelming under the weight of unsustainable circumstances. A servant asks, "What needs to be done? How can I help?" Friends who organize meals for a family suffering the loss of a loved one serve an intensely practical need. A youth group that takes on lawn care and snow shoveling for a family whose child is battling a terminal disease bestows a simple but significant service. A youth worker who doesn't possess the clinical skill to help a girl recover from sexual abuse makes a difference by driving her to therapy.

If at this point, you're thinking, *This all seems harder than it looked from a distance,* please relax. The good news is that relationship really matters—more than just about anything. Crisis interventions, and especially the prevention strategies in chapter 4.0, are not nearly so tied to expert technique as to the *therapeutic alliance*—the genuine connection that sets the context for surviving and thriving beyond the crisis. Remember what Robert Veninga discovered:

> Almost without exception, those who survive a tragedy give credit to *one person* who stood by them, supported them, and gave them a sense of hope.[4]

Maybe you don't have it all together. Reviewing the qualities of effective crisis helpers—humor, empathy, availability, emotional focus, approachability, resourcefulness, training, and a servant spirit—you may feel you possess only a couple of those attributes, and even those not as completely as you wish. Sure, there's room for growth, but don't underestimate what you bring to the table right now. You like kids, and kids like you. You can stand by them, support them, and give them a sense of hope. If you want to know how few people there are who render even that basic level of care, just ask a teenager to describe the adults in her life.

So, on behalf of young people everywhere, thanks for doing what you can. Keep after it; you'll get bigger as you go.[5]

2.3   DEEP **LISTENING**

We are surrounded by people who need help. Their needs range from the simple affirmation of a human encounter to complicated, layers-deep emotional and spiritual issues with life-and-death consequences. Our capacity to help begins with intentional acts of paying attention. That means watching, taking time to ask questions, and listening until we understand what people are really saying.

Given the ratio of ears-to-people in the world, listening is a surprisingly rare gift between folks who claim to care about each other. At this writing there's no reliable data on how much time parents and adolescents spend in meaningful conversation, but the common wisdom is *not much, not nearly enough.* Listening takes time. Good listeners pay a price. And many families simply can't or won't ante up.

RVP: I was an adjunct professor in youth and family ministry at Denver Seminary for more than a decade. One day I asked a class to talk about the most influential people in their lives and why those people were so important. In the middle of describing her dad, one student stopped talking, gathered her thoughts, looked me straight in the eye, and said, "I'm sorry, Rich, but you're making me really nervous!"

Obviously I was taken aback and concerned that some-thing about my demeanor made her feel uncomfortable. So I apologized.

"Oh no! It's not your fault! It's just that I'm not used to really being listened to."

Few young people ever have the experience of being *really* listened to by an adult—someone who takes the time, energy, and focus required to truly understand. The psychiatrist M. Scott Peck put it so well:

> The principal form that the work of love takes is attention. When we love another we give him or her our attention; we attend to that person's growth. When we love ourselves we attend to our own growth. When we attend to someone we are caring for that person. The act of attending requires that we set aside our existing preoccupations...and actively shift our consciousness. Attention is an act of will, or work, against the inertia of our own minds.[1]

JH: Rich is often asked to lead workshops on "Speaking So Kids Will Listen." I'm wondering if the more important subject to master might be "Listening So Kids Will Speak."

HOW TO DO IT

Here are five key elements in deep listening:

UNPACK YOUR OWN BAG

Some youth ministry wag said youth workers must view themselves as "missionaries to savages in a jungle." The metaphor is hopelessly old school, but if you can get past the Euro-trash arrogance, it's instructive.

To be effective, missionaries must learn to know:
- The "jungle"
- The "savage"
- The "missionary"

An effective cross-cultural worker learns everything she can about the people she crossed cultures to serve and the culture into which she's crossed—all the while continuing to learn about herself, including an enlightened examination of the cultural experiences and assumptions she brought with her from her native culture.

If you're 19 years old and working with students just a couple of years younger than you, the first two requirements are relatively easy. The range of developmental and sub-cultural factors will be relatively familiar unless you're serving in a context that's utterly unfamiliar (like if you grew up in a city center and you're working in a farm community). The older you get, the more homework it takes to stay in touch with the people and the context (the "savages" and the "jungle," sorry). The good news is, if you remain in the jungle and live among the savages, it's not that difficult.

The third requirement—knowing the missionary—is a more complex, long-term task. One way to learn about yourself, as the missionary, is to look at what's in your backpack. What you keep with you says a lot about who you think you are and what you think you're doing.

Your access to what's in your bag at any given time affects the style and substance of your ministry—especially your capacity as a listener. Unpack your bag, and see how the contents shape your listening skills.

Life Story. Who you are as a result of your cumulative life experiences can enhance or inhibit your capacity to listen. If you grew up in an alcoholic family system and never got help to work through anger and abandonment issues, you may find yourself emotionally overloaded when someone asks you to listen to a story that sounds a lot like yours. On the other hand, if you're a survivor of childhood sexual abuse and have received help in working through the myriad issues involved in recovering from that trauma, you're likely to be an empathetic listener to anyone with an abuse story.

Age. No use pretending you're younger or older than your actual age. It's just a distraction that causes you to pay too much attention to you and too little to the person you've agreed to attend.

Language. Your comfort zone of vocabulary and usage makes a difference in how many questions (especially follow-up questions) you must ask in order to understand.

Gender. The socialization of boys and girls in any culture influences the manner in which men and women learn to hear spoken messages and read nonverbal cues.

Education. If you're trained in psychopathology and theology, you will listen differently than if you're only trained in psychopathology.

Physical surroundings. Even if you tend to be a focused listener, a room that is noisy, hot, cold, or crowded can make it difficult to pay attention. If you're easily distracted, it's especially important to control the listening environment appropriately.

Personal condition. It pays to take account of factors like fatigue, illness, and unresolved personal issues in order to stay focused on listening.

Personal feelings. Don't be in denial about this: Positive or negative feelings about the person you're listening to *will* affect the quality of your listening.

LISTENING WITH ACCEPTANCE

RVP: I have a friend who has to be one of the most naturally gifted listeners on the planet. She has never studied human behavior or taken a graduate course in counseling psychology, but few people I know have Lindy's capacity to help others move so quickly into heart-to-heart conversation.

I've been privileged to be on the receiving end of her listening skills. I've also watched her do her listening thing with others in an effort to improve my own skills. But I have to admit, after careful observation I've concluded her ability is more a function of who she is than what she does. Lindy loves and cares for people. She accepts them as they are. Because what she does as a listener flows so naturally out of who she is as a person, people feel accepted and safe enough to share with Lindy who they truly are.

Teenagers need adults who receive them as they truly are. Youth workers have unleashed on the world a plague of spiritually schizoid youth group kids by teaching them to play religious games. Instead of celebrating the marvel of each person's uniqueness—fearfully and wonderfully made in the image of God—we are responsible for creating little "Stepford Christians" who act just-so around us, afraid that if we learn what they really feel, believe, and long for, we'll reject them.

Ordinary folks felt safe around Jesus. He treated them like people, not projects. Author Jim Petersen says, "If we are interested in people only because of what we might accomplish with them, then we have missed the point. When we think like that, we aren't loving others as our heavenly Father does. He loves with no strings attached."[2]

Proverbs 20:5 says, "The purposes of the human heart are deep waters, but those who have insight draw them out" (TNIV). People who take a pounding from life desperately need friends and helpers who will listen non-judgmentally to what they're thinking and feeling.

JH: The *judge* in me used to care a great deal about why people went wrong. Was it poor judgment? Compulsion? Irresponsibility? Immaturity? Weakness? Were they victims or perpetrators? Over the years I've come to believe that the details of how people got upside down doesn't make much difference in the outcome of their lives. Did she jump or was she pushed? Does it matter? She's broken—now what?

There's no question that broken people—however they came to be broken—need help evaluating their conditions, assigning responsibility where it belongs, and working toward a way of life that minimizes the likelihood of jumping or being pushed again. But it's no good making that evaluation until they've been scraped off the sidewalk *this* time. *Now* is when we can help by suspending judgment and offering acceptance.

LISTEN TO THE WHOLE PERSON WITH YOUR WHOLE PERSON

Kids are masters at spotting disinterest—at least they believe they are. That's why effective listeners take pains to project an inviting tone of voice, engaging eye contact, and a relaxed, attentive physical posture—all focused on encouraging a person to disclose, rather than conceal, the story behind her story. Your task is to listen to a student's whole person with your whole person.

Effective listening begins with the ears. Someone with a keen grasp for the obvious said, "The fact that God gave us two ears and *one* tongue should be our first clue." The same can be said for two eyes to take in the depth of the person before us (with still only one tongue to tell them what we see). How about if we agree to a general ratio of 2:1—where we look and listen twice as much as we talk? This assumes we can learn to exist without the constant sound of our own voices.

Why do we find it so easy to lose concentration when we're listening to others? Most listeners process information in the range of 300 to 500 words per minute (the rate generally declines with age). But most people speak at a rate of 100 to 200 words per minute, which means there's serious excess capacity on the listening side of the transaction. And with excess capacity comes the tendency to daydream, fret, plan, doodle, and—if we're not careful—lose track of what the other person is saying. Just being aware of this phenomenon can help us be more attentive.

Beyond mere awareness of the challenge lies the physics of deep listening:

- Using our eyes as well as our ears, watching for nonverbal cues, as well as making eye contact

- Vocalizing unobtrusive encouragement and requests for more information (mmm, yes, say more about that, ouch, talk about what you think that means...)
- Leaning toward the person from time to time to communicate intentional presence

This can be hard work. Scott Peck said, "Listening well is an exercise of attention, and by necessity hard work. It is because they do not realize this or because they are not willing to do the work that most people do not listen well."[3]

People sometimes say one thing with their lips and a very different thing with their eyes. Even in spoken communication, much is hinted at beyond the words through speed, intonation, pitch, breathing, flinching, flushing, eye-rolling, breaking eye contact, foot tapping, rocking, fidgeting, jaw-clenching, weeping, crossing arms and legs, slouching, slumping, rapidly shifting eyes, and staring into space. Forget about that 100-200 words a minute: A person in distress may speak much faster—or much slower—or not at all. There's much truth in the old adage: *The deeper the sorrow, the less tongue it has.*

Rolly Martinson had a girl in his high school group who was beginning to show signs of depression and withdrawal, but she was unwilling to admit she was struggling. Rolly believes one of the best ways to learn about kids is to visit their homes. So Rolly and his wife worked at getting an invitation to the girl's home for dinner. After the meal they asked her for a tour of the house, and she took them everywhere except her bedroom. That seemed rather strange, so Rolly asked her to complete the tour by showing them her room. Noticeably uncomfortable, she took them to a door that required a key. Inside, they found a space decorated and furnished for an infant. Rolly said, "Oh you must have misunderstood—we wanted to see *your* room."

"This is my room," she said.

Rolly's honest concern was enough to release the girl to tell her story. When she broke the news that she was pregnant, her parents demanded she have an abortion. She was whisked off that same night to a nearby city, and the procedure was performed the next day. Both parents were leaders in the Christian community and warned her it would smear the family name if she told anyone what happened. Two days later she returned to school with a note asking that her absence be excused due to a cold.

The girl's bedroom reflected her desire to keep the child alive. Rolly went the extra mile—listening to more than her words—to get at the story behind the story. His eagerness to see past the sanitized version of this young girl's life was the beginning of real healing for her.

LISTEN TO THE STORY BEHIND THE STORY

Hear the cry of one young person's heart in this anonymous poem.

Please Hear What I'm Not Saying

Don't be fooled by me.
Don't be fooled by the face I wear,
For I wear a mask, I wear a thousand masks,
Masks that I am afraid to take off,
But none of them are me.

Pretending is an art that's second nature to me.
But don't be fooled.
I give you the impression that I am secure,
That all is sunny and unruffled with me,
Within as well as without,
That confidence is my name and coolness is my game,
That the water's calm and I am in command,
And that I need no one.

Don't believe me, please!
My surface may be smooth,
But my surface is my mask,
My varying and ever-concealing mask.
Beneath lies the real me,
In confusion and fear,
In loneliness.
I idly chatter with you in the suave tones of surface talk.
I tell you everything that's really nothing,
Of what's crying within me.
So, when I'm going through my routine,
Please don't be fooled by what I'm not saying,
And what I'd like to be able to say,
But what I can't say.

Only you can call me into aliveness,
Each time you're kind and gentle and encouraging.
Each time you try to understand because you really care,
My heart begins to grow wings,
Very small wings, very feeble wings, but wings.
With your sensitivity and sympathy and your powers
of understanding,
You can breathe life into me, I want you to know that.
I want you to know how important you are to me,
How you can be a creator of the person that is me if you choose to.

Please choose to.
Do not pass me by.
It will not be easy for you.
My long conviction of worthlessness builds strong walls.
The nearer you approach to me, the blinder I may strike back.
I fight against the very thing I cry out for.
But I am told that love is stronger than strong walls.
In this lies my hope,
My only hope.
Who am I, you may wonder,
I am someone you know very well—
I am a hurting member of your family,
I am the person sitting beside you in this room,
I am every person you meet on the street.
Please don't believe my mask,
Please come behind it to glimpse the real me.
Please speak to me, share a little of yourself with me,
At least recognize me.
Please.
Because you care.[4]

A skilled listener learns to use questions to clarify what's been said and repetition to confirm that both parties are having the same conversation. As deep listeners, we bear the responsibility to remain engaged until what's being said and what's being heard are the same.

Author Paul Swets offers a helpful model he calls ACE (Attending, Clarifying, and Evaluating) for improving our listening skills:

Attending. We attend to people by giving focused attention. Attending requires the discipline to listen with everything we are—to take in and process what they say, how they say it, what they choose not to say, and what they find painful to say.

Clarifying. Our challenge is to hear what is being said—not more, not less, and not other than what's being said. That calls for clarifying statements and questions from the listener. The classic counseling phrase, "What I hear you saying is..." is just an attempt to clarify. Either we heard what was said or not; the only way to be sure is by asking. That said, it's possible to misuse the phrase. Learning guru Stephen Glenn used to tease: "If I hear you say, 'What I hear you saying...' one more time, what you'll hear me saying is 'Good-bye.'"

Evaluating. This is the action step. How should I respond to what I've heard? Swets says we have several options:

- Ask for more information
- Remain silent
- Express our feelings
- State our opinions[5]

Whichever we choose, the point is to keep listening until we reach understanding.

LISTEN WITH GOD'S HELP

RVP: I was raised as a mainline Presbyterian, very suspicious of those who claim to hear from God. But I have to admit, a careful examination of God's Word, in harmony with some personal experience, caused me to re-evaluate my position.

My duties as a chaplain in a long-term facility for juvenile offenders included organizing and conducting small-group Bible studies in several units. (I still say federal, state, and private facilities for juvenile offenders offer youth workers incredible opportunities to do ministry in one of our nation's most neglected mission fields and with some of our neediest kids.)

Toward the end of my time with the Department of Corrections, I began traveling a good bit, speaking about teenagers in crisis. One night I drove out to the jail to inform the guys we wouldn't be having Bible study that week because I'd be out of town. When I arrived at the unit, the shift supervisor met me at the door and asked me to join a meeting in the staff office. Bob explained that Steve (who was attending my Bible study) had been determined to be both homicidal and suicidal and would be held in his room on suicide watch until the unit psychiatrist arrived for a clinical evaluation. Bob instructed the staff to implement suicide watch procedures and insisted that no one but him be allowed to enter Steve's room. I was bummed, because I was interested in seeing if there was any way I could bring comfort or hope to Steve. But as a member of the staff, I had to respect the boundaries Bob established.

I spent a few minutes with the other guys in the unit; when it came time to leave, I asked Bob to let me out the door. That's when God spoke to me. That's the best I can say. I certainly didn't hear an audible voice, but I had very little doubt it was God instructing me to go to Steve's room. The very one who, minutes earlier, made it clear that no one was allowed in Steve's room was letting me out the door. I said, "Bob, I think I need to go to Steve's room."

"I've never been one to stop a man of the Lord," Bob replied, closing then locking the door and leading me to Steve's room. Bob opened Steve's door, motioned me in, and I heard the lock click behind me.

Steve was looking out his window and didn't glance back to see who was there. I had no idea what I was supposed to do. All I could think about was Bob's warning that Steve was suicidal and homicidal. Which meant Steve wasn't the only one at risk at that moment.

I saw a handwritten note on Steve's bed, which I assumed was a letter from his girlfriend. I picked it up hoping it would give me something to break the ice. What I read was his suicide note. Well, there was an opening.

"So...how are you going to do it?" I asked.

He turned, looked at me, and said, "I'll show you." He crossed to his closet, reached way back inside, and took out a butcher knife he'd pilfered from the main kitchen—so much for the knife count portion of our kitchen security.

All I knew to say at that moment was, "Steve, that tears me apart, because I love you."

He lunged at me, deliberately letting the knife fall. He threw his arms around me, sobbing and holding on for what felt like an eternity. When he began to regain his composure, he looked me in the eyes and said, "I can't remember the last time someone told me they loved me."

Then I got to tell him how I was on my way out the door when God stopped me in my tracks and redirected my steps, just so I could come to his room and let him know that not only did I love him but that he was loved just as he was by the God of the universe. Hearing that, Steve began sobbing again. It was the beginning of some incredible healing in his life.

Hebrews 13:20-21 reads:

> May the God of peace, who through the blood of the eternal covenant brought back from the dead our Lord Jesus, that great Shepherd of the sheep, equip you with everything good for doing his will, and may he work in us what is pleasing to him, through Jesus Christ, to whom be glory for ever and ever. Amen

We really are equipped "with everything good" for doing God's will. The God who calls us to "come alongside" those in any pain with the same "coming alongside" we ourselves have received from God, will *equip us and work in us* what is pleasing to God. We aren't called because we're qualified—we're qualified when we're called.

2.4   ACTION **PLAN**

You're not exactly shocked to hear from Carl's mother. She says Carl has been skipping church, which you knew, and missing church basketball practice, which you also knew. You didn't know about Carl's grades, which were inexplicably in free fall, or about the increasingly frequent arguments with his parents about anything and everything. Mrs. Stevens is convinced it's drugs. Her husband chalks it up to a phase (which you don't particularly buy as a concept, but you're mainly listening right now). Mrs. Stevens says, "It's time for tough love." Mr. Stevens says, "Give the boy some space." Mrs. Stevens seems relieved when you offer to spend time with Carl.

Carl, however, is less than thrilled. He arrives nervous and defensive. You lead with an assurance that you're not a secret agent for his parents. Carl crosses his arms and mutters, "Whatever." You ask Carl if he wants to talk about what has his parents all up in arms. He just shakes his head.

There is a long, awkward, fidgety silence when you say, "I'm worried about you, man. If something's gone wrong, I'd like to help you put it right."

A minute into the silence, Carl's right heel starts pumping and you know you're getting somewhere. Another minute passes and

Carl's jaw begins to work; he leans forward, forearms on his knees, and stares at the floor. Half a minute later he says, almost inaudibly, "I hate him."

You let the words hang in the air between you, finally saying just as quietly, "Tell me about that."

More jaw clenching, and a single tear drops to the floor between Carl's feet. "If she knew what he's really like, she'd leave him. Maybe I should just tell her. I'm just afraid she'd forgive him, and I don't know if I could handle that."

Once Carl decides to speak, the story is short and to the point.

After basketball practice one evening, Carl noticed his dad's car parked outside the family business and thought he would drop in to say hey. It was after hours, so Carl used his key to slip in the back door. His father didn't hear him come in or leave—he was preoccupied, making out with a woman Carl had never seen before.

Carl slipped out into the night, barely able to breathe. He dragged his key along the length of his father's car, gouging the paint from front to back as he passed—the only evidence he'd been there that night.

Carl was certain his mother's heart would break if she knew about this. He also feared confronting his father. So he decided to try and forget the whole thing—a strategy he now admits isn't working very well.

Your work is cut out for you. Carl is in survival mode. The anger toward his father will stay bottled up for only so long—it's already begun to leak.

Carl's decision to be honest gives you a place to start. Had he chosen to remain silent, inventing excuses for his behavior or simply denying there've been any problems, the path to resolution would be much more complicated. With your help, Carl will be able to identify how his behavior is making a bad thing worse without producing any hope of a solution. Before this conversation ends, Carl will agree it's impossible to go on pretending nothing is wrong.

You will guide him in brainstorming several plans of action, and ultimately Carl will accept your offer to help him confront his dad. None of this is pretty; it's just the first step on a redemptive path.

THE NEXT STEP

On a good day, crisis intervention opens doors to permanent resolution. Sometimes that won't be possible. The diagnosis of a terminal disease doesn't lend itself to solutions. The best a helper can do is work to lessen the impact—by developing coping strategies for living with a terminal illness, for instance. Which is *not nothing*. For people who believe in redemption, the hope of heaven is a big deal, as is the clear-headed opportunity to make amends for things done and things left undone.

In more ordinary (less terminal) crises, your role as helper is to assist people in determining what course of action *they will take*—because they're the ones who must act on their own behalf. Otherwise you've only postponed the problem for another day. If you make the decisions, you haven't helped people learn to work through similar situations in the future. That's *rescuing* rather than *coming alongside*. There are rare instances when a person must be persuaded to give up control temporarily because she is dangerously out of control, but those are exceptional circumstances.

Developing an action plan together pokes holes in the darkness, letting in enough light so the person in crisis can see a way out. The crisis helper facilitates the process but insists that people choose their own course of action. They, after all, must live with the choices.

So, once an immediate crisis has been neutralized, the next step is identifying and sorting the issues and options that have to be addressed to form a workable plan. The following flow sheet is helpful in determining an action plan. (It is reprinted in section 6.1.)

ACTION PLAN WORKSHEET

I. What is the identified problem (beyond the presenting problem)?

II. What are the possible outcomes (both negative and positive)?

A. Which is the most desirable outcome?
B. What general steps are required to move toward that outcome? (Return to more specific steps later.)

III. Who are the active participants, and what is their stake in the outcome?

IV. Who are the passive participants, and what is their stake? (And what can be expected from each stakeholder?)

V. What are the resources and roadblocks to reaching the goal?

VI. Who else should be involved in the solution?
A. Extended family?
B. Professional referral?
1. Medical doctor?
2. Psychiatrist and/or psychologist?
3. Social worker?
4. Law enforcement?
5. Lawyer?
6. Pastor?
7. School personnel?
8. Employer?
9. Friends?

VII. What specific steps must be taken?
A. In what order?
B. Who should take responsibility for each step?
C. Who should provide support?

VIII. What is the timetable?

IX. What other resources are required?
A. Money?
B. Transportation?
C. Temporary lodging?
D. Food?
E. Other?

X. Who will provide on-going support and feedback?

In *People in Crisis: Understanding and Helping,* Lee Ann Hoff provides a useful model for evaluating the potential effectiveness of an action plan. A good plan should be:

- Problem oriented
- Appropriate to the person's functional level and dependency needs
- Consistent with the person's culture and lifestyle
- Inclusive of significant others and social network
- Realistic, time limited, and concrete
- Dynamic and renegotiable
- Inclusive of follow up[1]

Problem oriented. A good plan focuses on and limits itself to the identified problem. The effective crisis helper recognizes her limitations and declines to engage in long-term therapy. The helper assists a person to design a plan to restore equilibrium, not to indulge in amateur psychoanalysis. Therefore, the plan is specific and limited.

Appropriate to the person's functional level and dependency needs. People function on a variety of intellectual, emotional, physical, and spiritual levels that may not exist in equilibrium (for example, a person may be physically mature but emotionally immature, or intellectually sophisticated but spiritually naïve). Youth workers, parents, and teachers sometimes forget what it's like to be an adolescent. A successful crisis plan is marked by awareness of the functional level of the one who'll be doing the work. Expecting the best of people should never translate into expecting more than they can deliver—that frustrates everyone involved.

Consistent with the person's culture and lifestyle. The effective youth worker is a student of youth cultures—at least those to which she has physical proximity. Few youth workers feel as comfortable in a student's home as they would on that same student's high school or middle school campus. As a result, many youth workers find it difficult to work with and understand the dynamics of families in crisis.

There is an emerging awareness that effective youth ministry, and especially crisis work, seeks to engage students *and* their families—whatever those families look like. Contextualized youth ministry is sensitive to the challenges of working with spiritually, ethnically, racially, and socio-economically diverse family systems. All options should be considered in developing an action plan, even though most will be discarded with cause.

The values and religious belief system of the helper will certainly influence, but should not dictate, the process of planning for action in a crisis. (Translated, this means you may not get what you want.) Because a helper is personally opposed to the use of birth control by adolescents is not cause to ignore its viability when sorting through the options in the action plan for a sexually active teenager. Painful as it may be to contemplate, birth control may be the most responsible near-term course of action for a student who does not share the helper's moral compass. If you can't live with that, refer quickly and bow out gracefully.

Inclusive of significant others and social network. Effective plans of action understand the need we all have for support and encouragement from those who matter to us. This is especially sensitive for the young person who believes no one gives a rip whether he lives or dies. A letter to Ann Landers illustrates this well.

Dear Ann Landers:

Last week I attended a funeral visitation. It was extremely sad. A 13-year-old girl had committed suicide. "Sally" was 5'2", thin, petite, blonde, and wanted desperately to belong. She tried out for cheerleading and didn't make it. In fact, she failed to get in a single club she signed up for. The girl looked so unhappy, my heart ached for her. A few weeks ago Sally won a raffle. It was a certificate from a pizza place that entitled her to invite 14 friends to a pizza dinner. She turned down the prize, because she said she didn't have 14 friends. At the funeral home I sat and watched the school kids come through in droves. I counted well over 100 in the 45 minutes I was there. Later I learned that more than 100 had been in and signed the guest book.[2]

Whoever said, "Friends are the lifeblood of adolescence," was onto something. When times are tough and we wonder how we can go on, who of us hasn't appreciated the encouraging words and physical presence of people we call *friends*? A good plan finds ways to rally the troops around the hurting person in authentic, appropriate ways.

That said, an effective plan also recognizes that a person's social network may be a contributing—even a precipitating—factor in the crisis. A young person struggling with drug dependency will have difficulty kicking a habit while she associates with friends who are users.

Realistic, time-limited, and concrete. What good is a plan that has no basis in reality? Making a plan look good on paper doesn't guarantee success. Why construct false hopes and raise expectations that can never be realized? That's why it's important to account for the possibilities *and* the limitations of the plan so the established goal is attainable in a reasonable time.

Agreeing to a time line is an effective means of motivating people to action. A plan with no dates attached is more *notion* than plan. A time line grants mutual accountability.

Make certain the plan is concrete—meaning specific and easily understood. If, for example, a family lists "learn to cooperate" as one of its goals, help them translate the fuzzy "learn to cooperate" into concrete, measurable skills like "learn to listen respectfully to each other" and "learn to find win-win solutions when we disagree."

Dynamic and renegotiable. Life is never static. As people and situations change, the action plan may need updating or replacement with a new and timelier plan. Let's put a smiley face on it: Sometimes folks "get it" faster than anyone thought possible. If that happens, help them skip ahead in the plan, as long as everyone is confident it's true progress and not just a bluff.

Inclusive of follow up. Follow up is important for several reasons. If you help people take the trouble to develop a responsible action plan, it makes sense to evaluate the process, shore up weaknesses, and celebrate success. You can communicate ongoing commitment to the relationship by including follow-up visits in the plan.

WORKING THE PLAN

The effectiveness of any plan of action is measured by the extent to which people reach their stated goals. The unimplemented plan is just a collection of nice ideas. If the overall goal of crisis intervention is resolution of the immediate crisis or a lessening of the impact of the crisis, the effectiveness of the plan can be assessed by the degree to which it moves everyone involved toward those ends.

It's frustrating to do the hard work of helping people construct a plan only to see them sabotage the strategy or fail to even try it. Here are some of the more common reasons people fail to follow through:

LACK OF CAPACITY

Crisis overwhelms people, short-circuiting normal functioning capabilities. Folks may have very good intentions but find themselves emotionally or psychologically incapacitated—in which case your job is to help them increase capacity rather than scrap the plan.

FEAR OF THE UNKNOWN

Some parents feel like hostages in their own homes, held captive by a teenage son or daughter who somehow managed to take control of the household. Generally, it's fear and not their little prince or princess that holds these people hostage. The chief fear lies in not knowing the outcome should they put their foot down and give their kid a choice between living as a fully functioning partner in the family or working on a new place to live. This is a terrifying scenario to many parents, because it invokes an unknowable future with the child they love.

Some people continue making the best of an awful thing because they fear an even greater loss of control if they take action.

The same is true for the abused child who is old enough to know what's going on and articulate enough to tell someone who could help, but keeps quiet because he doesn't know the end result of speaking up. "Better the Devil We Know" is the name of that sad tune. In such cases, you may be the one to encourage—to put the heart of courage into—a person whose heart is mainly full of fear.

DESIRE FOR CHANGE

Jesus once asked a man, "Do you want to get well?"[3] It's hard to imagine why someone as smart as Jesus would ask such a transparently ridiculous question. Or perhaps Jesus knew that people sometimes prefer sickness to the possibility (and responsibility) of health.

Don't read too much into it, but listen for subtle language cues like those given by people who speak of tragedy in the first person possessive: *my rape, my accident.* Most youth workers can identify at least one young person they can count on for a good crisis every six weeks or so. Kids who learn to fabricate crises as a way to get attention don't see much advantage in genuine resolution.

OWNERSHIP

Students who participate in designing their own action plan are more likely to engage and follow through and less likely to sabotage the plan. The greater their personal investment in the process, the greater the chance they'll work to make it succeed.

LACK OF RESOURCES

Implementing an action plan requires careful attention to financial costs, availability of helping resources, and time constraints. Do your homework on this early and often by keeping your crisis network up to date.

PERSONAL DISCOMFORT

There are situations when an action plan requires people to move well outside their comfort zones. Ask people to count the cost beforehand, while the plan is being written; then call on them to do what they promised—and support and celebrate their efforts to follow through.

3.0 THE BIGGER **PICTURE**

Repeat after us: *It's not about me; it's not about me; it's not about me.*

The impulse to control a crisis is understandable—and misguided. In the bigger picture there are laws governing the conduct of crisis helpers. What's more, there are ethical considerations for engaging people in crisis.

Beyond all of which is this: Being the right person to begin an intervention doesn't necessarily make you the right person to see it through to the end. You'll need to *be* there at the end, but you may not be in charge—by which we mean you may NOT be in charge. Please don't think you can control the crisis recovery path.

An effective action plan shifts responsibility and credit to the people in crisis. Along the way you may need to shift the intervention load to someone better prepared in individual and family therapies.

Nothing personal—you're not a counselor; you're a youth worker.

Say it again: *It's not about me; it's not about me; it's not about me.*

3.1 REFERRAL

Referral is a crucial component in any crisis intervention model. Just in case this is news to you, let's be clear: No one we know is capable of *knowing all*, *loving all*, and *healing all*. Effective crisis helpers figure that out sooner rather than later. Even experienced youth workers who've been involved with young people and their families for decades encounter situations that require more insight or understanding than their training and experience can deliver— or maybe the same skill set, just delivered by someone else. Take a deep breath and repeat after us: *It's not about me; it's not about me; it's not about me.*

Choosing to refer a young person, parent, or family to another helper is not an admission of weakness. It's a sign of strength—a statement that you are committed to helping people find the help they need (and the help they can receive), whatever the source.

To be effective, referral must be *responsible, timely, appropriate,* and *sensitive to financial and other considerations.*

REFERRAL SHOULD BE RESPONSIBLE

A referral is the result of a helper's awareness that another person or agency is better positioned to address the identified problem (or help identify what that problem might be). Young people may feel abandoned when you recommend a referral, so make every effort to assure them you'll be there for them, even though you believe someone else is better positioned to help in the present situation—you're not subtracting, you're *adding*.

JH: Responsible referral requires a crisis network of reputable therapists, specialists, agencies, and programs to which you can direct young people and their families—and, when appropriate, they'll return the favor. I've taken referrals from a variety of people helpers, not so much to come try my youth group as to come meet me and tie into my support network. It's definitely a two-way street if we want it to be.

As you build your crisis network, don't make assumptions. An academic degree (M.A., M.S.W., M.D., Ph.D., etc.) behind someone's name is promising, but it guarantees nothing more than that he has passed the right tests and jumped through the necessary hoops—it implies general preparedness without promising competence. Professional certification and a current license to practice likewise suggest conformity to certain standards of knowledge and regulatory compliance without ensuring the qualities necessary to help. That means you'll have to do some homework.

Ask a dozen people where they would go for help with a medical crisis, drug or alcohol dependency, an eating disorder, individual or family counseling, sex abuse, domestic violence, sexual conduct issues, and post-traumatic stress disorder (add to the list as you wish). Chances are, several names will come up more than once. Once you've narrowed your list, compose a half-page letter to each of them, explaining who you are and what you're doing (building a crisis network) and asking if you can schedule a brief appointment to introduce yourself and visit for a few minutes about her practice and how she prefers to take referrals from outside her field.

When you meet, don't try to pass yourself off as anything other than what you are. Ask questions and listen carefully. Answer questions briefly and honestly. You're not there to tell your life story, you're there to learn and start building rapport.

You'll get a vibe pretty quickly from those who agree to meet with you. Ask yourself:

- Did this person seem to know what she was talking about?
- Did she seem to care about adolescents?
- Did she engage me with openness or did she try to intimidate or bluff me?
- Would I be comfortable introducing her to someone who loves and trusts me?

At the end of this reflection, you'll have a pretty good idea about whether or not you're likely to call on her in a pinch.

You may wonder if therapists and professionals will agree to meet with you—they will. The best of them are genuine people helpers. Almost all of them depend on referrals to one degree or another to pay the rent, so it's to their advantage to take half an hour to meet you and describe their treatment methods, faith perspective, payment structure, and referral and intake procedures.

It's fine to ask about a therapist's faith perspective, but don't be put off if the answer doesn't sound like what you'd expect from a pastor or youth worker. Some therapists decline to talk about their faith with clients, because the problem at hand is not about them and certainly not about their personal theology. (Therapists are more likely to ask questions than make statements about a client's faith.) The important thing to learn in your introductory meeting is whether or not a person seems likely to intentionally undermine the faith of someone you refer.

The helpers who never need referrals for business are people who work in non-profit and publicly funded settings. You may be surprised at the personal alliances you can nurture with such people in the broader community. Youth workers who have endured mass crisis report the significance of relationships with youth workers they already knew when the fat hit the fire. After the Columbine High School massacre, a youth worker said, "We had never agreed about everything theological, but we had been meeting because we knew everyone agreed about loving and caring for kids. The day after the shooting we got together for a few minutes to get our bearings and get organized a little bit. It was amazing to walk into the room that day and embrace each other. That was no time to be reading nametags and asking, 'So what do you do?'

There was a sense of belonging as things got underway. There was no competition. There's no competition to this day."

You don't have to do all this in a week, but keep chipping away at it until your list of intervention resources includes these elements:

- Counseling services—psychiatrists, psychologists, family therapists
- Psychiatric hospitals or specialized units for adolescents
- Crisis telephone lines (include national toll-free hotline numbers)
- Poison control center
- General hospital special care units
- Drug and alcohol abuse programs and support groups
- Adolescent stress units and support groups
- Eating disorder treatment programs and support groups
- Community-health and mental-health centers
- Crisis pregnancy programs
- Police departments (juvenile officers)
- Hospital emergency units
- Family mediation and legal services
- School counselors and administrators
- Psychiatric social workers
- Drug- and alcohol-abuse counselors
- Department of Social Services/Child Protection Services
- Department of Mental Health, community services
- Crisis help centers
- Alcoholics Anonymous
- Narcotics Anonymous
- Church-related support groups
- Anti-abuse programs

It's helpful to compile the following basic information about each program:

- Name of program or individual
- Address
- Telephone number (24-hour crisis number)
- Services rendered
- Admission requirements
- Referral procedure

- Costs
- Name of a specific contact person

Not to put too fine a point on it, but building a crisis network *before* you need it is like backing up your computer files—nobody ever wishes she hadn't done that.

One more thing about responsible referral: There aren't many people who are willing to just look the other way because you work for a Christian organization. Like everybody else, churches and nonprofits are vulnerable to legal action. Sorry to bring this up in the middle of a crisis, but it's important to note that you could face some level of liability if you refer a student and/or family to a specific person or agency later found to be negligent. So, when making referrals, try to suggest more than one therapist or program from which a person or family can choose.

When that's not possible (and if you live in a small town, it almost never is), it's probably wise to describe your recommendation as the best resource you know of locally, as distinct from calling them "The best in the country or I'll eat my hat!" It feels a little silly to even say that in the context of life-and-death interventions, but that's where we are at the moment, so there you have it. (For more on legal considerations, see section 3.2.)

REFERRAL SHOULD BE TIMELY

Consider a referral—

- As soon as you sense a situation is beyond your capabilities
- As soon as you believe specialized treatment may be warranted
- As soon as you believe the person you're helping may be dangerous to himself or others

That said, it's important to remember the difficulty adolescents have forming trusting attachments to adults—especially adults who wear clinical labels. When you decide to refer, take special care to make the transfer as seamless as possible, including the effort to make a face-to-face introduction yourself.

On occasion you'll work with a student who openly resists a referral. That sort of resistance can often be traced to a fundamental fear: "If I need to see a therapist, I must be crazy!" The image of a client lying on a couch, spilling his guts to a therapist who is bored and slightly crazy himself, is enough to send most adolescents right over the edge.

Adolescents, like most of the rest of us, don't want someone playing with their heads. This is why it's important to know as much as possible about those to whom you make referrals: So you can make the introduction in a way that suggests you are asking one friend to meet another friend you believe can offer more help than you can at this time. (Remember: Addition, not subtraction.)

Sometimes young people are resistant or embarrassed, and the only way you'll get them to agree to see someone else is by volunteering to go with them. We've both had experiences helping male victims of sexual molestation who were adamantly opposed to telling their parents or the police until we agreed to go along and support them through the ordeal. Van Pelt says it's how he came to understand what the apostle Paul meant when he talked about weeping with those who weep.

Be aware that parents and guardians may not always support your efforts to see their daughter or son receive professional care. Sorry, but it's naïve to assume all adults will behave in the best interest of their children. In *People of the Lie*, Scott Peck talks about evil parents—those who use and abuse children for their own sinister purposes.[1] Some parents resist outside help because they fear personal exposure. A counselor may discover that their child's presenting problem conceals parental abuse.

If you face sustained resistance from a parent and you have continuing concern for the physical or emotional welfare of a minor child, you may need to solicit the involvement of a social welfare worker who can intervene and order treatment. We'll talk about how to do that in section 5.12.

But the truth is, most parents are heartbroken when they discover their child has been the secret victim of abuse. For most parents the revelation makes sense of behavior that was baffling before. They are saddened but grateful for the hope of getting their child back.

REFERRAL SHOULD BE APPROPRIATE

Since most parents and guardians won't know what to do or where to go for assistance, if you recognize the need for more extensive or specialized help, you can provide an invaluable service by putting them in touch with the right helping resources. The adults, too, may need assurance that you're not ditching them, that their child is not off-the-charts-crazy, that you're *adding* to the team of helpers, not subtracting.

The referral must be appropriate in terms of the circumstances and action plan. A young person battling a cocaine addiction should not be referred to a program that specializes in alcoholism. A therapist who specializes in geriatric issues is probably not the right choice for helping an adolescent struggling with an eating disorder. If you're diligent about maintaining a current crisis network, you'll be prepared to make a responsible and appropriate referral when the time comes (or at the very least, you'll know whom to call for advice).

REFERRAL SHOULD BE SENSITIVE TO FINANCIAL AND OTHER ISSUES

RVP: I took a call from a youth ministry colleague looking for an appropriate treatment facility for a young man in her group. I asked a bit about the boy's history and his present situation in order to zero in on a suitable recommendation. A facility in another state seemed to offer exactly what he needed, and it included a wilderness adventure component that was a perfect match with the boy's love of the outdoors. I agreed to talk with the boy's mom and share what I knew about the program. We had a great conversation, and the more I told her about the program the more excited she became. It seemed like a perfect fit.

Unfortunately, I made a terrible assumption. Because I had visited their church and had a good feel for the socio-economics of their community, I assumed there would be no problem with insurance. Wrong. The boy's father had been out *of work for more than a year, and the family was without medi-cal coverage. Without insurance, the program I recommended would cost them $1,000 a day out of pocket—far more than they could afford. In my naïve enthusiasm I set the mom up for a terrible disappointment. Our conversation shifted from considering a world-class treatment facility to brainstorming community-based programs. I sure wish I could start that one all over again.*

Once you know you need to refer, square one is finding out about financial resources. It doesn't matter how many successful pro-grams exist in your community if the cost is more than a family can afford. Some therapists and specialized treatment programs offer a sliding scale where cost of services is determined by salary level, number of children in the home, and extenuating circumstances (that's why costs and payment structures are part of the introduc-tory conversation when you're building a crisis network—so you know who is positioned to work best with uninsured families).

Many congregations offer pastoral counseling services, and some have full-scale Christian counseling programs to respond to church-family and community needs. Services are typically pro-vided free to parishioners, or fees are determined on an "ability-to-pay" basis. Other churches and helping ministries may provide financial assistance so that individuals and families in need can receive professional counseling. There's a pretty good chance your head of staff knows about these resources or can find out.

Whatever the case, families should always have a clear under-standing of the costs, and arrangement for payment should be in place before treatment begins. It's not your responsibility to nego-tiate those details, but it is your responsibility to learn the gen-eral cost and payment structures on the treatment side and the general insurance and out-of-pocket capacity of the family so you don't add sticker shock to the list of crises.

3.2 LEGAL & ETHICAL **CONSIDERATIONS**

January 1, 2005. Three dozen adolescents are transported to a Minot, North Dakota, emergency room for treatment of injuries suffered during a New Year's Eve party. Three are hospitalized; the rest treated and released. The injured represent close to one-third of the 12-to-19-year-olds who attended.

The injuries are the result of snow sledding—actually, not sledding so much as piling onto cardboard boxes and careening down a hill in quick succession. There is a NO SLEDDING sign posted.

Local police say the sleds hit rocks, a light pole, and each other.

The local chapter of a Christian outreach organization sponsored the party and the director explains that some of the celebrants went down the wrong hill. But, he says, parents of the injured are "gracious." He says most parents believe his organization's intent is to love and help kids grow mentally, physically, and spiritually.

Well—maybe not so much physically.

FIVE REASONS WHY

Why do so many youth workers do so many dumb things? Why are there so many breaches of safety followed by expressions of hope that parents will be "gracious" because, after all, *we mean well*?

Here are five nominations:

IGNORANCE

Most youth workers are volunteers and may be understandably naïve about the legal and ethical responsibilities of working with minors. These people are not building ministries; they're serving kids and families by sponsoring a youth group or chaperoning outings. They've never heard the term *mandated reporter.*[1] They haven't read a booklet or attended a seminar on legal liability, because they don't know there are such things. They're good-hearted folk who might be excused for what they don't know.

There's no excuse for officers and employees of 501(c)(3) tax-exempt corporations who are expected to know that churches and parachurch organizations are required by law to comply with the same legal requirements as, say, schools and camps. Many paid youth workers, church boards, and organizational leaders have a practical awareness of those responsibilities. In fact, at this stage, those who remain clueless do so willfully—as if what they don't know can't hurt them.

For the record, this is an area in which ignorance is not bliss. If something goes wrong because of negligence, youth workers and their organizations are liable *whether they know the law or not.*

THE PERSONAL FABLE

Some youth workers embrace what professor David Elkind calls *the personal fable*—the insidious notion that bad stuff only happens to other people.[2] It often takes a bad experience to motivate such people to proactive and preventive measures. (See also, *hubris, arrogance,* etc.)

ENTITLEMENT

We've known our share of youth workers who regularly and unapologetically break every rule in the liability book, because they believe the rules are excessively restrictive and unrealistic for working with adolescents. Consequently, many of their group activities are lawsuits (and maybe tragedies) waiting to happen.

This is not to say we think youth workers are obliged to play it safe—only that all of us are obliged to do everything we do in the safest possible manner, whether it's dodge ball or technical rock climbing.

DESIRE TO BE LIKED

Who doesn't want to be liked? Most youth workers would rather say yes than no; would rather be seen as cool than conventional; would like to be known for creating adventure and fun. That's fair enough, unless it means placing greater value on being liked than on looking out for the people we serve. At best that's immature; at worst it can be criminal.

UNWILLINGNESS TO PAY THE PRICE

There are fiscal implications attached to responsible youth ministry. Some ministries are simply unprepared to pay the cost of background checks for paid staff and volunteers. Requiring a reasonable student-to-staff ratio at events requires more planning and may involve marginally higher costs. Some folks would rather take their chances.

TAKING OUR CHANCES

The trouble is, taking our chances is riskier today than it's ever been. If attorney Carl Lansing is right, "The numbers of lawsuits and other legal actions being brought against those in Christian ministry have caused this field to emerge as one of the most rapidly expanding "growth industries" for lawyers."[3] Well, in this economy, who couldn't use a growth industry?

Youth workers can't just plead ignorance on legal and ethical issues. Jesus prayed that his followers would be *in* the world but not *of* it.[4] Being *in the world* has always included living as responsible citizens.

If that makes you want to say, "Hey! I just want to love kids for Christ's sake," that's wonderful. We certainly affirm the role of nurturing friendship between adults and students. We also affirm that it's essential to realize those caring friendships don't take place in a vacuum. When you intentionally choose to help another person, you take on the risk of liability if things go badly.

Perhaps it shouldn't be this way, but it is. The unhappy reality is that some people file capricious or malicious lawsuits. To that number, add criminal and civil actions based on evidence of negligence or wrongdoing, and you begin to see the big picture.

Jesus knew that people called by his name would be subject to malice, accusations, misrepresentation, and slander, because that's how our enemy operates. The name *Satan* actually means *accuser*. Casting doubt on the goodness of God by discrediting the people of God must feel like a double win to the accuser. This is not new news. When he dispatched the 12 disciples on a mission trip, Jesus said, "I am sending you out like sheep among wolves. Therefore be as shrewd as snakes and as innocent as doves. Be on your guard ...."[5] Shrewdness and innocence work together in the disciple's tool kit.

Youth workers are notoriously simpleminded when issues of legal responsibility are raised. The only time most youth workers think about legal matters is when students arrive for a retreat without medical release forms (and, hoping for the best, still allow them to climb into the church van). Few of us have really thought through the implications of working with young people in a cultural context where most people seem suspicious of religious leaders and their "product." To most youth leaders, being "wise as a serpent" means protecting themselves from sophomoric practical jokes, not cultivating a functional awareness of how a minor misstep becomes a federal case.

The sledding misadventure at the head of this chapter was reported, with attributed quotes, by the Associated Press and picked up by dozens of media outlets. Was it just a slow news day? No, the sledding story squeezed its way into a news cycle dominated by the Christmas tsunami that killed more than 200,000 people from South Asia to East Africa on December 26, 2004. People are paying attention to what youth workers do when what youth workers do is unnecessarily dangerous.

So then, sheep among wolves, shrewd as snakes, innocent as doves—how does all that play out in our daily involvement with young people and their families? The full scope of legal and ethical issues is broader than we can cover here. There are excellent books on the subject that should be required reading for anyone who manages or supervises a youth ministry program. We are particularly taken with Jack Crabtree's *Better Safe Than Sued*.[6]

Here are four ways to ensure that you act responsibly and cover the legal bases as you respond to the needs of young people and their families.

BE WHO YOU SAY YOU ARE

Advertisers sometimes use a technique called *intentional ambiguity* to create an impression that isn't exactly false, but isn't quite true either. They spin the truth in order to sell products and services. You see this a lot in movie trailers, political campaigns, and, unfortunately, evangelism. This is not okay.

Christian ministries should be distinguished by a reputation for being who we say we are. This is especially important in the way we represent emotional, psychological, or mental services.

No use whatsoever of the term *counseling* should be permitted unless staff (paid or volunteer) are formally trained and currently licensed (where licensing is required) to provide clinical counseling services. Saying that you provide "counseling" or referring to a helping relationship as a "counseling relationship" establishes an expectation of professional competence you should avoid unless you're prepared to back it up. People who present themselves as counselors are accountable and legally liable for that representation.

Terms like *helping relationship, discipling relationship, mentoring relationship, spiritual advisor, coaching, pastoral care,* and perhaps even *pastoral counseling* more accurately represent what most of us do. So unless you are a conventionally qualified counselor—in addition to being a youth worker—avoid misunderstandings or legal entanglements by intentionally calling what you do something *other* than *counseling*.

STAFF SELECTION, SUPERVISION, AND TRAINING

A relatively small percentage of church and parachurch youth ministries fully exploit the potential of a formal application process. We are too often driven to fill empty slots with warm bodies (which is reflected in what most of those positions pay). That said, there is a growing awareness of legal vulnerability among ministries that hire full- and part-time staff members and recruit volunteers to work with minors. Every organization that puts children in contact with adults must show due diligence in determining whether or not the adult has a record of criminal behavior toward young people.

Some administrators fear that making the process too demanding will discourage good people from applying. These people avoid written applications, personal references, background checks, and required orientation classes that might spook new recruits.

All we can say is these cautionary measures are a small price to pay for protecting children from predatory adults, some of whom seek opportunities to prove to themselves that their compulsions are under control—sometimes producing tragic results.

In addition to the typical information requested on a written job or volunteer application, the following questions should be asked of anyone whose responsibilities will include involvement with minors. (For more on state sex offender registries, see section 6.5.)

- Have you been convicted of a criminal offense? If yes, please explain.
- Have you been convicted of child abuse or sexual abuse or been involved in any activity related to molesting or abusing children or teenagers? If yes, please explain.
- What moving violations are on your driving record? Please list and explain.

A surprising number of ministries require personal references but fail to follow up. Design a form that will help reference providers understand the role you are asking youth workers to fill in relation to students and provide a confidential means to express concerns or hesitation. Be certain to protect the confidential nature of these forms.

Some ministries choose to do formal background checks on all present and prospective child and youth workers. Understand that such checks must be uniformly applied. If you choose to do background checks as a requirement for employment or volunteerism, you must first check present staff, then consistently check new applicants. Failure to do so could be grounds for a discrimination suit.

But protecting children only *begins* in the recruitment and selection process. It is the responsibility of a church or youth ministry to provide ongoing training and supervision to ensure the safety of minors in its care.

CONFIDENTIALITY

Most of us assume that something shared in confidence will be kept in confidence. Breaking confidence represents the betrayal of trust—a fundamental element in human relationship and a critical factor in pastoral ministry.

Most men and women involved with young people lack formal training in counseling and tend to approach confidentiality from an extreme position—either overestimating or underestimating its importance in helping relationships.

Youth workers who can't resist the urge to share confidential information won't have to worry about it very long. One major breach of confidence is all it takes for word to spread that you can't be trusted.

On the other hand, don't make unwise promises. Consider:

Karen doesn't make eye contact when she says, "Remember when we were talking about families and how sometimes parents have problems and then as a result their kids have problems too?"

"Sure," Sue replies, "I've seen a lot of that."

"Well..." a tear forms and rolls down Karen's cheek. Sue says nothing but offers Karen a napkin. "I'm sorry," Karen whispers.

"This is really hard for me. Sue, if I tell you something, will you promise not to tell anyone?"

Sue's response comes quickly: "Of course. You know you can trust me. I promise."

Karen takes a deep breath. "Well...for about a year now..."

Karen will fill the next 40 minutes describing a series of incestuous encounters with her stepfather and the self-hatred that drives her increasingly frequent thoughts of suicide.

And Sue will be faced with a monstrous dilemma. Though Karen assures her that just being able to talk about it is very helpful, Sue doesn't believe anything will change at home. What's more, Sue wishes she'd never promised to keep Karen's secret, but she can't imagine violating her commitment. As a result, Sue will be miserable, knowing Karen needs more help than she can possibly offer.

Sue will ask Karen to talk with the youth pastor, and offer to go with her. It's an idea Karen won't even consider. It would cause embarrassment to her mother and might even cause a divorce. Karen is determined to do anything necessary to keep peace at home. But she won't promise not to hurt herself.

Well-intentioned helpers like Sue face this kind of situation all the time. With training in crisis intervention and a balanced understanding of confidentiality, Sue would know it's unhelpful, unsafe, and unnecessary to make blind promises.

Imagine Sue's conversation with Karen taking a different tack at the critical moment:

"I'm sorry," Karen whispers. "This is really hard for me. Sue, if I tell you something, will you promise not to tell anyone?"

Sue takes a deep breath, never breaking eye contact with Karen. "I think you know me well enough to know I care about you; is that right?" she says. Karen looks away. Sue leans forward: "Karen, do you have any question about my willingness to help you with whatever this is—and do it in a way that protects you to the best of my ability?"

"I guess not," Karen says quietly.

"Then I'm going to ask you to trust me with your story. I promise I won't talk about it with anyone else unless I believe we need more help—in which case I'll tell you what I'm doing and why I believe that person can help us. I just have to be sure you're safe. Can you live with that?"

There is a long silence as Karen considers this. Finally she murmurs, "It was hard enough deciding to tell you."

"Tell me what made you choose to tell me," Sue says, and the conversation begins to take off, gently guided by Sue to accomplish what Karen most wants and needs:

• Getting this off her chest
• Finding help to get free of the abusive entanglement with her stepfather
• Getting her mother the help she needs to survive the shock of her husband's wrongdoing
• Getting her stepfather the help he needs to start turning things around

It won't be easy and, as Sue suspects, it will be more than she and Karen can handle on their own. Looking back, they will both understand why Sue had to frustrate Karen's initial desire for confidentiality in order to get the healing started.

RVP: *On occasion a young person has asked me why I won't promise not to tell anyone. My response is simple and straightforward: "Because it may not be in your best interest, and there are certain situations in which I'd be violating the law by keeping that promise."*

JH: I can't remember ever being challenged on that. I volunteer the information; I say, "Look, I can't keep a secret if I truly believe you're in danger. That's not fair to you or me. If you got hurt and I didn't do anything to stop it, I would have to live with that." So far, that's been enough to break the ice. And it gives me a chance to gauge how serious the kid thinks the problem is. Most offer some reassurance that they're not going to do anything stupid. At which point I say, "So tell me the story, and I promise I'll do everything in my power to help you—or help you get to someone who can. We'll limit the number of people who know about it to those who can actually help. Hopefully, that's just me. Does that sound fair?"

The assurance that we understand how difficult it is to say some things and the promise that we won't treat their experiences lightly are all most teenagers require before plunging into the dark waters of trust.

MUTUALLY CONFIDENTIAL RELATIONSHIPS

All this said, it's wise to have a mutually confidential relationship with someone who can help you when you need a reality check, feel stuck, or need referral help. Most licensed therapists have a colleague (often with more advanced training and experience) with whom they regularly visit for consultation and professional supervision. Keeping the identities of the people involved anonymous, they review specific cases and talk about how to proceed.

Some churches have staff therapists who review difficult cases with youth workers. Churches and parachurch groups sometimes contract with a local therapist for consulting services. Access to some level of professional backup is in the best interest of the entire church community as long as information remains confidential.

A parent's right to know what's going on in the life of a minor child demands careful consideration in crisis situations (suicidal or homicidal thoughts or behavior, crisis pregnancy, substance abuse, etc.). This is especially complicated when a young person fails to recognize the need to involve his parents in the solution or adamantly refuses to cooperate if they are involved. There are times when acting in the best interest of a minor means frustrating his short-term desire to keep something from his parents. These times are few-and-far-between, but you have to be prepared for them.

Kids generally fear hurting their parents and want their support. When that's not the case, it signals a deeper (or at least another) problem.

JH: I have a fortunate history of being in the right place at the right time to help students reveal hidden crises to their families. Mostly that's meant being with someone when she broke bad news to her parents. Occasionally it's meant telling the story on her behalf. The situations where I spilled the beans to protect an adolescent's safety have been few, extraordinary, and far between.

Giving young folks a chance to tell their own stories springs from a conviction that our job includes helping them regain an appropriate measure of control. If we seize control of their stories, we contribute to keeping them off balance.

There's also a parent-oriented benefit. Being present when a student discloses his dilemma to a parent reassures the adult that the story has already been filtered through the perceptions of another caring helper. It provides an emotional buffer to keep everyone focused on solving the problem, and it reassures both parent and child that they are not alone in addressing the crisis.

Most youth workers would prefer never to violate a student's wishes by revealing a toxic secret. Indeed, in the rare case when you must go over a kid's head, he may choose to withdraw from you, which is to say he may not like (or trust) you anymore. Since your first obligation in a crisis is to preserve life, this is a regrettable, but worthy, tradeoff. You can work at restoring the relationship over time.

Once you've determined that it's in a young person's best interest to involve her parent or guardian, it's only right to inform her of your decision (except in extraordinary circumstances when it might further aggravate the problem and put the young person at greater risk). This is a last opportunity to urge her to be an integral part of the process. "If I do it, I'm taking control of your story, which I don't want to do. If you do it, *you're* taking control of your story, which is what I think you're hoping for anyway. Let me help you do that by being there to help you deal with your parents."

By informing the student of your intentions, you communicate several important messages:

- I respect you and will not do anything behind your back. I won't be part of a conspiracy to seize control of your life.
- I have nothing to hide. I want you to hear me say what I believe your parents need to know and give you a chance to add to that.
- I love you enough to risk our friendship, which I value very much, in order to keep you from harm.

There are few, if any, aspects of youth ministry that require greater sensitivity. Friendship is a fragile balance—the "lifeblood" of adolescence. Doing what friendship *requires* won't always be understood or appreciated by teenagers—or their parents, for that matter. But if a young person's life is spared or a family is restored in the process, it's worth whatever price you pay.

THE LAW REGARDING CONFIDENTIALITY

If you are an ordained member of the clergy or if you are licensed as a professional counselor, there are laws in nearly every state that protect your rights and monitor your responsibilities as a pastoral counselor or therapist. Those laws also protect the rights of those who seek your counsel. It is your responsibility to know the law, any exceptions to that law, and to abide by it. Generally speaking, exceptions requiring and permitting disclosure include:

- The duty to warn others of imminent and real danger of physical harm
- The duty to report child abuse to proper authorities
- Discussion within the context of formal supervision by a licensed mental health professional
- Informed, voluntary consent to disclosure by the client[7]

If you're not ordained clergy or a licensed counselor, you may not be covered by your state's confidentiality rules. That means it's possible you might be required by a court to divulge information shared in a confidential manner. It's not common, but it can happen.

The other side of the coin is that counselors, teachers, medical professionals, and the police have historically been *mandated reporters* with regard to suspicion or knowledge of child abuse of any kind (physical, emotional, or sexual). Mandated reporting laws now include pastors, youth workers, and childcare providers in most states.

We think you should assume you're required by law to report evidence of abuse. How to go about that reporting is covered in section 6.2. This is another area in which it is *your* responsibility to be familiar with the law of your state and abide by it. The "I didn't know I was required" defense will not hold up in court. If you're a mandated reporter and fail to comply, you place yourself, your ministry, and its leadership in jeopardy.

DOCUMENTATION

A landmark clergy malpractice suit in the '80s was taken all the way to the California Supreme Court and ultimately dismissed, because the pastoral staff was able to demonstrate they'd acted responsibly in caring for a parishioner who sought their help but ultimately chose suicide. As soon as the staff recognized the gravity of the young man's emotional condition, they referred him to professional counseling. Because they carefully documented the steps they took to get him professional care, their defense was strong.

Much of the people helping in youth ministry happens on the fly. Students who are reticent to set up an appointment to talk about their struggles may simply walk up to you after youth group and blurt it out. Occasionally, people requesting your help will be strangers to you. Whether you know people before they approach you for help, and whether the interaction is formal or informal, it's a good idea to make and discreetly save notes about the date the conversation took place, what was disclosed, and any recommendations you made. This kind of documentation can be helpful should you be required to provide testimony in a court of law. A simple intake interview form is provided in section 6.8.

It's worth underscoring that documentation of a confidential nature must be stored under lock and key. If you maintain records on a computer, protect them with a password. When you leave a church or parachurch ministry, take the records with you. Just as documenting your interactions can be vital if you are called upon to defend your involvement, failing to protect confidential documents can also get you in hot water.

4.0 PREVENTIVE **PARTNERSHIPS**

Apart from acquainting them with the God of mercy, there's not much you can do to prepare the young for an asteroid strike. It's just one of those things. To a slightly lesser degree, this is also true of hurricanes, tornadoes, earthquakes, blizzards, fires, and floods. Add catastrophic disease to the same list. And divorce, plane crashes, and train derailments. And serial killers, car bombers, and kidnappers.

These are the things that come out of nowhere to disrupt life-as-we-know-it. Even one of Job's *comforters*—pausing in the middle of hammering Job with the bad news that bad things happen mainly to bad people—had to admit that, as surely as sparks fly upward, our sort are born to trouble.[1] Or as a Hemingway character said in *A Farewell to Arms*: "The world breaks everyone."[2]

Sometimes rocks fall from the sky, and there's nothing a teenager or a youth worker can do about that except thank God she's alive when the dust settles. And try to figure out what to do next.

In other cases, preventive measures are in order. Youth workers are uniquely positioned to prevent all manner of heartache. This is not to say a youth worker can head off every disaster, but she can do a lot if she knows how. And the *how of prevention* is much like the *how of intervention*: It is relational, and it springs from partnerships with students, parents, schools, and sometimes law enforcement.

PREVENTION IS RELATIONAL

Arthur C. Clarke is a double hyphenate: scientist-novelist-inventor. Clarke wrote *2001: A Space Odyssey*; he also wrote the basic theory upon which satellite communication technology is built. He must have been one of the most frustrated scientists on the planet at the end of 2004.

Clarke, a resident of Sri Lanka since 1956, was working on Project Warn with the Japan US Science Technology and Space Applications Program.[3] The project was scheduled to test a tsunami warning system for the Asian region (like the systems already in place elsewhere). He was working on the warning system, because he knew the vulnerability of coastal populations along the Indian Ocean from Thailand to East Africa. He was working on it, but it wasn't complete when a 9.0 earthquake disrupted the water off the northwest coast of Sumatra, kicking out two giant waves that surged in a 360-degree pattern that killed more than 200,000 people outright from Indonesia to Somalia.

Clarke knew, perhaps better than anyone, that satellites were limited in detecting tsunamis, because the waves surge more than swell (there's no obvious surface change to signal what's happening). In this case the water level rose and moved at the speed of a commercial jetliner without generating anything to *see* until it was too late to respond. Project Warn includes data based on *proximity*, because that's what it takes to detect a tsunami. *Proximity* in the form of a network of sensors spaced across a wide expanse of water to measure change patterns.

The system was scheduled for a test simulation in 2005.

In youth work, relationship is proximity. We can't prevent a crisis in a kid's life if no one is close enough to sense a disturbance. Effective crisis prevention engages a network of friends and caring adults who look out for each other and know each other well enough to sense when something is going wrong.

What sorts of crises can such a network prevent?

- **Addiction:** By observing and responding to patterns of self-medication, impulsiveness, compulsiveness, suggestibility, and poorly developed refusal skills
- **Bullying:** By creating safe environments where no one is permitted to harass or demean another
- **Co-dependency:** By observing and addressing unhealthy attachments, people pleasing, and rescuing
- **Cutting** and **Self-mutilation:** By observing and responding to anger, frustration, anxiety, victimization, and efforts to cover up or display wounds and scars
- **Eating Disorders:** By observing and responding to unhealthy body images and unwholesome attitudes toward food
- **Running Away** or **Flight:** By observing and responding to patterns of family conflict, frustration, and anxiety
- **Sexual Exploitation:** By observing and responding to evidence of low self-esteem, eating disorders, or peer-like attachments with much older or much younger people
- **Suicide:** By sensing and responding to depression, heartbreak, anger, or hopelessness
- **Truancy:** By observing and responding to poorly developed or declining learning patterns, perceptual difficulties, and a noticeable lack of motivation
- **Violence:** By observing and responding to signs of victimization, frustration, anger, vandalism, animal cruelty, and self abuse

PREVENTION SPRINGS FROM PARTNERSHIPS

In most cases, the network of relationships that makes prevention work is natural and obvious to the casual observer. It's a network of the family, friends, and caring adults who are near enough to notice when something goes wrong.

Sometimes that's not enough. Sometimes what's required is a network of partnerships that includes other students, friends, siblings, parents, teachers, and school staff—and, occasionally, law enforcement, physicians, and social services. Keep in mind that:

✦ **The Youth Worker's Guide To Helping Teenagers In Crisis**

- Students engaged in peer mediation do an enormous amount of good for each other
- Friends are generally the first to sense signs of struggle
- Siblings often see what parents miss
- Parents (if they're functional) are the principal stakeholders in any child's welfare
- Teachers' almost daily contact with students enables them to track the ebb and flow of social interaction and emotional well-being
- School administrators can bring focus and urgency to an emerging problem if others are slow to act
- Physicians may be able to diagnose and treat physical disorders before they reach crisis proportions
- Local law enforcement personnel would rather prevent people from criminal activity than arrest them after the fact
- In extreme circumstances, child protective services can act to remove a minor from harm's way

4.1 YOUTH **GROUPS**

No one is closer to kids than other kids. That's why peer-to-peer evangelism is better than outsider evangelism; it's a proximity thing. It's also why mobilizing students to create a preventive community makes so much sense.

Students engage their peers even more than teachers, and at potentially greater depth and across a wider range of life issues than any adult. We say *potentially greater,* because it's possible to keep things at the level of video games and pop culture gossip. Plenty of kids do just that, which is exactly what effective youth ministry works to overcome.

The age in which *fun* was the primary tool for youth ministry is well past. *Engagement* is king, but engagement in what? Our answer is: Engagement in *wholeness* (including quite a bit of fun, since you mention it).

To put it in more or less biblical terms, youth workers are charged with making *disciples*, and making disciples is communal by nature. This isn't the place to explore holistic disciple making; we bring it up only to contextualize the priority of engaging students in community, because community is where crisis prevention happens. We don't think the most effective peer-to-peer prevention happens between just two kids. We think it happens in healthy youth ministry communities.

So, without suggesting that prevention is the point of community (which it certainly is not), here are four ways healthy youth ministry communities accomplish crisis prevention.

OPEN ENVIRONMENTS

You can tell a youth group is open when everyone isn't the same. This isn't easy. Youth groups tend to look a lot like the neighborhoods where they reside, and most neighborhoods are not multicultural. That will take however long it takes. Meanwhile, it's worth remembering that just because everyone we know descended from grandparents who came from the same part of Africa or Asia or Europe or Central America doesn't mean they're all the same. Here's a proposition: If you're not close—really close—to someone who disagrees strongly with your politics, loathes your music, and can't fathom your taste in fiction, there's something wrong. We're not kidding; it's in the Bible.[1] And there's something wrong with any youth group that isn't open enough to be inviting to people from a wide range of tastes and perspectives on life. This too is in the Bible.

JH: When our daughter Kate was a sophomore in high school, we took her to a youth group that was definitely not open. Kate was post-punk at the time: black clothes, eight-hole Doc Martens, *very* black hair. When she showed up at church, the other students seemed friendly enough, but they kept their distance at school. It didn't matter that Kate loved Jesus; nobody knew that, because to them she didn't *look* like anybody who would love Jesus.

The only students who reached out to her at school were people who thought she looked like someone who might party with them. It was pretty discouraging. It wasn't until the Easter break mission trip that folks were forced to spend enough time with Kate to find out what a treasure she is. If she'd been less resolute about building relationships with Christians, the final score might have been Partiers: 1, Youth Group: 0.

Look around your youth room. You should see someone approaching genius and someone who's a borderline dunce. You should see a hard-core jock sitting next to a propeller-head. You should see someone who doubts more than she believes arm-in-arm with someone whose faith puts yours to shame. There ought to be a punk, a popster, an opera freak, a wigger, and a goat roper who get along really well unless the conversation turns to music. If you're the leader and you don't see that when you look around the room, it's your responsibility to work on that. If you're not the leader, it's still your responsibility to work on it; you'll just have to approach it differently.

RVP: *A while back I did a student training day at a church that frankly baffled me. I don't think I've ever been in a place that was more caring, more energized, more attentive, or more diverse (by a long shot) in every measure of diversity for both students and adults.*

When I got a chance to ask the youth ministry leader what in the world was going on, he just smiled. "You're not the first to notice," he said. "The only answer I can give you is in the prayer our pastor prays every day: 'Jesus, send us the people no other church in town wants.'"

I admitted I hadn't heard anybody pray that before, because that's precisely what most of us don't want.

"Yeah," he said, "and we have our share of crazies around here. But I'm convinced that's why we have this amazing community."

I wonder what would happen in our youth ministries and churches if we were all that open. And I wonder if we'll ever find out.

SAFE ENVIRONMENTS

It's your job to see that nobody gets hammered by anyone in your group—physically, emotionally, intellectually, socially, or spiritually. Healthy communities create the kind of safety that draws people back over and over, because, really, where else would they go to get that sort of unconditional love and acceptance?

Creating a safe room begins when you break the code of silence. The code of silence revolves around the pretense that everything is fine when everything is not, in fact, fine. Some days are wonderful. Some days are better than others. The rest suck. Everyone knows this. When the social norm in a group is pretending no one has any recent failures and nobody is facing anything they can't handle, there's just no way that's a safe room. It takes a safe room to create a safe group, and that what's required to help people with small problems instead of being frozen out of their lives until things fly apart.

No one can wish a group to safety. Safety is engendered bit by bit through storytelling. Your group is safe when *any* story can be told without fear of retribution—and, perhaps more importantly, with hope of getting help if that's what's required for a happy ending. That doesn't mean going around the room and putting everyone on the spot every time you're together (which is actually a good strategy for *emptying* a room). It means communicating that each one's story is welcome. That includes listening compassionately, withholding judgment, and keeping confidence appropriately. (For more on confidentiality, see section 3.2.)

By and large, teenagers know when things are upside down, because they suffer everything from attention deficit to weight loss to relational meltdowns. Some kids try to numb the pain with more of what's causing the pain—like smokers who have to step outside to light up because their lungs are killing them. It doesn't take long to figure out that's not working. What it takes is a safe place to get a grip on that reality and decide what to do about it. Judgment from your group won't speed that up. But honest, inviting questions will: "Is this behavior really working for you? Because you seem miserable (or desperate, manic, out of control, scared, or whatever fits)."

So hear us when we say safety is not about taking an "It's all good" attitude. It's just that the less you judge, the more students will reveal, which will lead a healthy group to ask—and get—more honest replies to harder questions than you can get otherwise.

Teach your group the practices of deep listening from section 2.3. When your group learns to ask good questions and listen well, when your group learns to withhold judgment without surrendering wisdom, and when your group learns to keep confidence appropriately, the result is trust—and out of trust grows safety.

Safe rooms make space for silence. If you ask a question and no one answers, it may mean everyone is confused. Or asleep. Or gone. Or the silence may mean everybody's thinking. If you can't tell which, ask (one sign that a room is becoming safe is that someone will give you a straight answer).

Safe rooms make space for the unexpected.

JH: I was trying to get through my curriculum with a peer leadership group the night I learned this for good. It was a highly motivated group of student leaders—except that night, when they were going nuts. I know I was irritated, because I got sarcastic with them. Nothing. They settled for two minutes, and then they were off again. Finally, I closed my Bible and asked, "Is there something else we should be doing tonight?"

"No, we'll be good, sorry," somebody said. "It was just a weird day, that's all. Sorry."

I asked about the weirdness.

"Well, there was a suicide after school yesterday, and another last night. And this morning two more kids tried."

Oh, well then. Maybe there *was* something else we should be doing.

I learned to ask this question when otherwise focused groups go fuzzy: "Is there something else we should be doing now?" It's an honest question. Usually the answer is no, the group pulls itself together, and everything is smooth from that point.

And every once in a while I learn what it is that we should be doing instead of what I planned.

Take the time required to create a genuinely safe group. When you do, they'll become partners in prevention by looking out for each other during all those hours when you're not around.

CULTIVATE EMPATHY

Empathy means identifying with what another person feels. Empathy is a standard feature in healthy groups, because everyone knows the truth about everyone else. And knowing the truth opens the door to understanding that we're all in it together.

When we get close enough to each other, it turns out no one is better or worse or really all that much different from the rest. This is the oldest lesson in the book: "All have sinned and fall short of the glory of God."[2] "...through the disobedience of the one man the many were made sinners."[3] "There is no one righteous, not even one."[4] The only differences between us are not in the facts of our brokenness and wrongdoing but in the *details*. It's the old joke from the exceedingly large and talented comedian Louie Anderson, who said he saw a picture of a guy who weighed 1,200 pounds. "Twelve hundred pounds!" Anderson mugged, his jowls going slack. "Now *that* guy has a weight problem!"

The empathetic group has stopped trying to divert attention from their weakness by pointing out the weakness of others. The result is...you guessed it: Ever-increasing health.

It's probably not a wild assumption to guess that most students get lost on the emotional map once they move outside their comfort zone. Since empathy involves identifying with another person's emotions, it's good to have a shared language. Use the emotional map in section 6.3 to help your group build their empathic vocabulary.

It's worth noting that all the language in this chapter is provisional. That's because your group is always changing, kicking older kids out the top end to try what they've learned on the rest of the world, and importing new classes of students who, chances are, know very little about safe rooms and healthy groups. Add to that the likelihood that students will gladly bring friends to a healthy group, and you're looking at a job that's never quite complete. So—there's your job security.

GROUP INTERVENTION AND REFERRAL

You can teach students the art of crisis intervention. Mostly this kind of intervention won't be called *intervention*. It will simply be called *friendship*.

Help students learn that calling someone a friend means more than saying, "I like you." Friendship is a commitment to look out for the best interests of another person. That means helping her get what she wants—unless what she wants is not what she needs. It means making it difficult for her to engage in self-destructive behavior. It means asking tough questions when she gets too big for her britches.

If an enemy is someone who stabs you in the back, a friend is someone who stabs in the front, surgically holding you accountable to get the help you need to keep growing. Help your students understand that a friend does this not because he's better than you but because he is so nearly the same as you. Teach your students the principles of *intervention* in section 5.12.

Then you can teach them to go get help for a friend when they're both in over their heads. Referral is hard for young people for the same reasons it's hard for youth workers: pride, fear, ambition, wishful thinking... Help students learn to let go by helping them understand there's no failure in admitting a friend needs more than they can deliver, just as there's nothing heroic about keeping it to themselves once they have reason to believe their friend is in deep trouble.

The confession we asked you to repeat after us earlier is worth passing on to your students, as well: *It's not about me; it's not about me; it's not about me.*

The methodology of student referrals is much the same as it is for youth workers, minus the crisis network. That's why they have you. Teach students how to send or bring their friends to you for the next level of help. In addition, help them identify the staff member at school who's mostly likely to pitch in if they need help fast. And give them the Boys and Girls Town National Hotline number (800-448-3000) as a go-to resource in a pinch. They're not just knowledgeable about defusing emotional time bombs; they also have a terrific database of helping resources in every area code.

4.2 PARENTS

Don't you hate it when people paint all adolescents with the same brush—when they make unfair generalizations about all teenagers because of the misbehavior of a few? Yeah, well, we used to do that with parents.

It was easy. We were inexperienced and unsure of ourselves, easily threatened and often intimidated. So we saw parents as clueless at best and quite possibly malevolent, and we acted as if those things were true until proven otherwise. That was a bad thing. We didn't know what we didn't know. Or we knew and were just arrogant.

We know better now.

PARENTS AS PARTNERS

Most parents mean well (those who don't mean well are in a special class reserved for psychopaths and the evil).

Most parents do the best they can under the circumstances. Those circumstances may include: Mediocre to lousy preparation for parenthood, occupational and financial stress, personal unhappiness, weakness, brokenness, distraction, addiction, confusion, misinformation, fatigue, anxiety, immaturity, poor relational skills, and spiritual rootlessness—not to mention the naïveté, arrogance, fear, ambition, and wishful thinking they share in common with students and youth workers and, uh...us.

Parents are human, with all the positive and negative characteristics attached to that blessedly maddening condition.

Some parents view their children with contempt, but most do not.

Some parents are relentlessly self-absorbed, but most are not.

Some parents are unreasonable, but most are not.

This means most parents can be partners in prevention—if only because they have the proximity to pay attention to their kids. Far beyond that, a lot of parents are looking for partners to help them in the task that's uniquely theirs: Preparing their children to be women and men.

Here are nine ways to engage parents as partners in prevention:

REALITY CHECK

If you think something may be out of balance with a student, check with his parents. Don't alarm them, and don't create suspicion; just ask how he's doing. If they want to know why you're asking, say you're not sure (unless you *are* sure, in which case you may be having the wrong conversation). Tell them something just feels slightly off and you wondered if it was just you.

If they seem worked up by your question, remind them that episodic short-term depression, anxiety, anger, attention deficit, fatigue, weight fluctuation, and general goofiness are all pretty common in adolescence and nothing to be distressed about. Invite them to give you a call if they see anything that worries them.[1]

EARLY WARNING

Ask parents what teenagers and other parents are talking about around the neighborhood. Your sub-cultural awareness may alert you to something another adult would miss. This notion is borrowed from epidemiology in which clustered health events may be an early warning of a larger public concern.[2]

For instance, if your casual questioning turns up an unexpected number of references to fighting, pregnancies, eating disorders, runaways, hospitalizations, car accidents, or exploding trailer homes—that may tip you off to an increase in sexual activity, drinking, rage, gang activity, or the influx of a new drug to your community. As in epidemiology, such clusters usually turn out to be coincidental and unrelated; but every once in a while they point to something significant.

ADVISORS

Ask a few parents to join an advisory group. It doesn't matter whether it's an official committee or a *kitchen cabinet* with no official powers. Your willingness to ask questions and listen will score points throughout the system. The parents who join your band will be a conduit for information you need to know and a channel for communicating with other parents. Be on guard against hijackers looking for undue influence, and beware of stacking the group with people who are such fans they can't be trusted to give sound advice. Other than that, knock yourself out.

NETWORKERS

There are parents in your network who can introduce you to people you need to know. A parent may be able to get you a meeting with city officials, school district personnel, or hospital staff. That way, you don't have to start from scratch in building your crisis network. Let parents help you get where you need to go in the larger community. The same wisdom applies to big-church politics. If you need support from committees or staff in other parts of a complicated congregational hierarchy, get parents to smooth the way for you.

INTERPRETERS

You can't give up any details if you're doing crisis work, but don't fail to let some parents know the broad strokes of what you're doing. This means cultivating relationships with parents who have a grasp of what you're up against and what you're doing about it. There's a good chance you're the first youth worker in your organization to take prevention and intervention seriously. That may translate to more time with your office door closed than the youth workers who came before you; or it may mean more time away from your office altogether, engaging students at school, in their homes with their parents, or problem-solving over soft drinks at a nearby restaurant or public park. It helps to have parents who can vouch for the value of these work patterns.

JH: A church leader who raised two perfect children couldn't understand why I spent so much time over at the school with troubled students. She asked, "Shouldn't you be spending more time here, with our kids?" My rather heated defense was that three of my last five campus interventions were with the children of church leaders. In a cooler moment it was nice to know there were parents who knew enough about what I was doing to back me up on the value of my relationship with the schools—if only so I could be there when a church leader's daughter was in trouble.

BENEFACTORS

Bottom line: Parents can help get crisis prevention and intervention work funded. The more parents know about crisis, the more helpful they'll be in trying to get what you need for the job.

CRAP DETECTORS

Bounce your ideas about prevention off parents who see the world a bit differently than you do. When you say, "This is what I'm planning to do. What am I missing?" they will help you refine, expand, refocus, or scrap your plan.

ADVOCATES

Parents are natural stakeholders in your prevention efforts. Turn them into advocates by asking them to help you get from where you are to where you believe you need to be.

INNKEEPERS

There will come a time when you need to arrange temporary housing for a student who needs a time-out from her household—or a parent in the same situation. There are parents who can give you a *yes* on that in real time. In your crisis network, be sure to include a few families who are willing and able to do that.

The only things that can prevent you from engaging parents as partners in prevention are:

- Your own pride, fear, shortsightedness, or inertia (sometimes experienced as laziness)
- Mutual misunderstanding
- Organizational politics

You are responsible for the first category. If you can't overcome your pride, fear, shortsightedness, or inertia, get some help. If you can't bring yourself to get some help, get some help for that. Here are some ideas to overcome misunderstanding and political resistance.

- Form that advisory group now. It doesn't have to be fancy. It can be a monthly coffee klatch at Denny's. Make time for it now.
- Ask questions and listen. Keep a running list of things you'd like to know from parents, and ask around. Fill awkward silences, and divert meaningless chatter with meaningful questions. Turn your list into an occasional survey for adult groups in your community. Learn this truth: *People listen to people who listen.*
- Offer periodic live briefings for parents. Pick a subject you know parents need to hear about, then wrap that in a subject you know parents *want* to hear about. Offer a live briefing twice a year or once a quarter or every time there's a blue moon or a fifth Sunday (excluding holiday weekends of course). You don't have to do all the heavy lifting on this. Bring in an expert from time to time—a practitioner in a specific area of crisis intervention—for a 15-minute talk and a 30-minute Q&A. Caution: Agree in advance that this is not the time for a sales pitch, and offer to distribute brochures and business cards to interested parents yourself.

- Offer an opt-in parenting newsletter via hard copy or e-mail. A good example is the *YS Student eMail Newsletter* from Youth Specialties.[3] When you see who opts in, you'll know who's interested in what you're trying to do (which is much more valuable than blanketing every parent on the mailing list).
- Develop a peer-to-peer learning and support network. We're partial to a process called *Developing Capable Young People.*[4] Get training for yourself and a couple of parents, and go to town. This kind of thing is also a nice community outreach to parents.
- Declare yourself available and capable for intervention. If parents don't know you're available and capable, why come to you for help? Tell your prevention and intervention story directly and humbly. Better yet, get parents to do that for you.

4.3 SCHOOLS

If we hear one more person-who-ought-to-know-better bad-mouth teachers, there's gonna be trouble. Nobody has more contact with students than teachers. School administrators and staff are right behind them. Does anybody think they're in it for the money? Or the short workday? Yeah, right.

There are exceptions, and much of the system is broken, but most of the teachers we know are dedicated to students, and they're surprised and hurt when their devotion is questioned. The same goes for administrators and staff, most of whom are committed professionals. That makes them natural allies, once it's clear you share their commitments.

One of those commitments—right behind safety—is to see that nothing keeps students from learning. That's the real motive behind closed campuses. Administrators aren't trying to keep youth workers off campus; they're trying to keep *anyone* off campus who might be a distraction to their core mission of educating students. If you can show that you will consistently and unselfishly contribute to that mission, you'll be welcome because *you'll* be the ally.

HOW TO FORM PREVENTIVE PARTNERSHIPS WITH SCHOOLS

1. Understand what Jesus meant when he said he "did not come to be served, but to serve, and to give his life as a ransom for many" (Matthew 20:28, Mark 10:45). Take that attitude with you when you go to school.

2. Get familiar with the language of crisis prevention and intervention as it relates to school-based prevention and intervention programs. Section 6.7 is a glossary of terms to help you follow the conversation. School-based prevention programs have about as much jargon as religious folk do, so be patient and do your homework—or carry this book in your car so you can look up terms you didn't quite catch while you're still able to remember the words and abbreviations you heard.

3. Align yourself with a community-based organization dedicated to helping schools. Don't start something new, and don't affiliate with a religious organization. Look for local chapters of Parents for Drug-Free Youth or the National Family Partnership or Mothers Against Drunk Driving or whatever the equivalents are called in your community. These organizations are always in need of fresh blood.

- Go to a couple of meetings, and do a lot of listening.
- Once you figure out who the old-timers are, schedule a lunch appointment with one or two of them so you can ask them about the history of the organization in your community. (There's a good chance there have been ups and downs along the way.)
- Take on a small project and over-deliver.
- Offer to host the next meeting at your facility, if that's appropriate.
- After you establish yourself as a willing and thoughtful participant, tell them you'd like to visit with a couple of site administrators to see how they feel about their prevention programs and resources.

4. Ask students which school administrators have a reputation for caring about kids, and make an appointment with those indi-

viduals so you can introduce yourself and ask on behalf of your community organization (number three above) what they wish they had for prevention and intervention at their site. In the initial meeting—

- Listen more than you talk.
- Promise to report your conversation to the community organization you're aligned with—ask if there's anything from the conversation that the administrator wishes you wouldn't include in your report.
- Offer your services, especially if the school should ever have concerns about a student whose family is a part of your congregation. (This is a little more complex if you're in a parachurch organization with no recognizable parent membership, so choose your words carefully to be sure there's no hint of misrepresentation.) This is a fairly vague offer, since you're not going to provide a directory of your members (nor should you); but it's interesting to see how student-friendly administrators put two and two together when they're looking for community support.
- Ask if you can call them if you ever have knowledge of issues that may affect a student's performance at school— nothing confidential: Things like a family crisis that a student might not think to mention to his teachers.
- This is why God gives us business cards: Leave one (but don't leave information about your program or organization. If such information is requested, promise to bring it to them, then do so within 48 hours).

5. Don't cry wolf, but when you have a student in crisis, with his and/or his parent's permission, let the administrator you identified know he may not be at 100 percent for a few days and how you know that. Ask if she would be kind enough to inform the student's teachers of what's going on. Let her know she can call you if things get rocky for the student. Later, let her know when things are resolved, and thank her for being part of the solution.

6. Find out what the school has done in the past to highlight the annual Red Ribbon Week (dedicated to awareness of drug and alcohol abuse the last week of October), and offer to help with the

next one. Then blow their doors off with cool, kid-friendly stuff that makes the administration look good.

7. When the time is right, offer to support a Students Against Destructive Decisions chapter as an off-campus sponsor. (SADD was originally founded as Students Against Driving Drunk and may still go by that or a similar name where you live.)

8. Don't ever abuse the trust. Go back to number one above.

RVP: *A few months ago two suicides in quick succession rocked one of our high schools. A mutual friend asked if I would meet with the principal to see if I could help. I went to the meeting with a load of the best resources I knew about, expecting nothing in return. I just wanted to honor our friend's request and serve the principal as well as possible. After the introductions I asked specific questions about what they'd already done with faculty, staff, and students; he asked how I knew to ask about those things, and I told him a little about my work with students.*

Finally, the principal asked, "Do you ever speak to students? Would you be willing speak to our students in an all-school assembly? I think you could really help us." Reflecting on the conversation later I thought: You know, if we spent half as much time building relationships and credibility through serving people as we do dreaming up ways to get noticed, we would have more involvement on school campuses than we would know what to do with.

✚ The Youth Worker's Guide To Helping Teenagers In Crisis

4.4 LAW **ENFORCEMENT**

There's probably an officer at your local police department or sher-
iff's substation who is the point person for adolescent issues—there
may be more than one. This person maintains the departmental
link to Child Protective Services, Child Welfare Services, Children's
Services, or whatever it's called in your area. Someone in the
administration at your local middle school or high school knows
who that person is and will introduce you. Over time learn:

- What law enforcement officials think about the school-
  based prevention and intervention programs in the
  community.
- About the level of cooperation between the department and
  school administrators. Mention administrators you know
  by name, but don't reveal what you think of them until you
  know what the officer thinks of them.
- About the Student Attendance Review Board (SARB) or
  whatever is in place to address school truancy and
  associated issues.
- About the department's attitude toward SADD and Red
  Ribbon Week.

SERVE THE PUBLIC SERVANTS

Here's what you can do to serve local law enforcement:

- Help law enforcement have an appropriate presence during Red Ribbon Week.
- Discourage the kind of involvement that makes officers look bad.
- Help them dissociate from older students' attitudes about DARE—the heavily funded Drug Awareness Resistance Education program that is so-very-grade-school, if you know what we mean. In general, it has a childish association for a majority of high school students. And if you want our advice, don't become a DARE volunteer. Leave that for people in children's ministry (even if your responsibilities include younger grades. DARE is just a tough association to shake off for high schoolers).

STUDENT ATTENDANCE REVIEW BOARD (SARB)

If there's an SARB in your area, ask if you may observe a morning of interventions, then consider offering your services as a community representative.

JH: If you don't already have SARB or something like it in your community, keep your eyes open; I suspect it's the wave of the future (whatever name it travels under). Truancy, as a precursor to dropping out, is a very big deal. The 2000 census found high school dropouts had only a 52 percent employment rate, earning 35 percent below the national median earnings. And then there's the crime. Kids who are supposed to be in school commit an extraordinary percentage of juvenile crimes.[1]

All of this brought the U.S. Departments of Justice and Education to the table looking for solutions. A couple of quotations from that dialogue suggest someone may soon welcome your involvement:

The education system can't do it alone; our collective challenge must be to address truancy prevention in an aggressive manner. We must invest in strategies that enlist schools, families and community leaders and empower them to take charge.
—Deborah J. Daniels, assistant attorney general for DOJ's Office of Justice Programs

SARB brings together representatives from law enforcement, school, and community organizations to intervene in cases of chronic truancy, thereby reducing the risk factors and criminality that ride the wake of truancy. SARB's legal teeth are in the State Compulsory Education Laws and reflect this definition of *neglect* from the U.S. Department of Health & Human Services: "*Educational neglect* includes failure to provide appropriate schooling, special educational needs, or allowing excessive truancies."[3]

SARB confronts referred students and their parents or guardians and enforces school attendance by whatever means are at hand, including arrest (in cases of belligerence or chronic noncompliance).

The commitment generally takes half a day every other month (give or take), and it's no fun whatsoever. But it performs a service for the community and it places you in a cooperative relationship with the very people in law enforcement and public education you most want to know and serve for the benefit of prevention and intervention with the students and families you serve.

The cooperative relationship you develop with law enforcement is a service to your community and an investment against future needs. Honestly, what it may accomplish as much as anything else is making you comfortable phoning and walking in the front door at the local station. Add to that knowing whom to call to get referrals and advice when you really need it, and it's worth the time and effort.

5.0 WHEN & IF: **SPECIFIC CRISES**

Stick around youth ministry long enough and you'll encounter crisis in just about every flavor. In many cases it's a question of *when* not *if*.

This section lays out background issues and basic action plans for some of the most common crises.

5.1 ACCIDENTS

The burning questions when there's been an accident with injuries and death are: *Why? Why did this have to happen? Why were they so stupid? Or careless? Or unlucky? Why would God allow this kind of thing?* Accidents ignite profound doubt and exploration. They also generate blame.

The usually quieter but equally pressing questions are *Why not me? Why did I decide not to go with them? Why did I survive? Why wasn't I injured?* This is the beginning of *survivor's guilt*.

Glib answers about *everything happening for a reason* are good for filling an uncomfortable silence but not much else. Adolescents require more direct, thoughtful, and honest responses than that. "I don't know why this happened—it was an *accident*" is better than "I guess his time was up."

JH: Twenty years after his death in a plane crash, I interviewed most of the people who were closest to the rock-and-roll evangelist Keith Green. Almost all of them were clear that Keith was at fault. He was the pilot. He didn't do the math. He overloaded the small plane. He was cocky. But it was an accident; he didn't set out to do harm. He was a smart guy who made a fatal mistake. After two decades, nobody tried to convince me it was part of God's plan and no one viewed it as a victory for the evil one. Certainly, no one was glad about it; but everyone acknowledged God's mercy in the middle of the pain.

ACTION PLAN: ENGAGE THE PAIN

God doesn't waste pain. We shouldn't either. Don't over-explain, but when the time is right—with gentleness and respect, and without exploiting people to gain converts or personal power—engage students in exploring and learning for themselves.

- Help people work through blame by examining responsibility. Doing stupid stuff isn't evil; it's just stupid. But that doesn't make the pain go away. An accident that occurred under the influence of alcohol wasn't really an accident; it was a dumb (and possibly criminal) act by someone who knew better. What we know isn't as important as how we choose to behave.
- Open up the realities of cause and effect in the physics of life. Few cars and even fewer drivers can take a 30-mile-an-hour curve at 60 miles an hour. Fatigue increases the likelihood of errors in judgment.
- Deconstruct the *myth of invincibility* many adolescents believe so thoroughly. No one is smart, strong, *blessed*, or lucky enough to be exempt from accidents.
- Gently resist the narcissist who wants to make everything about him (*I wonder what God is trying to teach me through this*). Affirm the sober truth that God causes the sun to rise on the evil and the good, and sends rain on the righteous and the unrighteous.
- Comfort survivors with God's kindness and patience. Be present with them through the ordeal of recovery. Assure them it's okay to still be alive. Encourage them to live with purpose.
- Declare God's mercy. Offer to mediate in relationships broken by an accident.

5.2 ANGER

Behind most anger is fear. Fear of failure; fear of losing control; fear of being victimized, looking bad, missing out, being wrong, being *wronged*, ignored, dismissed, diminished, or disrespected; fear of abandonment, pain, or dying.

Fear doesn't generally get young people in trouble, though; anger does. Angry kids break, scratch, and deface things. They hurt people, animals, and themselves. Angry kids argue and brawl; they use baseball bats, automobiles, and their own strength as weapons. And sometimes, angry adolescents use weapons as weapons. All these behaviors stretch along a crisis continuum from relatively minor to terminally lethal.

ACTION PLAN: ESTABLISH LINKAGES

In most anger crises—the ones that don't involve crimes—youth workers can intervene (and maybe even prevent further crisis) by helping a student link his angry behavior to the underlying cause. That linkage is most readily accomplished by getting face-to-face, asking questions, and deep listening. A person who addresses her fear and directs her anger into creative action can move beyond her sense of helplessness and into a growing experience of personal capability to generate change—not merely dole out punishment.

The same is true for the student who has crossed the line into legal trouble. At that point, access becomes more difficult, and the stakes are higher. So, pay the price to gain access. Don't count on the juvenile justice system to help a kid resolve his anger. It could happen, but don't count on it. Do what you can to get time with the person whose anger has gotten him in serious trouble (do it by mail if you have no other option), and help him with the same kind of deep listening you would employ under less severe constraints.

5.3 BULLYING

Bullying and hazing have a great deal to do with anger, but also with entitlement—it turns out bullies tend to have a relatively high opinion of themselves.

The best data we have identify five parties to bullying: Bullies, victims, bully/victims, bystanders, and inattentive adults.

BULLIES

Between 7 and 13 percent of school kids bully others at school but are not bullied themselves. Compared to non-bullying peers, bullies:

- Have an inflated opinion of themselves
- Enjoy high social status
- Experience high levels of avoidance by peers
- Want to be the center of attention
- Have trouble taking criticism
- Are more likely to abuse alcohol and other drugs
- Are at greater risk of being victimized themselves (about half become victims at some point)
- Are more likely to express conduct disorder, ADHD, and other mental health problems
- Are more likely to carry a weapon in and out of school (43.1 percent versus 52.2 percent)

- Are more likely to fight frequently and be injured in fights (38.7 percent versus 45.7 percent)
- Are more likely to display antisocial and criminal behavior in adulthood

VICTIMS

About 10 percent of school kids are bullied at school but do not bully others. Compared to non-victims, bullying victims:

- Are at greater risk for physical and mental health problems like stomachaches, headaches, and depression
- Miss school more frequently because of fear
- Experience higher levels of anxiety into adulthood
- Struggle with feelings of low self-worth
- Express high levels of depression, social anxiety, and loneliness
- Experience high levels of avoidance by peers
- Have low social status
- Have few friends (whether they tend to be victims because they have few friends or have few friends because they are victims is unclear)
- Feel that control of their lives is in the hands of others

BULLY/VICTIMS

About six percent of school children *both* bully others and are bullied at school. Compared to their classmates, bully/victims:

- Have higher levels of conduct and school problems
- Are less engaged in school
- Report high levels of depression and loneliness
- Experience the highest levels of avoidance by peers

BYSTANDERS

About 3/4 of school-aged kids neither bully nor get bullied at school. About 22 percent live along the margins of bullying without being substantially drawn in.

ATTENTIVE AND INATTENTIVE ADULTS

Bullying requires motive and opportunity. Adult intervention narrows the range of opportunity. Benevolent, attentive adults reduce the motivation to bully, which appears to be otherwise self-sustaining.

ACTION PLAN: PAY ATTENTION

- Be one of the benevolent, attentive adults who reduce the motivation for bullying by engaging students in transformational experiences. Much of a youth worker's task tends to prevent bullying, but that's no guarantee. Watch and listen to find out who may be a bully. (Remember the percentages: If you know 30 kids, you probably know at least two bullies.)
- Don't let bullying—in *any* form—go unchallenged in your relational web. Youth workers are mandated to create sanctuaries for the poor, the weak, the blind and lame and sick—just the kind of people who are targets for bullies. Christmas is coming; don't make the baby Jesus cry by allowing anyone (ANYONE!) to harm those he came to redeem.
- Pay special attention to middle schoolers. Bullying festers in sixth through eighth grades.
- Watch and listen to find out who may be a bullying victim, and engage those students in healing relationships, including necessary intervention with school, parents, and law enforcement. (Remember the percentages: If you know 30 students you could easily know two victims.)
- Mobilize the bystanders. Bullies enjoy unaccountable levels of social status at school. Other kids fear, hate, and avoid bullies, but for some reason don't strip them of their social power. Unless you can think of some reason why junior oppressors should be rewarded for their treachery, mobilize the 20+ percent of student bystanders who regularly witness bullying to pronounce such behavior as childish, troubled, and surprising from someone most people seem to think is cool. Then get the other 50+ percent to back them up on that.
- Take an annual survey on bullying as a jumping-off point for group learning and decision making about what behaviors will be tolerated by the peer group. Be clear about what you mean when you talk about bullying:

- Hitting, slapping, kicking, pushing, tripping, spitting, or otherwise assaulting another person
- Name-calling; unwelcome teasing; ethnic, sexual, racial, or body-type insults; threatening, menacing, cursing, or otherwise verbally attacking another person
- Theft or intentional damage to property belonging to another person
- Insulting or threatening notes, e-mail, text messages, graffiti, instant messages, or other forms of communication meant to harm another person
- Spreading rumors, marginalizing, excluding, or otherwise intimidating another person socially or psychologically

• Engage students in developing a sophisticated emotional vocabulary so they can express themselves with vivid clarity and depth across a broad range of human experience. For a starting point, check out the emotional map in section 6.3.

• Mobilize adults. If the athletic teams in your community have developed a culture of bullying, address that with students (especially athletes), parents, teachers, administrators, and coaches. Offer your services to develop content for team meetings, classroom sessions, parent meetings, and school assemblies about how to make your community a bully-free zone.

• Check yourself. Could anyone argue convincingly that you've used your position as a youth worker to bully students, parents, friends, other youth workers, or your significant other? If so, do whatever it takes to make amends and get that turned around.

5.4 CHEATING

Some students cheat because they are over-challenged; others do it because they are under-challenged—at least in the beginning.

The over-challenged student probably cheats to save face, or, oddly, to please his parents who have persuaded him that grades are important but may not have let him know that they value learning even more. So, if push come to shove, he may cheat in order to secure his position in the classroom and at home. Except, of course, that he can't hope to sustain the illusion of academic success indefinitely. When the deception unravels he'll be in a bind for sure.

The under-challenged student may cheat because she's bored and distracted. Actually, she may not be under-challenged so much as *unengaged* compared to other learning experiences where she can't seem to get enough. Chances are the wheels will come off her wagon as surely as if she were failing the subject for lack of capacity.

It's probably a mistake to assume that either of them started cheating because they were lazy—*unmotivated*, perhaps, especially the under-challenged student, and possibly *demotivated* in the case of the over-challenged one.

The important thing to note is that there's more than one reason for cheating, and the eventual crises will be very different in nature.

ACTION PLAN: ADDRESS ROOT CAUSES

The over-challenged boy will need extra help, perhaps in the form of tutoring or an accomplished study partner. Find out if he's behind in more than one subject. If so, explore the possibility of deeper or more extensive problems. How is his eyesight? Does he process information effectively, or does he struggle with auditory or visual input? This will take a professional evaluation, because kids with lifelong process disabilities—dyslexia for example—probably don't have the language to compare what they see and hear with the capacity enjoyed by most others. The over-challenged student may also need assurance that the struggle he faces is not a character flaw, even if his attempts to cover it up were less than honorable.

The under-challenged student presents a different kettle of fish. A student who under-achieves may need to be fast-tracked. This is, of course, the kind of thing that must be assessed by school personnel. But that doesn't mean you can't ask the question. She may also be distracted by issues that aren't readily apparent, even to people who know her. Find out what else is going on: Is her family in flux? Is she being harassed or bullied at school, on the job, in the neighborhood, at home, or at church? Has she had a big disappointment? Is she grieving a significant loss (significant to *her*—it doesn't matter if it seems significant to others)? Is she feeling anxious about growing up in general or leaving home in particular? Most of the time things like this make sense once they're on the table.

Two other things: (1) Some students take cheating in stride because so many others do it.

JH: A group of bright, high-achieving students once told me it was really hard to earn a *B* while other students were stealing *A*'s. I heard other students casually admit to cheating on subjects that didn't matter to them. "I wouldn't cheat on something important," they'd say, "but I'm not going to major in geogra-

✦ **The Youth Worker's Guide To Helping Teenagers In Crisis**

phy, so what does it matter?" I think it matters plenty, but I don't always get a vote.

Persuading a student that learning is more important than grades may take some doing, and the doing may have as much to do with persuading parents as anything else. But that's a story for another day.

(2) Cheating can be habit-forming. For some people, there's a rush in getting away with cheating. Compare it to the buzz some folks get from shoplifting things they can readily afford to buy, and you may be in the neighborhood. The solution to that kind of small-time thrill seeking has much to do with resolving issues of compulsion and addictive behavior.

5.5 CUTTING & SELF-INJURIOUS **BEHAVIOR**

Why in the world would anybody cut, burn, scratch, hit, bite, bang, brand, or carve her body? Or yank out her hair?

Well...she may be diagnosed with mental retardation, autism, or bipolar disorder. She may suffer depression, anxiety, or post-traumatic stress disorder. Most likely, she's the victim of abuse and/or sexual assault.

Self-Injurious Behavior (SIB) is the repetitive but non-lethal destruction or mutilation of tissue without conscious suicidal intent. In fact, a person may engage in SIB to keep from killing herself. She inflicts physical pain to express interior pain, to contextualize and perhaps manage fear, rage, emptiness, isolation, and sorrow. Victimized adolescents who lack the capacity to talk about their pain may express their pain and depleted self-esteem with self-injurious behaviors. Eating disorders often co-exist with SIB.

GIVE ME A SIGN
- Lots of bracelets stacked at the wrist or ankle
- Razor blades, box cutters, paring knives, open paper clips, or broken glass stashed in their bedroom or among their belongings
- Peeled skin
- Scratched skin

- Patchy hair loss
- Many self-mutilators choose out-of-the-way places no one can see, which is a good reason not to wear a bathing suit or go see a medical doctor
- Most adolescents will continue self-injurious behavior until the underlying problem is resolved. Medication may alleviate symptoms of anxiety, stress, or depression, but the main treatment for self-mutilation is uncovering and addressing the root cause of the pain

ACTION PLAN: OPENNESS

- Acknowledge that you know about cutting and other forms of SIB and that you aren't shocked to learn that people try to manage their pain that way.
- Don't confuse SIB with moderate body piercing or tattooing. Excessive piercing or tattooing is worth looking into.
- If you suspect that an adolescent suffered assault, sexual abuse, or another considerable trauma, don't hesitate to ask, gently but directly, if he ever feels like hurting himself in times of high stress. If you get a yes or a soft no, ask directly if he has done anything to hurt himself.
- If you're not sure, don't be afraid to ask if he was ever assaulted, sexually abused, or had some other traumatic experience and link that to SIB.
- Same thing if you see signs that may indicate self-injury: Ask gently and directly if the injury is what it looks like. If you don't buy the response, press for a clearer answer.
- Check out the other chapters on violence, bullying, rape, incest, sexual abuse, and post-traumatic stress disorder for more on processing these categories of crises. If you believe the SIB is not a substitute for doing greater damage but a prelude to suicide, check the chapter on suicide.
- By all means, if you feel like you're in over your head, refer the student to a trained professional sooner rather than later. (See section 3.1.)
- Teach students who express SIB a rich emotional vocabulary. (See section 6.3.)
- Encourage journaling, poetry, drawing, music, and filmmaking.

- Ask students to call you before hurting themselves (that means a 24/7 commitment during an acute phase of SIB).
- Teach coping tactics such as:
  - Seeking companionship rather than isolating
  - Meditating on The Serenity Prayer
  - Practicing self-distraction techniques, such as short bursts of exercise or controlled breathing
- Press students to keep working on the underlying causes until they're resolved.
- Be aware that some people return to self-mutilating behavior during times of disequilibrium, so return to the top of this list and assume you're with them in this for the long run.

5.6 DEATH

RVP: *One of my greatest fears as a seminary student was the realization that I would eventually be called on to help people cope with death. The dreaded call came late one evening while the senior pastor was on vacation. An elderly parishioner was not expected to live through the night. Family members were on their way to the hospital and hoped I could meet them there. I arrived at the hospital ahead of the family and just moments before the woman died.*

I'll never forget the experience. I had the incredible privilege of praying for this dear saint while watching her slip from this life into the presence of the One she had served for so many years. I felt humbled that I was able to share that moment. I also felt panicked that I would be the one to inform her family of her death.

As the nurses prepared the body for a brief family viewing, I joined the family in the critical care visitor's lounge. I suspect my face told the story before I ever opened my mouth. My voice trembled as I said, "Grandma just passed away. It was very peaceful; she had no pain." We cried together, and then I invited the family to join me in Grandma's room where we shared more tears, some memories, and a prayer, giving thanks for her life and the way she had touched everyone present. The ecstasy and the agony of ministry...seminary didn't prepare me for this.

You may be called on to deliver the news that a loved one or close friend has died. Here are a few recommendations.

- Try to share the news in person. Don't use the telephone unless you've exhausted all other possibilities.
- Consider other flesh-and-blood options when you're too far away to share the news in person. Call a pastor or layperson who has a relationship with the family or friends, and ask her to go to their home or place of business on your behalf.
- Share the basic facts in a straightforward manner. The gravity of your message probably will be communicated in your demeanor long before any words are spoken. Provide details only as they're requested. It will take time for the reality of what you've shared to sink in. Recognize that people respond to tragedy in a host of different ways.
- Stay with the survivors. After you've shared the news, stay with surviving family members or friends until you feel confident they are stable and able to function. If you simply must leave before you feel that confidence, ask another crisis helper to stay with them.
- Be sensitive to their need for privacy. Some people have difficulty letting down their hair in front of others. Volunteer to wait in another room, or suggest that you'll be just outside the door should they need you.
- Look for practical ways to help.
- Offer to help with phone calls, funeral arrangements, transportation, meals and such, then get others involved from the helping ministries of your spiritual community.

ACTION PLAN: PREPARE STUDENTS FOR DEATH

We live in a death-denying culture. Prepare students for the looming possibility of death by:

- Talking plainly about death when you teach
- Taking students to funerals—one or two at a time—and talking afterward about their perceptions
- Taking a few students at a time to visit a funeral home, including a "viewing room." For many young people this will be their first encounter with a dead body. It may sound morbid, but when you invite their questions and demythologize

their misconceptions about the process, discussions about death and eternity will have new meaning.

STAGES OF GRIEF

Teach the stages of grief articulated by psychiatrist Elisabeth Kübler-Ross: Denial, anger, bargaining, depression, and resolution.[1] Preparing students to grieve with those who grieve also prepares them for their own inevitable grief.

Denial. A common initial response to news of someone's death is to deny the possibility; as if we believe that somehow our denial will make the loss go away. Funeral services go a long way toward finalizing the knowledge that it's really happened—there's the body of our loved one right there in that box. This is not to say a memorial service can't serve the same function. The important thing is to gather and acknowledge the loss *together*.

Anger. Anger over abandonment. Anger at the one who caused premature death. Self-directed anger. Anger at the dead. Anger at God. We are most helpful when we create an environment in which people have permission to verbalize their anger as a normal part of working through grief.

Bargaining. Be aware of the attempt by some—especially the young—to bargain with God. "God, if you'll bring back my mommy, I promise never to disobey again." The hope that they might have even the slightest control over the return of a loved one is all some kids have to hang on to. Bargaining is a desperate reiteration of denial.

Depression. The numbness that may protect people in the beginning of grief may trap them later as the magnitude of the loss sinks in. Part of that is the perception that everyone else has moved on and a person is alone. That's when your presence may be most significant. Keep checking in.

Resolution. Resolve happens when it happens. Bit by bit things get back to normal. There's still a hole where the lost love is supposed to be, but it becomes possible to function without him.

Review the part about taking care of survivors in section 5.20.

5.7 DIVORCE

Divorce shakes you off the ground
Divorce whirls you all around.
Divorce makes you all confused
Divorce forces you to choose.
Divorce makes you feel all sad
Divorce pushes you to be mad.

Divorce makes you wonder who cares
Divorce leaves you thoroughly scared.
Divorce makes a silent home
Divorce leaves you all alone.

Divorce is supposed to be an answer
Divorce, in fact, is emotional cancer.

—Ten-year-old Chicago girl[1]

IT HAPPENS IN EVERY NEIGHBORHOOD

When Rebecca was just five years old, she startled her mom with a simple but pointed question, "Mommy, when are you and Daddy gonna get a divorce?" Nothing at home had given Becky any cause to believe her parents' marriage was in trouble. No couples in her extended family or in her parents' circle of adult friends were separated, divorced, or even moving in that direction. Still, she assumed it was inevitable. At age five.

It turned out Becky had been watching a television program dedicated to helping kids with divorced parents; it was an episode of *Mr. Rogers' Neighborhood*.

And that about covers it. The dissolution of families is a fact of life today.

The impact of that falls heavily on children, who tend to internalize four kinds of messages from a family breakup: Humiliation, guilt, distrust, and lowered expectations.

HUMILIATION

Imagine being torn between "ex-lovers." While friends continue with the normal developmental tasks of childhood and adolescence, these kids must contend with the adjustment issues that result from family disruptions:

- Custody—who will live with whom and when and where?
- Emotional upheaval in the custodial parent
- Hostility between parents
- Personal grief
- Financial stress as a result of maintaining two households
- Increased responsibility for day-to-day household operations
- Anger toward parents, dates, and stepparents
- New household rules and roles

Many children are embarrassed to talk about their parents' separation or divorce. Some would rather suffer the agony and loneliness of silence than risk ridicule or rejection. All this conspires to undermine a child's sense of balance. The result is an unpredictable mix of dispositions that can range from shame to blame.

GUILT

Lots of children and teenagers in divorce feel responsible for their parents' choices. They struggle with questions like, "What did I do to cause it?" or "What could I have done to prevent it?" In rehearsing the past, they construct scenarios that point fingers of blame back in their direction. In thinking about the future, they concoct schemes to bring their parents back together again.

In families where the announcement of divorce comes as a total shock, children are more apt to assume personal responsibility than in families where war has been raging for some time and sides have been clearly drawn. In the latter case, children may feel guilty if they're relieved by the cessation of open hostilities.

Parents who wait until the last minute to tell children about their intention to separate or divorce minimize the opportunity for kids to process what's going on, ask important questions (*Will we still see you? Do you still like us?*), and receive vital assurances from *both* parents (*We still love you. This has nothing to do with your behavior. It's between us.*). Without processing, the likelihood that children will own responsibility for the separation increases significantly, making their adjustment that much more difficult.

DISTRUST

You know the old saying: *Fool me once, shame on you; fool me twice, shame on me.* Kids who endure divorce frequently show signs of losing faith in adults.

In an attempt to justify their actions, one or both parents may share grisly details that make the other parent look bad, irresponsible, and primarily at fault. The games parents play are further compounded by relatives and friends interested in helping the children see who's really at fault. The courts, whose purpose is to protect the best interests of children, often draw them into an arena where they're used by one parent against the other.

When the smoke clears, kids are left wondering if there's *anyone* they can trust. David Elkind again:

Consider for a moment what divorce does to the teenager's sense of parental wisdom, competence, and experience. This event not only confronts teenagers with difficult problems of self-definition, but it also changes their perceptions of adult authority. Many teenagers think, for example, that because their parents have messed up their own lives, they have nothing to teach the teenager about life and love. And when, in some single-parent homes, teenagers are treated as total equals to the remaining parent, this also contributes to the decline of parental authority. (Such equal treatment is particularly perilous in early adolescence, when young people badly need the guidance and direction of a more knowledgeable adult.)[2]

LOWERED EXPECTATIONS

It's not unusual to hear teenagers from disrupted families express the fear that they may never enjoy a happy marriage—or the opinion that there's no such thing.

ACTION PLAN: REALISTIC HOPE

- Expose students to realistically healthy relational models. Teach problem solving, sympathy, empathy, negotiation, conflict resolution, forgiveness, and restoration.
- Teach students to understand the limits of adulthood. Deconstruct the myths of adult omnipotence and omnicompetence. (This isn't that hard; they're already waking up to the fact that their parents are as goofy as anybody else—the trick is helping kids be generous instead of cynical about that.)
- Be present for kids whose parents are separating. Don't assume that information about divorce is a substitute for relationship. Investigative reporter Warner Troyer interviewed hundreds of American and Canadian children, youth, and adults who shared one thing in common: They were all children of divorce. "The most essential insight," Troyer observes, "is simply that parents, after divorce, aren't all that great. Other adult company and friendship is needed."[3]
- Recruit other adults, and devise organic ways for them to befriend and mentor students—especially the ones who live with single parents.
- Encourage divorced parents to engage in a church-based divorce recovery group. If there's no adolescent component to the divorce recovery groups in your community, get together with other interested folks and design one.

- Offer appropriate expressions of affection when kids are going through divorce. The experience of wholesome touch can be scarce during family blow-ups. It should go without saying that affection must be welcome to be appropriate (but we'll say it anyway). Beyond that, a child in emotional crisis may initiate inappropriate expressions of touch. Disengage from uncomfortable clinging and pelvic hugs gently and quickly.
- Take the initiative. When you know a family is in trouble, don't wait for a kid to initiate. Take steps to communicate your concern and availability.
- When you begin to see negative trends in a teenager's attitude or behavior, ask, "What's going on at home?"
- Don't hesitate to refer chronically depressed teenagers to professional care.
- Remind parents of the flight attendant's speech at the end of section 5.21: *Get your own mask in place, but check to be sure your child isn't turning blue.*

5.8 DROPPING **OUT**

Almost 90 percent of American teenagers finish high school or earn an equivalent degree. Adjust this locally—especially if you work with Hispanic students whose average graduation rate ran 20 percent lower than black, non-Hispanic students and 25 percent lower than white, non-Hispanic students at the turn of the century.[1] It's clear our work is cut out for us.

Most 16-to-19-year-olds who are not in school are also unemployed.[2] They tend to remain underemployed: Dropouts faced 48 percent unemployment in 1999; those who worked earned only 65 percent of the U.S. median income, meaning they earned 35 percent less than a middle-income worker.[3]

ACTION PLAN: CUT TO THE CHASE

- Find out what's behind a student's intention to drop out of school. The presenting problem is seldom the root cause. Address what's not obvious. Look for:
  - Anxiety about growing up and unfinished childhood business
  - Hidden addictions
  - Victimization at school
  - Learning disabilities
  - Extraordinary untapped ability
  - Pregnancy

- Income from illegal activities
- Family conflict
- Recommend appropriate alternatives. For many students, a high school equivalency is as good as or better than walking at graduation with a class of peers they care little about. For students utterly demotivated by the high school experience or profoundly motivated by another pursuit for which they show aptitude, suggest a General Education Development (GED) or High School Equivalency program. It's the learning (or at least the certificate) that matters, not the stereotypical high school experience. Help parents see the light, then help the student prepare to pass the test.
- Do what you can to help students find meaningful work, where meaning is measured by direct productivity or by income that supports personal growth and service.
- If a student chooses an alternative path, figure out how to involve him in the life of your group. Don't just kick him out of the high school group and send him to the college ministry—that's almost never a good fit. By the same token, think about altering his participation in your ordinary high school programming to suit his educational and life stages. Or not. It may be just as good to leave it alone and let him continue in the group as if nothing has changed (as long as nothing beyond the methodology of completing high school has changed). He is, after all, still a teenager. Negotiate something that works, and review the arrangement every couple of months until it's no longer necessary.
- Help students develop and work toward desirable scenarios for the future. Use the Plan of Action form in section 6.1 to develop a plan for the immediate educational crisis. Then work through it a second time to develop a plan to help the student get where he wants to go as a creative, productive worker.

✚ **The Youth Worker's Guide To Helping Teenagers In Crisis**

5.9 EATING **DISORDERS**

Americans have a remarkable emotional connection to food. Current science suggests that a combination of genetic and behavioral factors conspire in the startling increase in the incidence of *obesity* (body weight more than 20 percent higher than recommended for height) and *morbid obesity* (body weight more than 100 pounds over the recommended weight for height). The behavioral side of the equation is subject to emotional factors, including the use of food as a mood-altering substance.

At the other end of the food chain[1] are the eating disorders known as *anorexia nervosa* and *bulimia nervosa*.

The *anorexic* suffers from extreme weight loss caused by emotional, not physiological difficulties. Translated, *anorexia nervosa* means "nervous loss of appetite." In fact, the anorexic may suffer extreme hunger pains, but the fear of gaining weight overrides the appetite for food.

Bulimia is a condition characterized by "binge eating" or eating incredibly large quantities of food in a short period of time, after which the eater induces vomiting or abuses laxatives in order to purge the food. The term *bulimia* derives from a compound Greek word meaning "ox-hunger" (as in, "hungry as an ox"). So *bulimia nervosa* translates roughly as "nervous hunger."

The whole range of disordered eating is damaging to a person's health and may be deadly.

The wide majority of anorexics and bulimics are middle- and upper-middle-income females. Obesity is an equal-opportunity employer. The onset of anorexia and bulimia tend to happen near puberty, but their roots may go much deeper into childhood body-image issues. Puberty may be a trigger (among several) as the thickening and curving of the female form raises fears about fatness, leaving childhood, performing in adult contexts, failure, loss of control, sexuality, and generalized angst.

GIVE ME A SIGN

In *Walking a Thin Line,* Pam Vredevelt and Joyce Whitman identify key characteristics of anorexia and bulimia.[2]

ANOREXIA NERVOSA	BULIMIA NERVOSA
• Voluntary starvation often leading to emaciation and sometimes death • Occasional binges, followed by fasting, laxative abuse, or self-induced starvation • Menstrual period ceases or may not begin if anorexia occurs before puberty • Excessive exercise • Hands, feet, and other parts of the body are always cold • Dry skin • Head hair may thin, but downy fuzz can appear on other parts of the body • Depression, irritability, deceitfulness, guilt, and self-loathing • Thinks, *I'm much too fat,* even when emaciated	• Secretive binge eating—can occur regularly and may follow a pattern (caloric intake during a binge can range from 1,000 to 20,000 calories) • Binges are followed by fasting, laxative abuse, self-induced vomiting, or other forms of purging (or person may chew food but spit it out before swallowing) • Menstrual periods may be regular, irregular, or absent • Swollen glands in neck beneath jaw • Dental cavities and loss of tooth enamel • Broken blood vessels in face • Bags under the eyes • Fainting spells • Rapid or irregular heartbeat

ANOREXIA NERVOSA	BULIMIA NERVOSA
• Obsessive interest in food, recipes, and cooking • Rituals involving food, exercise, and other aspects of life • Perfectionist • Introverted and withdrawn • Avoids people • Maintains rigid control	• Miscellaneous stomach and intestinal discomforts and problems • Weight may often fluctuate because of alternating periods of binges and fasts • Wants relationship and approval of others • Loses control and fears she cannot stop once she begins eating

Add to those characteristics these hints of anorexia and bulimia:

ANOREXIA NERVOSA	BULIMIA NERVOSA
• Looks not just lean, but abnormally thin • Extreme attraction/avoidance language and behavior regarding food • Obsessive weighing throughout the day • Baggy clothing to hide shape	• Abnormally frequent trips to the bathroom • Abnormal fixation on exercise, no matter what • Cuts and calluses on knuckles and backs of hands • Car or closet smells of vomit

ACTION PLAN: ENGAGE

- Teach students to self-identify eating disorders. Your reasoning: It's damaging behavior that can be dangerous and even deadly.
- If you have food issues, identify them and take steps to regain health.
- If you have snacks at youth group meetings, include healthy selections.
- Open your doors to students struggling with food.
- Teach students to bring friends for help if their eating is troublesome.

- Engage students in generous, open conversation when you see clustered characteristics and signs of eating disorders.
- If you're certain an unacknowledged eating disorder is wreaking havoc in a kid's life, consider an *intervention*. (See section 5.12.)
- Get to the story behind the story. If an eating disorder is the presenting problem, the core issue may be:
  - Sexual threat. There is an uncanny coincidence between eating disorders and sexual abuse. By some accounts, more than 80 percent of women treated for eating disorders self-identify as victims of molestation and sexualized violence. Obesity and starvation may be attempts to desexualize. Bulking may amount to gaining protective strength against further abuse. Deal with the sexual abuse, and the eating will tend to take care of itself.
  - Fear of fatness. Some children have been hammered about their weight to the point of obsession. Deal with self-image and self-esteem needs.
  - Fear of leaving childhood. Some children find adolescence threatening. Find out why.
  - Fear of performing in adult contexts. Some children are intimidated by adult expectations. Find out why, and seek to relieve the pressure.
  - Fear of failure. There's a high incidence of perfectionism among anorexics and people pleasing among bulimics. Find out what meaning a young person assigns to failure and why.
  - Loss of control. Some anorexics and obese adolescents are staking out a personal space where a despised and feared adult cannot go. "They can push me around all they want, but they can't make me eat." Find out why a kid feels bullied, impotent, or out of control, and help her deal with that.
  - Generalized angst. Many people have experiences and perceptions of the world that make them anxious and afraid to take responsibility. Food is an amazing, cheap, and legal mood-altering substance. This is food as self-medication. Like the abuse of alcohol and other drugs, they wouldn't do it if it didn't work. Find out why the student is afraid, and help him tackle and overcome his fear.

- Don't hesitate to refer a student when you believe you're in over your head. That said, there are no miracles in treatment, and many teenagers bluff their way out of counseling relationships and treatment programs. So:

  - Plan to be in it for the long haul. Everybody has to face food pretty much every day. Thus, the presenting problem can't be isolated from normal life. The recovering food addict needs to know you understand the struggle.
  - Teach parents to understand eating disorders. Acknowledge their fear (often mixed with frustration and expressed as anger). Help them come to see that eating disorders frequently include a family component that lies beneath the presenting problem. That means solving food issues often requires addressing family issues.
  - Teach your student community to embrace kids who have eating disorders with grace, sensitivity, and the knowledge that the fix takes time.

5.10 HAZING

JH: There was an angry ritual at my high school 35 years ago—
it had been going on as long as anyone could recall. On the
last day of football practice (the day before the last game of
the season), once the coaches left the field, the seniors lined
up between the goalposts and made the younger boys pass
through them. It was the seniors' last chance to express their
appreciation for their teammates.

As a sophomore I watched older boys beat the hell out of
younger boys. I remember Charlie Pope on top of me, pounding on my facemask before letting me up. As a junior I got off
easy because I was a starter. We'd had a frustrating season, but
apparently none of the seniors were too frustrated with me.

The next year, Ted Strauss and I were co-captains of the
team. It was the last day of practice, but this year our final
game would be for the state championship. In 24 hours we
would be in the Florida State Seminoles' locker room, preparing to go out in front of a capacity crowd and win or lose the
state title.

Before that last practice, there was a brief discussion among
the seniors about the value of tradition. As the tide turned from
tradition toward teamwork, a couple of guys expressed frustration that they wouldn't have the chance to do to someone else
what was done to them in previous years. Ultimately, though,
no one wanted revenge more than he wanted a state championship. When the coaches left us alone on the field that day,

we called the team into a huge huddle, churned the worn-out sod with our cleats, hollered, cheered, and mainlined adrenalin like the junkies we were. The scrum ended with a mighty shout, and we all ran through the goalposts together.

As far as I know, the goalpost beating tradition died that day. The next day, we won the state title.

I don't know that organized sports are inherently flawed, but I believe I have ample evidence that *people* are. The anger many of us felt in those days didn't just go away because we chose not to beat up our younger teammates. It went somewhere else. I'm glad we didn't generate more anger for those younger guys by victimizing them, which is what we do on a regular basis in this culture. We do the things that were done to us—the things that made us angry and crazy—and our victims do those things too. It just about never ends until somebody swims against the tide just enough to ask, "Is this gonna help us win the state championship? Because if it isn't, I don't think we should do it."

THE FACTS

That said, here are a few things we know about hazing: 91 percent of high school students join at least one group. 98 percent of them have positive experiences in their group activities, and half of them have *only* positive experiences.

- 48 percent engage in initiation activities that are considered hazing—humiliation, substance abuse, and dangerous activities (though only 14 percent use the term *hazing* to describe what happens to them).
- 43 percent endure activities ranging from mildly to profoundly humiliating.
- 30 percent perform acts they believe are illegal as part of the initiation.
- 71 percent of those hazed suffer negative consequences as a result—fights; injuries; conflict with parents; hurting other people; disrupted eating, sleeping, and concentration; confusion; embarrassment; feeling guilty; trouble with the police; broken friendships; considered suicide.

- Dangerous hazing is as common among high school students (22 percent) as it is among college athletes (21 percent).
- Substance abuse is part of 23 percent of high school hazing, increasing to 51 percent in college.
- 40 percent of students say they wouldn't report hazing—36 percent of those mainly because "There's no one to tell," 27 percent because "Adults won't handle it right."
- Students who know an adult who claims to have been hazed are more likely to be hazed themselves than students who don't know an adult who claims to have been hazed.
- Most are not able to distinguish degrees of seriousness in hazing (when those who specified "other" were asked to list the other humiliating or dangerous activities they were required to perform during initiations, those acts included stealing, locking or being locked inside school lockers, self-inflicted pain, beating others, having multiple sexual partners, and performing oral sex on mentors (the researchers were prohibited from asking direct questions about sexual behavior in the study).
- A total somewhere near 1.5 million American high school students experience hazing every year, over half of whom are athletes.
- Even groups considered "safe" haze students:
    - 286,000 music, art, and theater students
    - 235,000 church youth group members (particularly dangerous hazing; nearly half are expected to engage in illegal activities)
- 61 percent of hazing occurs in eighth, ninth, and tenth grades.
- Reasons for going along with hazing:
    - It was fun and exciting (48 percent)
    - We felt closer as a group (44 percent)
    - I got to prove myself (34 percent)
    - I just went along with it (34 percent)
    - I was scared to say no (16 percent)
    - I wanted revenge (12 percent)
    - I didn't know what was happening (nine percent)
    - Adults do it too (nine percent)

- 98 percent think dangerous hazing is wrong, 86 percent think humiliating hazing is bad, 35 percent think hazing is socially acceptable.
- High school students recommend the following means to combat hazing:
  - Strong discipline for hazing (61 percent)
  - Police investigation and prosecution of hazing (50 percent)
  - Offer positive, bonding activities as alternatives (43 percent)
  - More education about positive initiation and hazing (37 percent)
  - Adults who support positive initiation activities (34 percent)
  - Physically challenging activities (30 percent)
  - Adults who say hazing is not acceptable (27 percent)
  - Good behavior required to join the group (29 percent)
  - A "no hazing" agreement to be signed by students (23 percent)
- At this writing, 44 states have anti-hazing laws.
- Anti-hazing laws make little difference in high school hazing.[1]

Hazing is a strange, shame-based ritual in which strong (or privileged) people humiliate weak (or newly arrived) people in order to welcome them into a closed society. And isn't it fascinating that the privilege of membership includes consent to inflict pain on those who follow?

How is hazing supposed to make us better people? It's not. It's supposed to make us loyal. It's supposed to make us compliant so we're willing to take whatever's next; so we're ready to take one for the team.

Of high school students who, having been hazed, say they wouldn't report hazing, 24 percent agree with the statement: "Other kids would make my life miserable." Sixteen percent agree with the statement: "I just wouldn't tell on my friends, no matter what."

ACTION PLAN: BUILD BETTER RITUALS

As in the case of organized sports, it's not the *idea* of initiation that's broken; it's the people doing the initiating. You don't have to throw out the idea, just redeem it. Done right, initiation is a valuable rite of passage that welcomes newcomers by letting them in on the secrets of the organic human and spiritual culture, not just the cold facts of the organizational chart and mission statement.

JH: I went to work for a church that had a tradition of kidnapping the ninth grade class on a Saturday morning in order to initiate them into the high school group. Students with driver's licenses were dispatched with a couple of partners to fetch the young ones from their beds while it was still dark. Some of the older kids liked to wear camo and face paint and use a little duct tape as part of the kidnap. It was a blast.

Unless you were one of the abductees, who tended to be disoriented by the experience, sometimes a bit roughed up, and almost universally embarrassed (except for those girls who were tipped off by an older friend and sat fully dressed and made up, waiting for the kidnappers to arrive—for them it probably worked out all right). Asking around a bit, I heard enough stories of unpleasantness to understand why that was the last time some students came to the senior high group.

So I stopped it. I figured there must be a better way to welcome the incoming class than humiliating and scaring them half to death. A few older kids complained for about 30 seconds, before most admitted it never seemed quite right to them either and we got on with inventing some new rituals.

Effective initiations build relationships and a growing sense of belonging based on mutual respect and sharing. Any ritual that violates that spirit endangers your mission. Every ritual that enhances relationships and belonging in respectful interactions serves your mission.

- Gather a group of mature students and adults, and brainstorm a continuum of honoring, engaging rituals to help you initiate newcomers and involve old-timers in passing on your culture.
- Stamp out any vestige of hazing.
- Create something insanely counterintuitive, like a day on which seniors compete to outdo each other by serving freshmen.
- Reinvent the practice of confirmation for your own spiritual tradition.

- Create killer lock-ins, retreats, and road trips for each age group (escalating the sophistication and adventure as students grow through your program).
- Design serving projects.
- Facilitate student-to-student mentoring.

5.11 INCEST

No one working in a religious community wants to believe a relative would sexually victimize any kid. The spectre of incest is made more ominous by the layers of relational complications.

According to the most widely acknowledged research we know, about 16 percent of women are sexually abused by a relative before age 18 (part of the 38 percent who report childhood sexual abuse).[1] That's about one girl in six. A literature review suggests about half as many boys are incest victims, but it's widely believed that sexual abuse of boys is underreported, so the number may be higher.[2] So, if students trust you and you make yourself available to hear bad news, there's a pretty good chance you'll eventually be asked to walk with someone through a case of incest.

The stakes are high. Among adults who were victimized by their mothers, a study reported by the New York City Alliance Against Sexual Abuse estimates that 60 percent of the women and 25 percent of the men had eating disorders. Eighty percent of the women and all of the men reported sexual problems as adults. Almost two-thirds of the women said examinations by doctors or dentists were terrifying.

Other studies referenced by the Alliance report a higher incidence of intense guilt and shame, low self-esteem, depression, substance abuse, sexual promiscuity, and post-traumatic stress disorder—with symptoms of flashbacks, nightmares, and amnesia—among incest survivors than among those assaulted by strangers.[3]

Imagine the difficulty of talking with anyone about a sexual relationship you are having with a family member. Most incest situations involve father-daughter or stepfather-stepdaughter relationships. Mother-son or stepmother-stepson incidents are much more uncommon. However, when they do occur they are far more damaging and difficult to treat.

Because it is so terribly difficult to admit that a father, uncle, brother, or other family member finds you sexually attractive and has acted on that impulse, most kids live in what some have called a "silent shame."

ACTION PLAN: LISTEN

- Teenagers are much more inclined to tell a peer than an adult or another family member about an incestuous relationship. If you communicate openness, sensitivity, and compassion on the subject, there's a fair chance you'll learn about incest through the intervention of a caring friend.
- Admitting incest is an act of (sometimes desperate) trust. Don't fail to thank any student who trusts you with his story. And promise to help him get through it and move toward healing and wholeness. Victims of incest need to know that their victimization can and will stop.
- Be prepared to address sorrow, anger, and abandonment in victims of incest. Not only were they abused by someone who should have protected and nurtured them, but there's also a good chance the other parent failed to take action for too long (if ever).
- Be prepared to address denial or outright resistance from parents when you help a student bring incest allegations to light. Use the definitions of sexual abuse in section 5.16 to qualify the charge.
- Anticipate guilt, shame, and fear in the victim. Many kids are made to feel responsible for the incestuous relationship. Reassure the victim she is not to blame. No matter what

the situation, the adult perpetrator is responsible for what occurred—period.

- Fulfill your legal responsibility. Pastors and youth workers are notorious in intervention circles for wanting to handle incest themselves in an attempt to protect families and, on occasion, the perpetrator. In *The Common Secret*, Ruth and Henry Kempe write:

> Whatever the background situation, under the laws of *all* our states, and most countries abroad, sexual abuse of children is *always* a criminal act (generally a felony); major psychiatric illness in the perpetrator is a relatively uncommon finding in the vast majority of sexual abuse cases, though it may be more common in forcible rape by a sociopathic criminal; and "therapy" deals with only part of the problem.[4]

- In most states, health care providers, mental health care providers, teachers, social workers, daycare providers, and law enforcement personnel are listed among those who must report suspected or known incidents of child abuse. Church-sponsored schools and daycare centers are not exempt from the law. Nearly half the states include members of the clergy specifically (and child and youth professionals by inference) as mandatory reporters. In another third of the states, "any person" is classed as a mandatory reporter. Consult a lawyer if you have any question about your reporting duty, because you may be liable if you fail to act.
- Act in the child's best interest. Most states have multidisciplinary teams and carefully developed policies designed to protect the child's best interest and work to keep families intact in the intervention process. The performance standard stabilizes the health and safety of the most vulnerable first, then looks at restoring equilibrium to the family.[5]
- Consult with your supervisor. To effectively care for families, your staff must operate as a cohesive unit. Youth workers experience difficulty when they attempt to operate as a separate entity. In matters as serious as incest, it's wise to have the counsel and confidence of a supervisor. Confidentiality must be respected, and the incident must not become

an item for staff gossip. Establish a plan of action quickly, and take steps to intervene.

- That said, if you encounter resistance from your supervisor and the threat of delays that could further endanger the victim, act quickly to fulfill your obligation as a mandated reporter and pastor to the victim.
- Network with school personnel, who originate a significant percentage of abuse reports to law enforcement. If your supervisor won't help you protect a child from incest, bring a school administrator into your confidence. If your case is compelling, she'll help you in a heartbeat.
- Be prepared to offer temporary housing. The thought of being responsible for the breakup of their family is terrifying to most kids—regardless of the abuse they have suffered. One way to help keep the family intact is to facilitate the temporary removal of the offending family member—or, if it's safer, the victimized child—from the household during the risk assessment and action plan development. It is generally more difficult to find people who are ready to welcome a "perpetrator" into their home, but don't overlook the possibility. A Christian community's willingness to care for both victim and perpetrator makes a strong statement about its commitment to families.
- Refuse to play the blame game. It's easy to harbor resentment and foster bitterness toward a perpetrator; or the offender's spouse if she (or he) failed to stop the abuse; or the parents if the abuser was a sibling, cousin, uncle, or aunt, and Mom and Dad failed to protect their children. It's difficult to understand how any adult could perpetrate or fail to defend against such unspeakable acts against a child, which makes it easy to "cast the first stone." An incest crisis, though, furnishes an unparalleled opportunity to extend the redemptive justice, love, and mercy of Jesus who consistently brought forgiveness and hope to all the wrong people.
- Stay close to the victimized child or teenager. Revealing the sordid details of an incestuous relationship is a gruesome ordeal for almost anyone. Traditionally, the first time a victim told the story was only the first in a series of examinations and investigative procedures.
- These days, multidisciplinary intervention teams from Child Protective Services are responsible for reducing the

trauma some children and youth suffer as a result of a crime against them. The CPS team is trained for the legal, psychological, and familial aspects of a thorough investigation. The result is that kids are spared the agony of having to tell their horror story over and over again to a host of different people. But don't depend on that. Do what it takes to remain close for the duration.

• Be alert for the signs of Self-Injurious Behavior (SIB) listed in section 5.5. Once they've told someone about incest, it's not unusual for young people to enter a period of high risk for suicide, drug abuse, and other self-destructive behaviors. Families don't always respond the way we hope. Instead of surrounding the victim with loving concern, families sometimes respond in disbelief, anger, shock, or paralysis, leaving the child without support. Step into the gap; "come alongside" with God's love, comfort, and assurance.

5.12 *INTERVENTIONS*

Alan I. Leshner, former director of the National Institute on Drug Abuse, says the essence of addiction is "uncontrollable, compulsive drug seeking and use, even in the face of negative health and social consequences."[1] This echoes a line from the pastor Don Finto: "What you can't get enough of, that's your god."[2]

There is an element of idolatry in addiction. Given the chemical effects of drugs on the brain (apparent in the withdrawal symptoms if nothing else), there is also a strong element of *desire* in the user's drug seeking. Addicts are willing to leave father, mother, home, and friends for the drug. They will lie, cheat, and steal for it. And they'll surrender their bodies to the drug in a complete act of worship.

All this is easier to see if we set aside chemical reactions for a moment and focus on addictive *behaviors*. Sex addicts, co-dependents, and the eating disordered don't have physiological withdrawal symptoms from abstinence. But they certainly experience powerful emotional and spiritual suffering that an alcoholic or cokehead would recognize.

Getting the attention of a person so thoroughly given over to a substance or behavioral habit isn't easy.

Most addicts don't really contemplate giving up their drugs until they are confronted with the high likelihood that they will have to give up everything else—family, job, home, car, friendships, personal dignity...everything—in order to keep using. Or the realization they already have. Faced with that, an addict really has to think about cutting back.

There's a story going around addiction circles that says the average alcoholic in recovery (whatever "average" means) gets about 54 wake-up calls before he finally admits that his life is unmanageable and only a power greater than himself can restore him to sanity. We can't tell whether that's a real number, or if it's just a good story about how hard it is for an addict to get that the drugs don't work (because they certainly appear to) and how worthwhile it is to hang in there (non-co-dependently of course) with a user who may be on wake-up call number 51.

ACTION PLAN: *INTERVENTIONS*

54 car accidents, blowups, breakups, black eyes, moving violations, STDs, divorces, missing teeth, lost jobs, and...interventions.

We'll italicize the word *intervention* here, because everything you do in response to a crisis is an intervention. What we're talking about here, though, is a well-defined process that's come to be known by the name *intervention*.

Interventions are designed to break through denial in people struggling (or maybe not struggling enough) with chemical dependencies and addictive behaviors. *Denial*, as the old joke goes, *is not a river in Egypt;* denial is an elaborate patchwork of excuses, adaptations, rationalizations, and reasons why everything is working much better than it appears to be and it's the people who are worried who are the ones with the problem. Until a user acknowledges her need, she won't be motivated to seek help.

User has two meanings here, because addicts tend to use people as well as substances. An *intervention* is a structured time in which people close to the user present her with factual data to underscore the severity of her behavior as it affects them.

Just to be sure we're clear about this: *interventionists* tell the addict how her behavior affects *not her* but them. This can be infuriating to an addict, so be prepared. *Interventions* divert the focus from the ego of the user to the impact of her behavior on people who are important to her. *Interventions* should include a minimum of two affected people—and more is better because there's safety in numbers. But not too many. If the user feels like you're piling on, she may respond with stubborn defensiveness (which she might do anyway). Or she may simply shut down, believing you'll wear yourselves out and leave her alone if she just goes limp on you.

Effective *interventions* are story-based and non-judgmental—a facilitator within the group referees to make sure they stay that way. But successful *interventions* are in no way shy about speaking into the life of the user with specific and detailed personal accounts of what her behavior has cost each person in the room—that's the whole point. The *interventionists* aren't accusing the user of being selfish; they're demonstrating through true stories how selfishly she is behaving (possibly without ever using the word *selfish*).

This is tough going. Sometimes the only thing that keeps an *intervention* from getting out of control is true love and the hope, however faint, that the user could live instead of die. Premature death is the eventual outcome of addiction. Check out the lost years of potential life at the beginning of the Substance Abuse and Addiction feature in section 5.19.

The facilitator may be a mediator asked to help out, or she may be one of the circle of friends. Her job is to make sure each participant has ample opportunity to give specific examples that demonstrate the negative effects of the user's behavior in real life. In the process users often hear for the first time about something that happened while they were under the influence, how others truly perceive them, and how friends and family have been damaged by their behavior. The facilitation needn't be heavy-handed or even obvious. We've been part of *interventions* where the conversation was guided so subtly that an observer might have had difficulty picking out the facilitator.

The facilitator keeps bringing the subject back around to love, committed concern, and hope. The facilitator may encourage participants to describe the consequences they foresee happening should the person continue using:

Boss: "One more time and I *will* fire you."
Friend: "And you'll lose your car."
Father: "Because I won't pick up your payments and insurance."
Friend: "You'll have to sell it."
Father: "At a loss, because it won't bring what you paid for it."
Brother: "So she'll still owe money on a car she no longer owns? That sucks."

Don't rush it, but don't let an *intervention* go on indefinitely. If it's working, the user will probably be exhausted before the *interventionists* run out of things to talk about. If it's not working, there's no sense in beating it to death. There may come a moment when the facilitator must say, "I think we've done what we can do for now," at which point it's good to ask the user to summarize what she heard before you break it off for the time being. Her response may reopen the dialogue, or it may simply confirm what everyone in the room suspects: It's time to regroup and plan another approach. If that's the case, make sure everyone understands that you are putting a comma in an unfinished thought, not putting a period at the end of a sentence. There's nothing wrong with setting up another meeting then and there. If the user is still in the room, it's because she's trying not to burn any more bridges or maybe because the truth is beginning to dawn on her.

The goal of an *intervention* is breaking through denial and motivating the user to receive help. The *interventionists* should have a pretty good idea of what that help will look like when they walk in the room. This is not a good time for brainstorming. If mental health counseling or detox are part of the plan, the parent or guardian needs to know what's available, what it will cost, what it takes to get the ball rolling, and what to do during the hours (or more likely, days) before the treatment commences.

In evaluating the help available, help families grapple with these questions:
• Is hospitalization required for detoxification or other medical reasons?
• Is a medical specialty required?

- What level of family involvement is required in the process?
- Is inpatient or outpatient care preferred?
- Can treatment begin immediately? If not, how long is the waiting list?
- What is the duration and location of the treatment?
- What will treatment cost?
- What costs, if any, will be covered by insurance?
- What is the success rate of the treatment program we're considering?
- Will the program or individual counselors support or oppose the spiritual values of our home?
- Is a peer-based help program like Alcoholics Anonymous a possibility?

If the plan leans toward peer-based assistance, no matter where you are, there's a 12-step meeting starting in about two hours somewhere reasonably close by. In most places you can find a centralized number in the phone book for Alcoholics Anonymous, Narcotics Anonymous, and the like; and they'll be more than happy to send you a schedule or tell you about their meeting times and places. In some cities, meeting schedules can be found on the Web.

Since 12-step meetings are not all created equal, learn in advance when and where to find an appropriate meeting. If you don't know anyone working a 12-step program, ask around and someone will find you. That's not meant to be spooky. It's just that Alcoholics Anonymous, Narcotics Anonymous, Sex Addicts Anonymous and the rest are, in fact, all *anonymous*. They don't use last names, and they don't identify each other in public except by prior mutual agreement. So if you start asking friends if they know where you might find a 12-step program, pretty soon one of them will say he might be able to give you a phone number, and off you'll go.

If the user continues to deny the problem (or the *severity* of the problem, since she now knows she has relational problems with people who love but no longer trust her); and if she is a minor, her parents may have a legal rationale, and possibly an obligation, to arrange for treatment whether she wants it or not. This is a rare and difficult thing, and it's important to remind the parents that if they don't believe they're taking life-saving action, they should go back through the user's history and consider the *intervention* options one more time to see if there's another way.

If they're afraid of losing their child, encourage them to hope that, though the child may resist and resent their decision, it's not likely to significantly affect the outcome. There is little difference in rate of success between those who voluntarily submit to treatment and those who fight it tooth and nail. Many teenagers who were dragged into treatment end up expressing profound gratitude for their parents' tough choices. Remind yourself of this, as well. It's possible the user will see you as a betrayer. *You're first obligation is to preserve life, not friendship.* With a little grace you may save the friendship as well as the friend.

5.13 POST-TRAUMATIC STRESS DISORDER (PTSD)

Post-traumatic stress disorder is an anxiety disorder that sometimes develops in the aftermath of terrifying events in which assault or bodily injury was witnessed, threatened, or actually occurred. PTSD is not universal, by any means. Most people exposed to disaster, for example, don't experience major mental health effects, and those who do tend to recover within a couple of years. But it can be a tough couple of years, including flashbacks, vivid memories, intrusive thoughts and nightmares, emotional numbness or hyper-arousal, sleep disturbances, depression, anxiety, headaches, stomach complaints, dizziness, chest pain, irritability, outbursts of anger, and feelings of intense guilt. None of these is out of the norm in the immediate aftermath of trauma. When symptoms persist beyond a month, mental health professionals may diagnose PTSD.

Misery loves company. Full-blown PTSD may be accompanied by co-occurring addictive and self-destructive behavior; by self-doubt, paranoia and psychotic breaks, severe depression, excessive compliance, fear of intimacy, and an enveloping sense of helplessness, hopelessness, and despair.

PTSD can be triggered by a violent personal assault, rape, or mugging; by natural or human-caused disasters or accidents; or by military combat. About 30 percent of those who spend time in war zones suffer from PTSD. People who endured childhood abuse or other prior trauma are somewhat more likely to experience PTSD.

Back in the day, it was generally believed that emotional numbness following a trauma was a sign of resilience. The growing suspicion among researchers today is that people who exhibit emotional distance after trauma may be more disposed to PTSD.[1]

ACTION PLAN: TALK

The good news is that talking about it helps. Since the diagnosis was recognized in the American Psychiatric Association's *Diagnostic and Statistical Manual of Mental Disorders* in 1980, a body of research has established the effectiveness of cognitive-behavioral therapy and group therapy (both talk-based) for working through trauma. Medication may help ease related symptoms of depression, anxiety, and sleeplessness, but it's not necessarily indicated for long-term recovery.

Some studies show that sooner is better for talking through the trauma of catastrophic events. Following a hurricane in Hawaii, a study of 12,000 schoolchildren found that two years later, those who had received counseling soon after the storm were doing better than those who didn't get that kind of help.[2] If you suspect PTSD, you can be a significant helper to the one who's suffering by providing a safe place to talk. Chances are you'll be a bigger help by referring him to a mental health professional who has experience treating people suffering post-traumatic stress. That said, in the unlikely event of a mass disaster, you may be on point with large numbers of students who need group experiences to help them process their trauma and begin recovery.

5.14 PREGNANCY

At this writing, there is less adolescent sexual activity in general, and greater numbers of sexually active adolescents report using condoms and birth control pills to lessen the likelihood of pregnancy. These findings are interesting but essentially useless when a young woman sits across from you saying she's missed her period.

ACTION PLAN: PROTECT AS MANY LIVES AS POSSIBLE

- Don't rush to judgment. Listen deeply.
- Find out why she believes she's pregnant.
- How is her health?
- Has she seen a doctor?
- How far along is she?
- How is she holding up emotionally?
- Who else is involved? What is the nature of the relationship?
- What do her parents know? How are those relationships?

If she hasn't had a reliable pregnancy test yet, that's a good next step. Crisis pregnancy centers offer free tests and counseling for minors without requiring parental permission.

If a pregnancy has been verified through reliable testing, talk about the father, the nature of their relationship, options available to them, and whether their parents have been informed.

Encourage young people to risk the possible negative consequences of informing their parents of the possible pregnancy. If the parents react badly, at least they'll know where they stand. And perhaps they'll rally round the crisis and make the best of a bad deal.

If the girl is leaning toward abortion, directly and matter-of-factly explore her reasons and perceptions about the possible outcomes. Don't let your predispositions get in the way of understanding. Assuming the likelihood that you would counsel against abortion, we doubt you'll get your way by exerting pressure before you've taken the time to exercise some deep listening. As always, get the story behind the story. Abortion may seem to her like the only reasonable alternative, where *reasonable* means avoiding extended pain for her and/or her family and/or her sexual partner.

If the girl is leaning toward single parenthood, be just as direct and matter-of-fact about that as you would be while helping her think through abortion.

Ditto if she is leaning toward marriage.

If the pregnancy is new, there's time to consider all the possibilities. Help the young woman develop several scenarios that describe the paths to desirable and undesirable outcomes. Ask questions that will cause her to consider positive and negative effects on everyone involved. Acknowledge what's already begun to dawn on her: There is no easy way through her pregnancy. Every choice she makes has a ripple effect on other choices and on other people's lives.

Do your homework on birth and adoption alternatives. Your crisis network should include resources to advise you and provide direction or services to the young woman.

Be aware that if she goes to a crisis pregnancy center for testing and learns she's pregnant, she will also receive counseling regarding her legal medical options. Few, if any, crisis pregnancy programs are truly "values free," one way or the other. When options are presented and abortion is entertained, the philosophical bent of an agency or clinic will be reflected. At this writing, if the girl elects to have an abortion, a dozen states have no parental notification or permission requirements. The rest require that one or both parents be informed 24 to 48 hours before an abortion or grant their permission in writing.

Knowing there is no easy way through her pregnancy, recommend that she protect as many lives as possible and take the risk that the God of mercy and grace can use a very difficult circumstance for good.

5.15 RAPE

Rape is a violent crime behind which the offender leaves physical evidence in the form of DNA and other identifying substances. Since the majority of rapes and sexual assaults are committed by people known to their victims (70 percent is the baseline), capturing evidence is a key factor in getting convictions.

Everyone knows it's not quite that simple. Even with physical evidence, proving forcible rape can be made difficult by a vigorous legal defense. Timing is everything. Forensic medical documentation of bruises, abrasions, and DNA evidence in the hours immediately following an attack is vital to a strong physical case. And the few hours immediately following the rape are exactly the time when a victim is most likely to be emotionally incapacitated by the trauma.

If the crime goes unreported for half an hour, that can easily turn into half a day and every cycle of the clock makes it more difficult for the victim to report. The results are well known: Isolation, grief, fear, anger, self-doubt, distrust, regret, depression, and sometimes substance abuse, eating disorders, cutting, sexual adventurism—and on and on...

ACTION PLAN: BE THERE

- Teach boys that forcible sex is never, ever permissible in any form.
- Teach boys to teach *other* boys that forcible sex is unacceptable and criminal.
- Teach girls that forcible sex is a crime no matter who the offender is.
- Teach girls and boys to report the crime immediately. Give out your phone numbers, and promise to drop what you're doing and help them get medical attention and report the crime 24\7\365.
- Take victims to an emergency care unit as soon as possible after an attack. Adolescent rape victims may resist medical attention because it requires parental consent, and many are afraid the examination will be painful. Address that concern by acknowledging they may not only experience discomfort during the exam, but they may also have to face other potential medical issues, including the risk of sexually transmitted infections and the possibility of pregnancy. It's unpleasant, but it has to be addressed.
- Medical personnel are mandatory reporters in all states and are required to report sex crimes. Legal requirements may necessitate additional medical examinations. Stick with the victim through that process. You don't have to talk; you just have to be there.
- Be present in the months that follow. The medical and law enforcement systems have become fairly sensitive to rape victims and witnesses. Many police departments employ women to interview female rape and sexual assault victims. Victim assistance programs work to make court appearances more tolerable. You can assist by providing perspective, another set of ears, acceptance, and ongoing support through legal depositions, meetings with police, and court appearances.
- Consider referral to a psychotherapist with experience in sexual assault recovery.
- Consider suggesting she attend a support group of women who have survived rape.
- Prepare to help the victim work through lingering fears, spiritual doubt, social anxiety, and confusing emotions. Be there for as long as it takes.

5.16 SEXUAL **ABUSE**

The U.S. Department of Health & Human Services' National Clearinghouse on Child Abuse and Neglect Information defines sexual abuse on a child as:

> A type of maltreatment that refers to the involvement of the child in sexual activity to provide sexual gratification or financial benefit to the perpetrator, including contacts for sexual purposes, molestation, statutory rape, prostitution, pornography, exposure, incest, or other sexually exploitative activities.[1]

The USDHHSNCCA&NI glossary includes additional refinements:

> Sexual Abuse: Inappropriate adolescent or adult sexual behavior with a child. It includes fondling a child's genitals, making the child fondle the adult's genitals, intercourse, incest, rape, sodomy, exhibitionism, sexual exploitation, or exposure to pornography.[2]

Any of these acts committed by a parent, guardian, relative, or caregiver (youth worker, teacher, sitter, camp counselor, etc.) is classified as sexual abuse. For more specifically related to incest, see section 5.11. Sexual abuse allegations are investigated under the guidelines of Child Protective Services agencies in each state. In most instances these acts are criminal offenses, as well. Any of these acts perpetrated by someone not acquainted with the child is classified as sexual assault, which is always a criminal act handled by police and criminal courts.[3]

THREE CATEGORIES OF SEXUAL ABUSE OF CHILDREN

1. Non-touching—Voyeurism, exhibitionism, production or purchase of child pornography, exposure to adult sexual activity
2. Touching—Molestation, penetration, incest, child pornography
3. Forced or physically violent—Rape, sadism, masochism, child pornography

NON-TOUCHING SEXUAL ABUSE

Sexual abuse of children or adolescents doesn't require actual physical contact. Voyeurs or "Peeping Toms" are sexually stimulated by viewing naked bodies or people involved in sexual activity. A voyeur may masturbate while fantasizing or secretly viewing children or adolescents. Voyeurs sometimes seek jobs or positions as volunteers in daycare centers, schools, camps, church youth programs, after-school programs, and community centers frequented by children or adolescents.

Exhibitionistic pedophiles receive sexual stimulation by exposing their genitals to minors. At times, indecent exposure by men includes masturbation.

Child pornography involves producing or possessing any visual depiction of a minor in sexually explicit conduct as defined by U.S. Code § 2252:

- "Minor" means any person younger than 18 years old;
- "Sexually explicit conduct" means actual or simulated—
  - Sexual intercourse, including genital-genital, oral-genital, anal-genital, or oral-anal, whether between persons of the same or opposite sex;
  - Bestiality;
  - Masturbation;
  - Sadistic or masochistic abuse; or

- Lascivious exhibition of the genitals or pubic area of any person.[4]

Exposure to adult sexual activity includes situations in which children are encouraged, invited, or forced to watch adults engage in sexual activity with other adults or children.

TOUCHING FORMS OF SEXUAL ABUSE

Molestation includes inappropriate touch; fondling or kissing a child on the breasts or genitals; or enticing or causing a child to touch, fondle, or kiss the breasts or genitals of an adult.

Sexual intercourse, for legal purposes, includes genital-genital, oral-genital, anal-genital, or oral-anal, whether between persons of the same or opposite sex.

Even in the absence of physical force, sexual intercourse with a child is considered "statutory rape." Different states have slight variations in the age at which legal minors may consent to sexual intercourse. Most states set the age of consent at 18, some at 16, and a couple at 14 and 15.

Incest is sexual activity that occurs between family members. In a high percentage of child sexual abuse cases, the perpetrator is someone who is known, loved, and often related to the child. It can be a parent, sibling, grandparent, stepparent, uncle, cousin, or other family member.

FORCED OR PHYSICALLY VIOLENT SEXUAL ASSAULT

Rape is forced sexual intercourse or attempted sexual intercourse committed against a woman, man, girl, or boy against the person's will and without the person's consent. (For more on helping rape victims, see section 5.15.)

Sadistic or masochistic incidents are rare in child sexual abuse. The sadist takes pleasure from and receives sexual stimulation by inflicting pain on another person. Masochists are stimulated by having pain inflicted on them.

PEDOPHILIA

Pedophiles are people, predominantly men, for whom prepubescent children are objects of sexual desire. Pedophilia may have more to do with age issues than gender *per se,* as pedophiles may demonstrate same-sex, heterosexual, or bisexual attraction toward children.

An infrequently used term for an adult who demonstrates a sexually predatory appetite toward adolescent boys is *pederast.* The behavior is called *pederasty.* There is no corresponding term for those who demonstrate a sexually predatory appetite toward teenage girls—not surprising, given the generally predatory attitude toward adolescent females in this culture. The closest thing may be "Lolita Syndrome," borrowed from the 1958 Nabokov novel, *Lolita.* Or you could go with *lecher* or *filthy old man.*

ACTION PLAN: EYES WIDE OPEN

- There is no known method by which pedophiles, pederasts, or lechers can be screened prior to their apprehension for child abuse. So teach children and adolescents to recognize signs of sexual advance, including inappropriate touching, embracing, and kissing.
- Teach children and adolescents to recognize signs of seduction, including pleasurable touching; embracing and kissing; inappropriate gifts; and bribes in the form of gifts, special privileges, or favored-child status.
- Teach children and adolescents enough to understand how and why seduction works. This is important even if a child proves unable to avoid sexual abuse. One factor in post-abuse resilience among boys is a level of sexual knowledge that contextualizes any pleasure response to the abuse so as to reduce the likelihood of crippling guilt.[5]
- Teach verbal refusal skills.
- Teach parents to create an exit strategy by which a child is empowered to flee a self-defined threat and enabled to get to a safe place for pick up.
- Teach children and adolescents to call 911 and tell the dispatcher an older person is sexually threatening them.
- Teach children and adolescents to report sexual abuse no matter what.

- Pay special attention to preschool boys. According to Department of Justice statistics, boys are most vulnerable to sexual assault at the age of four.[6]
- Pay special attention to eighth and ninth grade girls. According to Department of Justice statistics, girls are most vulnerable at age fourteen.[7]
- Check for prior sex offense convictions against all staff and volunteers who work with children and youth. The U.S. Department of Justice Sex Offender Registry Web site is at http://www.ojp.usdoj.gov/bjs/abstract/sssor01.htm. All 50 states and the District of Columbia maintain searchable sex offender registries. A list of the state sex offender registries is in section 6.5. If you need assistance, local law enforcement officials will help you find out if a person has been convicted of a sex crime.
- All that said, do everything in a way that is even-handed and human. Nobody needs to feel like he's on trial because he wants to help kids grow up whole and healthy. No parent needs to feel her children are at greater risk than they are in fact. No youngster needs an incitement to undue suspicion or anxiety about people who truly care for her. Practice due diligence before you invite anyone onto your leadership team, then seek the balance of trust and supervision.
- Inform parents of your selection process for staff and volunteers who lead children and adolescents, including training, supervision, and evaluation.
- Train staff and volunteers with clear standards about how and under what circumstances they may touch children and adolescents (and inform parents of these standards). Don't prohibit appropriate touch. A hand on the shoulder, side-by-side (not pelvic) hugging, tousled hair, and noogies are usually appropriate if the younger person welcomes them. No touch is appropriate if it is unwelcome.
- Train staff and volunteers to recognize signs of sexual abuse in children, including undue displays of physical affection and physical clinging.
- Teach parents to be receptive to sexual abuse disclosures from their children and adolescents. Factors that influence the likelihood that kids will inform their parents about sexual abuse include: The age of the child, the relationship with the perpetrator, threats or bribes, how the incident is

perceived by the minor, the level of trauma, and the level of trust between parent and child. Kids are more likely to talk about sexual abuse when they are confident of their parents' unconditional love. Parents who don't want to hear bad news usually don't until it gets very bad indeed. Teach parents to nurture openness and deep listening with their children.

• Teach parents to be aware of children's play that suggests sexual knowledge beyond their years. Remember the peak year of vulnerability for a male child is four years old. Children that young may not verbally describe an abusive episode by an adult or older child, especially if they've been cautioned not to do so. If a parent sees behavior that may be a clue that something inappropriate has occurred, an inviting question like, "Tell me how you know about that," can get the conversation going (even if the child's first answer is evasive, which may be another clue).

• Teach children and adolescents to disclose instances they believe are sexual abuse. The lists of behaviors at the beginning of this chapter form a list from which questions can be judiciously formed by parents and youth workers to explore the magnitude of a child's report. Unlike the past when children were more easily victimized because they didn't know they could say no to the sexual advances of an older child or adult, lots of kids now learn early to say no, to get away and tell someone. Nonetheless, parents may not hear about abusive episodes, because a young child fails to recognize the behavior is wrong or abusive. It may not "feel" right, but a child will tend to comply if he knows the perpetrator through family relationships, civic activities, or church involvements. When the child trusts the person, he will tend to assume the activity is normal even though he hasn't encountered it elsewhere.

• Adolescents may conceal sexual abuse for precisely the opposite reason: Because they recognize the behavior is wrong; and, for reasons of their own, they respond with guilty compliance instead of justifiably angry defiance. (And "reasons of their own" may include bribery and threats.)

• In cases of incest, offending males have been known to warn children that their mother may die if she discovers what they've been doing. Threats of physical harm to other family members or the victim are enough to keep kids in psychological bondage indefinitely. Special favors and the promise of gifts or privileges may be leveraged in an attempt to keep children quiet, though such tactics become less effective as children mature.

• It's also possible that a naïve adolescent may not know that what was done to him was sexual abuse. Age-appropriate learning about physiology and sexuality are important to the whole-person growth of children, including their recovery should the worst happen.

• Shock must be added to the list of reasons adolescents might not disclose sexual abuse, especially sexualized violent assault—all the more if it comes at the hands of someone they know. In 2003, seven of ten female victims of rape or sexual assault identified a significant other, a relative, a friend, or an acquaintance as the attacker.[8] The *unknown assailant* accounts for no more than a quarter of all rapes, but the stereotype leads many victims to underreport sexual abuse and assault. Just because the guy was a boyfriend doesn't alter the legal fact that forced penetration is rape. Just because it was Uncle Bud doesn't change the fact that forced fondling is sexual abuse. Too many young women and men accept incidents that should be reported as crimes, and they may even accept responsibility for what happened. A girl who believes she was raped because she "led her boyfriend on" may not risk further retribution by telling her parents.

• Some parents only learn about a sexual assault because the physical trauma of the attack requires medical attention—giving kids who might not otherwise risk telling their parents no recourse, since medical clinics and emergency units require parental consent before they will treat a minor child.

• The task of youth ministry includes teaching students the truth about sexual abuse and assault and providing a climate for disclosure.

  - Use questionnaires like "Where in the World Are You?" in section 6.6 to survey your students' attitudes and discover the needs within your group.

  - Consider devising a survey (or series of surveys) to learn about your group's involvement in and attitudes about high-risk activities like suicide, alcohol and drug use, eating disorders, Self-Injurious Behavior (SIB), sexual adventures, gender issues, and abuse (emotional, physical, sexual). Well-executed surveys are response vehicles for students who are struggling or "have a friend who is struggling."

- The manner in which a survey is introduced is as important as the survey itself. Students must *hear* (Communication is what's heard, not what's said.) that you take their responses very seriously and welcome the opportunity to follow up during personal conversations with anyone who's interested. Once you've opened the door, students will find it easier to tell you they want to talk further.

JH: I don't know whether I heard this somewhere or just recognized the pattern; I only know there was a shift in the depth and breadth of my work with adolescents when I figured out that almost any significant adolescent issue I mentioned in a serious manner was followed—usually pretty quickly—by a student who wanted to talk with me about that. I never knew a kid struggling with an eating disorder until I mentioned in a youth group talk that a lot of people struggle with eating disorders. After that I never ran out of people who wanted help with an eating disorder. The same is true of sexual abuse in all its forms, sexual identity issues, violence, substance addictions, and sexual compulsions. Adolescents (and their siblings and parents, for that matter) are looking for open doors. I would rather they walk through our doors than some others I can think of.

SIGNS OF SEXUAL ABUSE

It is somewhat easier to identify signs of abuse in small children than in teenagers.

• Be aware of children who, by their language and behavior, indicate awareness and experience in sexuality that exceeds the curiosity displayed when little kids play "doctor."
• Children who have suffered recent sexual abuse may show physical signs such as soiled underwear or pain when sitting or walking.

- Abused children may be excessively physical in displays of emotion.
- Abused children may be notably fearful of what they interpret as advances toward their bodies (a simple hand on the shoulder, for example).
- Emotional and physical withdrawal from relationships is common among sexually abused children.

Adolescent victims usually want someone to intervene on their behalf but find the risk of disclosure very difficult to take. Things to watch for in combination:

- Numbing out
- Post-Traumatic stress symptoms including flashbacks, nightmares and terrors, unprecedented zoning out, disengagement, and emotional hypersensitivity
- Self-Injurious Behavior (SIB)—including cutting, burning, or scratching
- Unprecedented sexual activity
- Undue and inappropriately sustained affection and clinging to adults
- Unexpectedly deep depression
- Unprecedented nervousness, anxiety, or edginess
- An unusually high percentage of women suffering eating disorders (80+ percent by some counts) are the victims of sexual abuse or assault

5.17 SEXUAL IDENTITY **CONFUSION**

What a young person believes about his sexual identity affects everything—his feelings and opinions about himself and others; what he will and won't do with his body (or another person's body); how he takes care of himself; his comfort level with God and the people of God; where he thinks he fits in the world; his dreams, aspirations, and expectations—everything.

So where does sexual identity come from? How do girls come to think of themselves as girls? And how do boys become comfortable as boys—however comfortable that may be? It's a big question.

NATURE **VERSUS** *NURTURE*

In a long-running debate, those on one side of the argument believe it's all about *nature*—plumbing and wiring determines sexual identity. The other side believes it's all about *nurture*—boys and girls are made, not born.

The nature proponents say sexuality—maleness or female-ness—is determined strictly by the amount of testosterone and other hormones in the womb at critical developmental stages. They insist the conversation should stick to biochemistry and steer clear of the messy social sciences.

The nurture camp claims boys and girls *learn* to be boys and girls in their families and communities through a process that overrides the effects of biochemistry.

These days, there aren't many purists in the nature versus nurture debate. Just because the plumbing and wiring are in place doesn't mean people know how to act. Biologically complete males and females learn the fine points of behaving like boys or girls from role models and trainers. By the same token, when there's a gender irregularity, naturally occurring body chemistry appears to overrule psychology and social relationships.

In 1997, the benchmark case for infant sex reassignment was publicly and embarrassingly discredited when researchers revealed that, at age 14, "Joan," the poster child for infant sex reassignment, declared "Enough is enough!" and demanded a reversal of the hormone treatments and surgeries that created the appearance of femininity. Joan then opted out of psychiatric treatment and, from a research perspective, dropped out of sight. Seventeen years later, a determined researcher located Joan, now living as "John"—a married man raising three stepchildren and living a quiet middle-American life.[1]

Still, it's families, communities, and cultures that nurture the *nature* of male and female children into the *behavior* of boys and girls. Over time, that socialization blossoms (or calcifies) into the adult patterns of women and men.

Sexual identity has gotten a little murky in the last half-century or so—a long story better covered elsewhere. Suffice it to say people have come to speak as though sexual identity had less to do with what makes people male and female and more to do with what females and males do sexually.

In the mainstream, folks treat sex as though it is one thing—a physical act—and sexual identity is something else—the kind of physical acts a person prefers (most recently the language has turned from sexual preference to sexual orientation, suggesting a predisposition). Sexual identity is understood as a person's sexual compass. Most people seem to assume that:

a) Everybody will have erotic encounters of one sort or another,
b) They'll begin those encounters sooner rather than later, and
c) The only question is: With whom?

The current notion is that people's sexual identity determines which of three ways they'll answer that last question:

• Heterosexuals want sex with people of the other gender.
• Homosexuals want sex with people of the same gender.
• Bisexuals want sex with whoever is available.

This is a somewhat confused way of thinking about things. From the biological point of view, sex has to do with reproductive capacity and nothing else. In the biological realm, there are two large categories and one small one:

• Females (about 50 percent) contribute eggs containing X chromosomes.
• Males (about 50 percent) contribute sperm with X or Y chromosomes.
• Sexually ambiguous persons (a fraction of a percent) are born with indistinct, mixed, or non-functioning sexual organs and therefore contribute nothing to the gene pool.

Remember, we're talking reproductive biology here, so males and females are categorized as a matched set. Sexually ambiguous persons are considered case by case and presumably don't reproduce.[2] So, as far as biology is concerned, there are two sexes—end of discussion.

But the popular notion about sexual identity treats homosexuals as a third sex, which becomes four if you count bisexuality and five if you subdivide homosexuals by gender. No one disputes that some of us (ballpark estimates range from four to ten percent) aren't sexually attracted to people of the other gender but are very attracted to people of the same gender. What's at stake is: *Why*?

Two answers dominate the conversation: Nature and nurture. And we're more or less back where we started.

Here's a hypothesis based on lots of field research. Just about everybody who pursues sexual fulfillment seeks emotional safety—a completely different kind of *safe sex* than we're used to talking about. Even people who prefer their sex rough or dangerous do so because it feels somehow safer than the alternatives—not unlike their friends who are tempted to cut themselves because at least it's a pain they feel they somehow control (unlike the uncontrollable pain they experience as the result of emotional, physical, and sexual abuse).

Some people are so afraid of—or so angry with—people of the other gender that if they seek sexual encounters at all, they certainly won't be heterosexual encounters, because there's no way that could be safe. So if they want sexual pleasure, they'll either go it alone or seek it in same-sex encounters or relationships.

And then there's sexual addiction. Some people are gripped by sexual addictions that work themselves out in heterosexual, bisexual, homosexual, or *autoerotic* behaviors.[3] Addictive behaviors are based on attraction, aversion, or a combination of both. People are attracted to what seems to work for them; they're repelled by what doesn't seem to work. So, to emotional safety, add sexual aversion and attraction.

All of this equals a confusing set of messages as boys and girls come of age sexually.

OUR BIG PICTURE

Whatever scientists may learn in the future about our genetic nature, we already know a great deal about the profound effect childhood and early adolescent experiences have on sexual identity. From those experiences we form a complicated picture of ourselves. How we perceive what we experience, what we think it means, where we consciously or unconsciously place each experience in the bigger picture, and how we behave as a result all play a role in our sexual identity.

When a boy is called a *sissy* because he doesn't throw a ball well, that experience becomes part of his big picture. When a girl is teased for being a tomboy because she possesses unusual upper body strength, the teasing becomes part of her big picture. When a child of either gender is touched inappropriately by an older person of either gender, that touch shows up somewhere in the big picture. When adolescents are repeatedly asked if they are gay or lesbian, those questions are introduced to the big picture—consciously or not.

And what do people do with the big picture? That's the puzzle. Why one person becomes promiscuous and another becomes sexually repressed and a third seems to function along entirely conventional lines is as difficult to explain as it is to predict. Why one person comes to be more attracted to the male form and another to the female form is an equally complicated mystery. Who knows where to begin unraveling the ball of twine that creates sexual attraction toward children or sheep or a list of sexual fetishes too long and complicated to catalog here, let alone explain?

THE STORY BEHIND THE STORY

We know this: Behind every story there's a story. Most of the time (not all the time, but most of the time) when we hear the story behind the story, what people do (or did) suddenly makes a certain amount of sense. Not that the story behind the story excuses illegal or immoral acts, but it helps interpret them.

So what does all this have to do with anything? For most of us, nothing. Even if we take the most enthusiastic estimate of the number of homosexuals and bisexuals, 90 percent of us will never make a single personal choice regarding homosexuality or bisexuality—though, realistically, quite a few of us will have experiences that are confusing, maybe even troubling, but have nothing to do with being homosexual or being bisexual.

That said, we all know there's no excuse for bad behavior. The boy who seduces girls is not better than the one who seduces other boys. Both are seducers. And that has something to do with all of us, because, quite apart from the conversation about sexual identity, no one has the right to seduce another person.

GIVE ME A SIGN

Sexual identity crises are self-defined. Apart from the most extreme behavioral affectations, there really aren't any signs of sexual identity confusion. Delicate men and tough women are all within the range of "normal" for their genders. Having a great sense of style or loving softball are ridiculous measures of a person's sexual identity.

ACTION PLAN: TALK STRAIGHT

- Don't make jokes about sexual identity in public or private.
- Don't listen to jokes about sexual identity in public or private.
- Don't put up with jokes about sexual identity in your group.
- Resolve your own sexual identity and behavioral choices, and get help where necessary to complete any unfinished business.
- Take it *very* seriously when a student is willing to talk with you about sexual identity issues. Self-identified bisexual and homosexual adolescents and those who have same-sex sexual encounters or report same-sex romantic attraction or relationships are at greater risk of:
  - Assault—45 percent of homosexual men and 20 percent of homosexual women report being verbally or physically assaulted in high school specifically because of their sexual orientation; they are twice to four times as likely to be threatened with a weapon at school
  - Dropping out of school, being kicked out of home, and living on the street
  - Frequent and heavy use of tobacco, alcohol, marijuana, cocaine, and other drugs at an earlier age
  - Sexual intercourse, multiple partners, and rape
  - Sexually transmitted diseases, including HIV (homosexual girls have the lowest risk of STD infection; but lesbian adolescents are likely to have had sexual intercourse with males, in which case the risk remains)
  - Suicide—they are anywhere from twice to seven times as likely to attempt suicide as self-identified heterosexual classmates
  - The data don't link these risk factors to sexual identity *per se*—but they are conspicuously coupled with negative reac-

tions to gender nonconformity, stress, violence, lack of support, family problems, peer suicides, and homelessness[4]

- Teach a whole-person approach to sexuality. Shameless plug: Take your group through *Good Sex: A Whole-person Approach to Teenage Sexuality and God* by Jim Hancock and Kara Powell (Youth Specialties/Zondervan, 2001).
- Don't use the Bible selectively to make a point or to back people into a corner—it's not that kind of sword.
- Make it clear that you are open to talking with any student about any issue of sexual behavior or sexual identity in a respectful, honest, and open way.
- Don't draw distinctions between heterosexual, homosexual, and bisexual lust. It doesn't matter what your sexual identity and theology are—lust is not permissible. The implication that your lust is somehow better than your neighbor's is just ridiculous.
- Draw clear distinctions between sexual experiences and sexual identity. Many children experience various levels of same-sex preadolescent sex play with other children. Later, most see such experiences as child's play. A few attach more significance to those experiences in retrospect and need the assurance that it's a fairly common experience of growing up. The introduction of a much older child, adolescent, or adult to the story changes an experience of child's play into a sexually abusive encounter. Some victims of childhood or early adolescent sexual abuse come to believe they may be homosexual because they participated in same-sex activities, or bisexual because they had sexualized encounters with people of both genders.
- Know this: You don't get to vote on a student's sexual attitudes, beliefs, and behaviors any more than she gets to vote on yours. You can listen, learn, advise, teach, seek to understand, and persuade, but you can't control. Nobody can. Apart from killing your young friend outright, your influence over her sexual identity and choices is limited by your humanity. So, if you can help it, don't slam doors (other than those that protect other young people). As long as you're still talking, there's hope for a positive outcome.

5.18 SEXUALLY TRANSMITTED DISEASES (STDs)

If the sexually transmitted infection data reported by the Alan Guttmacher Institute can be trusted, the following is a snapshot of adolescent disease risk:

- Each year, about three million adolescents acquire a sexually transmitted disease—that's about one in four who are sexually active.
- A single act of unprotected sex exposes adolescent girls to a one percent risk of acquiring HIV, a 30 percent risk of genital herpes, and a 50 percent chance of gonorrhea.
- Chlamydia is more common among adolescent boys and girls than adult men and women—as high as 29 percent of girls and 10 percent of boys tested positive for Chlamydia in some test settings.
- Adolescents have higher rates of gonorrhea than sexually active 20 to 44 year olds.
- Some studies of sexually active girls found infection rates up to 15 percent for human papillomavirus (HPV is often linked to cervical cancer).
- The hospitalization rate for acute pelvic inflammatory disease is higher among adolescent girls than adults. PID, most often the result of untreated Chlamydia or gonorrhea, can lead to infertility and abnormal pregnancy.[1]

All of which is interesting but may be of limited use, since it's unlikely you'll be the first person to learn about sexually transmitted infections in your group. So...

ACTION PLAN: SAY THE HARD THING (GENTLY)

- Teach students to report suspected STDs to a physician. The impact of failing to treat HPV, gonorrhea, Chlamydia, PID, and HIV range between awful and fatal. And the epidemiological implications are staggering.
- Teach kids to bring their friends to you for advice if they suspect an STD.
- Teach parents that a child can contract an infection from a single sexual contact, so an STD doesn't signal unbridled promiscuity.
- Teach everyone that STDs are a medical problem with profound family, social, and spiritual connections. Good triage demands treating the medical condition at the earliest possible date.

5.19 SUBSTANCE ABUSE & **ADDICTION**

Good news. At this writing adolescent substance abuse is trending down in most categories.

- Tobacco (all forms)
- Alcohol (all forms and including binge drinking)
- Cocaine (all forms)
- Inhalants (all forms)
- Methamphetamines
- Marijuana

All are lower than they were a decade ago among ninth through twelfth graders.

Bad News. There are notable exceptions to the downward trend.

- The number of ninth through twelfth graders who report using nonprescription steroids one or more times has tripled since the early '90s to about six percent
- The number of ninth through twelfth graders who report using heroin one or more times has edged up to around three percent
- Ecstasy use, measured for the first time in 2003, stands at 11.1 percent of ninth through twelfth graders (± 3.7 percent).

- Among sexually active ninth through twelfth graders, the number who report alcohol or drug use before their most recent sexual intercourse is trending up (near 25 percent)[1]

Behind the changes, both positive and negative, lies the truth that nothing much has changed. There is volatility across a decade of substance abuse numbers that reflects the rise and fall of drug use in general and the relative popularity of specific drugs. And, of course, regional and local patterns may be quite different from national trends. The Centers for Disease Control and Prevention report self-reported drug use among ninth through twelfth graders by state (and some cities). Go online at http://apps.nccd.cdc.gov/yrbss/ to check your local listings.

One thing you're sure to notice is that wherever you live, most of the drugs that are ever used by ninth through twelfth graders are small-time when compared to the regular use of the big three: Alcohol, tobacco, and marijuana.

- Alcohol—At this writing about 45 percent report drinking in the 30 days before the CDC survey. About 28 percent report binge drinking in the 30 days before the survey.
- Tobacco—At this writing about 27 percent report using some form of tobacco in the 30 days before the survey. About 10 percent report smoking cigarettes 20 or more of the 30 days before the survey.
- Marijuana—At this writing about 22 percent report use in the 30 days before the survey.

Of the three, alcohol and tobacco remain unchallenged for lethality and public health costs. The baseline for direct alcohol-attributable deaths in the U.S. is nearly 76,000 each year, at a cost of 2.3 million years of potential life lost.[2] The economic impact is estimated at more than $26 billion in direct medical and mental health costs; $134 billion in lost productivity; and $24 billion in motor vehicle crashes, crime, fire destruction, and social welfare costs. That's a grand total of about $185 billion annually.[3]

Every year about 440,000 Americans die of cigarette-attributable causes, costing 5.6 million years of potential life lost and $75 billion in direct medical costs, plus $82 billion in lost productivity. Total cost: Near $157 billion annually.[4]

WHY?

That data is interesting but useless unless we understand *why* teenagers use alcohol and other drugs.

CURIOSITY

Adolescents are all about the new experience. Seventy-five percent of high school students report having one or more drinks at least once by twelfth grade.

PEER PRESSURE

It's hard for an adolescent to say no if friends are the lifeblood of her experience. It takes a lot of ego strength to face ridicule and rejection for standing against the popular will. In his classic, *All Grown Up and No Place To Go,* David Elkind speaks of teenagers who develop a "patchwork self," a self constructed by the simple addition of feelings, thoughts, and beliefs copied from others. Teenagers "who have grown by substitution and only have a patchwork self are less able to postpone immediate gratification. They are present-oriented and other-directed, easily influenced by others."[5] That's not everyone all the time, but it's a big number much of the time.

FUN

It's possible that nothing holds greater value than self-defined fun. You know the gag:

> "Did you have fun last night?
> "Oh man, I was so tweaked. I don't remember where I was or what I did. I woke up in a pool of my own urine—at least I think it was mine."
> "Dude."
> "I have a chipped tooth."
> "Dude."
> "I found the beginning of a tattoo on my ankle. I think it was gonna be My Little Pony."
> "No way."

"I don't know how I got home or what happened to my car—
or my underwear."
"Dude."
"I never had so much fun in my life."
"Sweet."

Come on. You have to admit you can't have that kind of fun
sober. As long as that urine thing doesn't become chronic, and My
Little Pony doesn't get infected, and the car doesn't show up in a
crime report, and a 30-year-old dude doesn't show up in a Trans
Am with the underwear, it will remain a cherished memory—well,
not a *memory* exactly.

MIMICKING

Some wag said young people aren't much good at listening to their
elders but they almost never fail to imitate them. We are a drugged
culture—with an adult beverage in one hand and prescription pills
in the other—trying to make ourselves understood around the
hand-rolled cigar between our teeth. Jess Moody said if we ever
took the country off mood-altering drugs for one evening, we'd
have a national nervous breakdown.

Example has always taught more than *lecture. I need a drink.
Don't talk to me, I haven't had my coffee yet. I just need a quick cigarette; then I'll be a lot nicer. Just a little something to take the edge
off.* Many of us encourage rather than discourage self-medication.

DECLARATION OF INDEPENDENCE

One young man said he started smoking pot "because all my parents ever talk about is how bad drugs are!" Marijuana was a way
of letting his parents know that he intended to do whatever he
pleased. Therapist Gary Forrest was among the first to describe
the phenomenon:

Studies indicate that over 80 percent of families in which both
parents drink produce children who drink. To the contrary,
over 70 percent of parents who do not drink produce children
who abstain. However, there are cases where complete parental abstinence from alcohol actually encourages the teenager
to drink. If drinking is taboo in the family, then the contrary-

minded teenager may conclude that drinking must be fun. For some teenagers, drinking offers a great way to upset and control parents who are non-drinkers.[6]

DISINHIBITION

What youth worker, teacher, or counselor hasn't heard the justifications? *I drink because it helps me be myself. I'm more creative when I'm wired. Getting a little toasty helps me get so much deeper into the music.* Placebo studies in which college students were told a drink contained alcohol when it did not found that those who *expected* to experience disinhibiting effects from the alcohol tended to get what they expected (some even reported feeling drunk)—in spite of the absence of alcohol in the drinks.[7]

ESCAPE

Teenagers use alcohol and other drugs to escape the pain of fractured or abusive relationships, feelings of inadequacy, fear of the future, school pressure, parental expectations—almost any stressor can lead to self-medication. The biggest challenge of drugs is that they work! At least for a while. Many users affirm that temporary relief is better than none at all.

ADDICTION

Regular use of some substances creates dependency. The heavy caffeine user who goes off his beverage of choice for any reason (say Lent or a backpacking trip) knows something about withdrawal symptoms like headaches, irritability, and disrupted sleep patterns—and that's just caffeine.

Drug potency is measured by degrees of physiological and psychological impact, progressive tolerance that leads to increased use but diminishing effects, and increasingly disruptive withdrawal symptoms. Mixing drugs is an experimental exercise in trying to manage all those variables, a task that gradually turns into a full-time job for addicted people.

Former National Institute on Drug Abuse Director Alan Leshner says the essence of addiction is "uncontrollable, compulsive drug seeking and use, even in the face of negative health and social consequences."[8] Compulsive craving, seeking, and using, no matter what; that about covers it.

TOLERANCE

Tolerance is a key indicator in addiction. This is why there's a difference between an alcoholic and a problem drinker. There is evidence to suggest that everyone has the potential for problem drinking. Problem drinkers have problems when they drink, and lots of problems when they drink lots. One of the telltale signs of a budding alcoholic is his capacity to absorb large quantities of alcohol without obvious impairment—it's often the alcoholic who drives the problem drinker home from a party.

This is not good news. Tolerance to high blood alcohol levels is the first clue that it will eventually take poisonous levels of alcohol to produce a physiological effect. Later, it will take poisonous levels of use to just feel *normal*. No one can poison himself on a regular basis without sustaining long-term organic damage. Better to be a lightweight when it comes to alcohol tolerance; better to face the music if you're not.

ACTION PLAN: ENGAGE

Don't immediately jump to conclusions when certain things seem to indicate involvement with drugs. By the same token, don't deny what's right in front of you. The presence of one or two of the factors commonly associated with substance abuse may only indicate that a teenager is experiencing changes typical of adolescence. However, when they suspect there's a problem, most adults tend to err *not* on the side of overreacting, but in waiting too long to act. If the concerns are reality-based, it's better to be safe than sorry.

SIGNS OF TEENAGE ALCOHOL AND DRUG ABUSE

- Withdrawal—Spending significantly more time alone in their room (or another secluded place in the home) than before; uncharacteristic avoidance of interaction and fun with their family

- Inexplicable relational shifts—Dumping valued friends and rapid bonding with a new circle of associates; being secretive about names, times, and places
- Difficulties in school—Unprecedented truancy, uncompleted assignments, loss of concentration, unexpected decline in grades
- Unreasonable resistance to reasonable authority—Unprecedented sustained conflict with parents, teachers, police, youth workers, other adults
- Inexplicably shifting interests—Loss of interest in personal hygiene, grooming, neatness, play, creativity, friendships
- Behavior problems—Stealing, shoplifting, lying, or unexplained spending
- High-risk behaviors—Loss of regard for personal safety, frequent traffic violations, vandalism
- Persistent signs of depression—Suicidal talk or gesturing, actual suicide attempt
- Sexual promiscuity—Indiscreet sexual behavior, multiple partners
- Health complaints—Unprecedented frequent colds, flu, vomiting, constipation, abdominal distress, headaches, tremors
- Changes in eating habits—Unaccountable increase or decrease in appetite with accompanying weight gain or loss
- Obvious signs of being under the influence—Alcohol on breath, slurred speech, staggering, dilated pupils, exhilaration, hallucinations, panic, delusions, heart palpitations, unprecedented unself-conscious body odor, sleeplessness

Remember the qualifiers in these descriptions—*inexplicable, unprecedented, persistent.* You don't want to leap to conclusions, but you also don't want to ignore clusters of suspicious behavior.

If parents call to talk about substance abuse and addiction issues, meet with them at your earliest convenience (unless the situation suggests an acute crisis—e.g. overdose or suicidal gesture—in which case you'd better clear your schedule or make an immediate referral). It's probably best if the adolescent doesn't attend the first meeting (if it was initiated by a parent).

Begin by affirming the parents for seeking help (even if their fears turn out to be unfounded). Ask open-ended questions that will enable them to air their concerns while they give you a sense of the progress of their child's behavior. Let them know you'll help them develop a plan of action once you're clear about the scope of the problem.

Some parents will share the entire problem—as they see it—in a torrent from beginning to end. Others need coaxing in the form of follow-up questions and frequent feedback. Here are some questions to get the story going.

- When did you first start believing there might be a problem?
- How did you respond to that realization?
- Tell me about the conversations you've had with her about this.
- Does she admit to having a problem?
- What natural consequences has she experienced because of her behavior? (Lost and damaged property and hangovers are *natural consequences*.)
- How did she handle that?
- What logical consequences have you enforced? (Restriction from driving and curfews are *logical consequences*.)
- How did she respond?
- What indicators do you have that the problem is better or worse than it was 30 days ago?
- What does your gut tell you?
- What makes you trust or distrust your instincts about this?
- What would you like to see happen?
- Do you believe you have the resources to get there?
- What would you like me to do, if I can?

Once the parents have shared their concerns and what they would like to see happen, you can assist them in coming up with a plan of action. (For more on this, see section 2.4.)

If you agree there appears to be cause for concern but it still feels intangible to you, suggest that either you or one of the parents organize a daylong road trip that includes just you (or a parent) and the kid you're concerned about.

- Take him out of school for the day, leaving early enough so he can't sleep in.

- Drive for three or four hours with limited stops until you get to whatever destination you've chosen for whatever business you've elected to conduct. (For instance, take him to inspect a conference center you've never used—even if you're not looking for a new conference center. The inspection will give him something to contribute and stimulate your thinking about what you do at camp.)
- A couple of times throughout the day, thank him for accompanying you on what probably seems to him like a fairly pointless mission, and tell him it's nice to have his company.
- Ask open-ended questions that require stories rather than conceptual answers. Start with subjects that are personal but non-threatening, and move gradually and naturally toward questions that invite greater disclosure—music preferences, sports, favorite television shows and movies, his parents' background, his own family. He'll be wary, but you can almost certainly outlast him, especially as you reciprocate with stories of your own.
- Note his physical posture and endurance, his apparent emotional affect and vocabulary, his degree of tolerance for and engagement in conversation, and his ability to remain focused on a conversational thread.
- When you reach your destination, make sure you get out of the vehicle and walk around a bit, including stairs or a hill in your walk. Eat something. Make small talk comparing where you are and where you live.
- On the return trip, include open-ended questions that call for stories about his imagined future as well as his remembered past.
- Thank him again for the company as you say good night.
- Whether it was you or the student's parent who took the road trip with him, the next day—with due regard for things said in confidence—share the story with each other. Ask questions about his behavior and apparent attitudes upon returning home for the night. Ask questions about his getting up and out of the home the next morning.

This approach is relatively costly in terms of time, but it can help you qualify and prioritize your concerns. You'll almost certainly have a better notion of whether there's an emerging threat or not. If further intervention is appropriate, you'll be on the same page as his parent.

In the process there's a fair chance the student will reveal, or you will otherwise discover, what's behind the parent's presenting problem. (For instance, the presenting problem may be, "Something's up, but we're not entirely sure what it is.") Once you believe you understand the scope of the problem, you can help his parent develop a plan of action.

If the issue turns out to be alcohol, be aware that some parents underestimate the danger of alcohol abuse. It's not unusual to hear a naïvely relieved response like, "Oh, it's just alcohol? I was afraid he was doing drugs!" This happens in spite of the fact that, in practice, the consequences of alcohol abuse are far more lethal than other drugs. Many teenage alcoholics and problem drinkers are robbed of the opportunity for early intervention, because people close to them don't want to see what they're seeing.

If professional referral is indicated, one of the greatest ways you can serve families is by knowing what treatment options are available to them.

Fortunately, a host of effective, community-based outpatient and in-hospital programs exist to help people overcome dependencies on alcohol and other drugs. Most programs require family involvement in the treatment regime, because a user's potential for long-term recovery is much greater when family members embrace the important role they play in the process.

5.20 **SUICIDE**

Someone now forgotten called suicide a "biological, socio-cultural, interpersonal, dyadic, existential malaise." This is a fancy way of saying that—though any of a number of factors might push her over the edge—the "typical" suicidal individual is juggling a constellation of balls that keep increasing in the course of weeks, months, even years.

Adolescents who are by nature more impulsive sometimes pose a notable exception to this rule. An especially painful breakup may be enough to do in a 15-year-old boy all by itself. But not usually—most of the time it takes more than a single tragedy to drive a suicide.

Most suicides can be prevented. If there's a single word that describes the suicidal disposition, it's *ambivalence*. Most suicidal people hang in the balance between "I really, really want to die" and "I really, really want to live."

There's a great story about a rookie cop on his first suicide call. He makes his way onto the roof of a 30-story office building and finds a man teetering on the ledge. Instinctively, the young officer pulls his service revolver and shrieks, "Stop or I'll shoot!" At which the guy on the ledge throws his hands in the air and yells, "Don't shoot me!" as if to say, "If you shoot me, I might die!" This is the same person who, moments earlier, contemplated becoming one with the pavement below. That's ambivalence.

GIVE ME A SIGN

Here are some risk factors that may conspire to produce a suicidal act:

- A history of developmental problems
- Escalating family problems
- Acute experience of separation and loss
- Feelings of rejection and being unwanted
- Chronic communication problems
- Obvious and abrupt behavioral changes
- Sustained extreme moodiness and withdrawal
- Repeated involvement in high-risk behaviors
- Abuse of alcohol and other drugs
- Medically undiagnosed physical complaints
- Perfectionism
- Despair
- Giving away treasured objects
- Suicidal notes
- Suicidal language: *I'd be better off dead. You won't have to worry about me much longer. No one cares if I'm around; I'll just end it all.*
- A common thread in most suicides is a history of problems, piling up one after another with no end in sight. When helplessness combines with hopelessness, people are at serious risk.
- Sudden, unexplained emotional release from a chronic depression. Counselors working with chronically depressed people warn that a sudden, drastic elevation in mood may mask a suicidal intention. Depressed people sometimes muster just enough energy to conclude that suicide is the only way to end their pain. Because ultimate resolution is in sight, they may experience an extravagant emotional release. Such episodes may indicate heightened risk.

ACTION PLAN: DIG DEEPER

- Take people seriously—even if someone brushes you off with claims that he would never do anything that stupid.

Pay attention to repeated mentions of death, especially in the presence of a cluster of risk factors.

- Look and listen for unverbalized emotion. Suicidal people have difficulty articulating the pain they feel and the hopelessness and helplessness of their situations. What's more, they believe many of their cries for help go unheeded. For some, suicidal gestures are efforts to gain attention and get help. Suicide has been referred to as a "perverse language." It's as if the suicidal person says, "If you won't hear me, I'll make you hear me—because you can't ignore a dead body!"
- If you have the faintest reason to believe a person's use of suicidal language may be serious, engage him in a private conversation to investigate. Use the SLAP outline in section 2.1 to guide your questioning.
  - **S**pecific Plans: Does he have a plan?
  - **L**ethal Means: Is his method lethal?
  - **A**vailability of Method: Does he have access to his intended means?
  - **P**roximity of Helping Resources: Will his plan put him out of reach?
- If you believe the risk is immediate, don't hesitate to refer or otherwise call in reinforcements. If a student, friend, or colleague asks you to check her perception that someone may be suicidal, drop what you're doing and back her up. It honestly doesn't take long to gauge the seriousness of a person hinting at suicide.
- Ask the question: "Have you considered suicide?" There are two fairly typical responses—"No, things aren't that bad yet!" or "Yeah, I have." Even if the answer is no, you've opened a door for ministry. If the answer is "No, things aren't that bad yet," use the situation for preventive care. "I'm encouraged that it hasn't gotten that bad, but would you promise me that if it ever does, I'll be the first to know?" Don't miss an opportunity to let students know they're not alone and they can bank on the fact that at least one other person cares deeply about them.
- Believe you can help. Don't ignore obvious warnings like, "I'll just kill myself, and then he'll be happy!" just because you're afraid to get involved. You can be a bridge to life for kids and adults in suicidal crisis. A degree in counseling or specialized training is not required to make a difference.

Youth workers, parents, teachers, and even peers can be the critical link to help. When you recognize your place in the helping process, you are free from the anxiety of carrying the full weight of responsibility. Do your part.

• Share responsibility and recognize your limits. Your responsibility is to preserve life, not friendship.

RVP: Following the suicide of one of their best friends, several middle school guys came to me to confess that he had shared his plan to kill himself and asked them to keep his secret. They did, and in the process they loved their friend to death. Our challenge is loving our friends to life, and sometimes that means blowing the whistle on them. Don't assume more responsibility than is yours to assume. Recognize your limits, and involve others with more knowledge and experience.

CONTRACT FOR LIFE

Engage your friend in a *Contract for Life*. Suicide prevention programs across the country utilize contracting, because it has proven useful in saving lives. The contract represents a simple agreement between people. Although it can simply be verbal, evidence suggests that a written contract is more effective. A typical contract looks like this:

Contract for Life

I _____ promise not to harm myself or attempt to kill myself.
   Suicidal Person

If I feel like killing myself, I will call _____ at _____
                                    Crisis Helper   *phone number*
and if I am unable to reach him/her, I will call the Crisis Hotline at

_____ and speak with a crisis worker.
   Crisis Hotline phone number

_____
   Suicidal Person

_____
   Crisis Helper

People in crisis have been known to take the terms of the contract more literally than one would hope. In wording your contract, be sure it says, "speak with" not "*try* to speak with." More than one young person who has attempted suicide after agreeing to a contract has defended herself, saying, "You asked me to *try* to contact you first. I *did,* and you weren't available!" Also, make yourself available on a 24-hour basis if you use a contract, because people in crisis do not limit their times of struggle to your work schedule. Your willingness to have your life interrupted for a person in crisis is a highly believable message of compassion.

- Deal with the method. Ask if you can hold onto or dispose of the method of choice. Doing so will reduce the possibility of an impulsive act. Don't use physical force in attempting to take control of a lethal object, or the crisis may escalate to a point of danger for all involved.
- Be willing to involve the police if necessary.
- Develop an action plan. (See section 2.4.)
- Take care of the survivors. "Murder is a crime of violence against the murdered person," a Salman Rushdie character says, and, "Suicide is a crime of violence against those who remain alive."[1] Being the ones who remain alive in the aftermath of suicide isn't easy. Those who live on will experience many of the same emotions as those who lose a family member or friend by accidental or natural death: Shock, anger, guilt, fear, and relief are common to all losses. But emotions with the same names may be experienced in a different way and to a different degree after a suicide.
  - Those left behind must deal with *shock and disbelief* not only because of the loss but also because the death was self-inflicted. Questions like *Can I go on without this person?* are compounded by questions like *What in the world just happened here?*
  - *Anger* is frequently directed at the deceased for being so self-absorbed. Those left behind blame themselves for not being sensitive enough, for ignoring warnings, or for not saying or doing whatever would've made the difference. Even God is a likely target. *If God is so wise and powerful, why did he let this happen?*
  - Death brings out the *guilt* in people. We wonder if we should have done this or that and whether it might have

✦ **The Youth Worker's Guide To Helping Teenagers In Crisis**

changed things. Little children are notorious for wondering if they should have behaved better and if that would have prevented mommy or daddy from feeling bad enough to want to die.

- The ones still living wonder if they can go on investing in relationships and *fear* initiating new ones. They seriously question the saying: "Better to have loved and lost than never to have loved at all." The vulnerability required by a relationship may be more than they can handle.
- Few emotions create more conflicts in the hearts and minds of the living than the sense of *relief* that sometimes follows a suicide. The dead often had a history of difficulties that became a heavy burden for family and friends. The loss is tragic, but there can be an accompanying sense of relief that it's finally over.
- The *shame* associated with suicide is difficult for surviving family and friends to work through. It's not easy acknowledging that a loved one's death was a suicide. Some have trouble even saying the word.
- It's not unusual for physical and emotional difficulties to surface in the wake of suicide, among them: Headaches, bouts of uncontrollable crying, fatigue, sleeplessness—in short, the physical and emotional baggage that travels with any crisis.

RVP: A guest on a daytime talk show observed, "We all have skeletons in our closet. A suicide is someone who leaves his or her skeleton in someone else's closet." That's not bad. Skeletons are reminiscent of childhood fears that still frighten us every time the closet door opens.

I remember going to bed at night as a child, fearful that some other "thing" was present in my darkened room. I found great comfort in pulling the covers over my head. Of course, the covers didn't change the reality of what was or was not present in the room. I just found comfort in the fact that I couldn't see. Had danger been lurking in the shadows, I would've been blind to the attack. My decision to avoid rather than confront might have been deadly. But I was just a little boy.

Some things change very slowly. Many adults develop deep-seated emotional problems, because they've been unwilling or unable to confront the skeletons in their closets. Our challenge in helping survivors cope is in their willingness to face their skeletons, identify their continuing influence, admit their fear of getting too close, and then work to get rid of the blasted things.

- Well-meaning friends and family often avoid talking about the suicide or initiating discussion about the deceased altogether. Not helpful—survivors crave the openness of a helper who will take time to listen as they share their wide-ranging emotions. Crisis helpers have a chance to guide them back into the painful past while keeping their feet firmly planted in the present. That's how people embrace the hope that life will go on for them.
- Some survivors need the skills of a trained therapist to help them deal with their skeletons.
- Families may benefit greatly from family counseling where they can work through issues of grief together. In the process they'll learn new communication and listening skills.
- Some people find help in specialized post-suicide or child-loss support groups.

• Correct people's misconceptions about suicide:
  - *Anyone who tries to kill himself has got to be crazy.*

RVP: *I asked a gathering of students, "How many of you at one time or another have contemplated suicide? It may only have been a fleeting thought, or it could have been something you considered for a period of days or even weeks." Close to half of them raised their hands. Fortunately, they represent the majority of suicidal people who manage to regain balance and choose life.*

Which is to say, half the people in a given room may have felt sad, frustrated, alone, and depressed enough to consider death—but that doesn't make them crazy. The vast majority of people who commit suicide are ordinary people who didn't make it because they lost hope. Had they been a little more resilient or held on a little longer, who knows?

- *Rich kids kill themselves more often, because they're bored with life.* Suicide is a truly democratic phenomenon. Rich kids kill themselves; poor kids kill themselves. White kids, Black kids, Irish kids, Norwegian kids—all God's children kill themselves. But mainly it's adults who kill themselves. The suicide rate for 10-to-14-year-olds is less than 2 in 100,000; for 15-to-19-year-olds the rate hovers near 8 suicide deaths for every 100,000; and 20-to-34-year-olds kill themselves at a rate of nearly 13 for every 100,000. The rates then spike within the next two cohorts, which is important to note because many of the people within these age groups would be the parents of adolescents—about 15 out of every 100,000 among 35-to-44-year-olds, and 16 out of every 100,000 among 45-to-54-year-olds.[2]
- *Suicide runs in her family.* No genetic markers have been found to indicate an inherited predisposition toward suicide. That said, there are *suicidogenic* family patterns that increase the likelihood of suicide. If a parent, older sibling, or someone extremely close commits suicide when children are young, those children may grow to view suicide as an acceptable way of coping—after all, that's what Grandpa did. Suicide takes the standing of "learned behavior" for them. Later, they may be more inclined than their peers to view suicide as a coping tactic. There may be *suicidogenic* conditions in some communities and schools where cluster suicides give the impression of normalcy.
- *She killed herself on that gloomy Wednesday. The weather must have depressed her.* You'd think. But a higher percentage of suicides take place in nice weather—more in spring than winter, for example. When the weather is gloomy, many people are depressed, and misery loves company. But when nice weather comes along and most people's spirits are elevated, the misery of people who are depressed is intensified.
- *Better stay with her tonight! That's when most suicides happen.* Actually, most adolescent suicides occur after school, between three and six o'clock in the afternoon.
- *There was something romantic about their suicides. They loved each other so much—they wanted to die together.*

Anyone who has been at the scene of a suicide knows there's nothing romantic or beautiful about it.

RVP: At the end of a presentation on suicide prevention, a weeping youth worker approached me. He explained that he owned a carpet cleaning company and had recently been called by the police to clean up the basement of a home where a 17-year-old shot himself in the head. The police told him the funeral director only took "the large pieces." It was horrific. He hated thinking about the boy's parents seeing the mess that had been their child. Real-life suicide means you're dead—period. Then people have to clean up your mess. There's nothing romantic about that.

- *There were no clues. She didn't leave a note. It couldn't have been a suicide.* At most, one in four suicides leaves a note. When suicides increased in North America, police departments and researchers started conducting "psychological autopsies" to reconstruct the relational patterns and interactions of suicidal people. Their findings demonstrate conclusively that the majority of suicides were proceded by verbal or behavioral clues. Unfortunately, those clues were often missed until the postmortem.
- *Suicide is the unpardonable sin! She'll never be forgiven.* There's nothing in the Bible that represents suicide as a sin that God is either unwilling or unable to forgive. Some Christian traditions take issue with this position, but with due respect, their position tends to feel like a "single issue" concern founded on extra-biblical sources. We certainly don't welcome the news of any suicide, but we affirm the goodness of God who, even when we are faithless, remains faithful.[3] Taking it upon oneself to end life—whether our own or another's—is sin. But God's grace covers a multitude of sins, and suicide is one of them.
• Teach perspectives and skills that enliven resilience in adolescents. In no particular order, resilient kids learn:
  - Not to take hardship personally
  - Not to blame themselves for the choices of others
  - To adapt to change and recover from disappointment

- That every condition, pleasant or unpleasant, is temporary
- To endure difficulty and pain
- A rich emotional vocabulary
- Negotiation skills
- Empathy
- Adaptability
- To laugh at their own humanness
- Appropriate risk taking in hope of appropriate reward
- Flexibility

Opportunities to teach these lessons abound in the context of road trips, service projects, camping, creative play, small-group learning, and mission projects.

5.21 TERROR

Earthquakes...Terrorism...Fires...Hurricanes...Industrial Accidents...
Tornadoes...Mass Murders...

These are the nightmare experiences from which people wish they could awaken. Smart people argue about which is worse, natural or human-caused disasters. There is some research suggesting trauma symptoms may be somewhat more persistent in the wake of human-caused events.

But that may be splitting hairs. When the dead are dead, the injured broken, the buildings tumbled, communications scrambled, dreams dashed, and hope dimmed, it doesn't make much immediate difference what caused it. Later, maybe—but not until the terror subsides.

Terror is that overwhelming fear that all hell is breaking loose and there's nothing to be done about it. The most expansive terrors leave high body counts and lots of people injured, dislocated, and exposed to secondary health and safety dangers. These nightmare scenarios continue to reverberate, wrecking economies and social networks—leaving the survivors shocked, then skittish, then afraid and sad for a very long time.

Are these wide-ranging terrors worse than the intensely personal trauma of rape or murder? Who knows? The post-traumatic stress symptoms are similar. The big may just be bigger, visited upon more victims.

Here's the gotcha: Regardless of its nature, no matter how public or private it may be, by the time terror hits, it's too late to prepare for it and too late to stop it—otherwise it wouldn't be terror.

If we've learned anything, it's that we can't get away with bluffing kids—not for long. We can't really promise to keep them safe, because once they find out that's beyond our capacity, they'll stop trusting us. If kids come to believe we are untrustworthy, that's just one more loss in a world that already feels pretty dangerous.

Here's a partial list of terrors parents and youth workers can't promise to prevent:

- Weather-related disasters
- Earthquakes and tsunamis
- Asteroid strikes
- Communicable diseases
- Physical and sexual assaults
- Terrorist attacks and acts of war
- Criminality, school shootings, and random acts of violence
- Economic and financial ruin
- Accidents
- Genetic defects
- Our own deaths

Here's a fairly comprehensive list of what parents and youth workers can promise:

#1 I'll do my best to protect you every day.

#2 ...There is no two. It's too bad the list can't be
    more extensive, but this is reality—so there you have it.

ACTION PLAN: PREPARE AND RESPOND

Before terror strikes, here are some things parents and youth workers can do to prepare students for the worst:

- Promise to do your best to protect them every day.
- Develop a mass disaster plan together.
- Make sure everyone knows how to:
  - Dial 911
  - Reach extended family and trusted friends by phone
  - Turn off the gas and reset the electrical breakers
  - Locate and use flashlights, batteries, portable AM/FM radio, candles, matches, fresh water, and nonperishable food
  - Locate their homes on a map
  - Walk to the nearest medical facility
  - Locate and preserve insurance policies, wills, and financial records
- Identify a meeting place in case you're separated and can't get home following a disaster.
  - Identify a secondary meeting place if you can't get to the first one.
  - Identify a third place to meet if you can't reach the others.
  - Agree on who will stay put at whichever meeting place they can reach and who will move from location one to location two to location three until everyone is reunited.
- Develop a *personal disaster* agreement.
  - Parents and youth workers should communicate convincingly that no event can destroy their loving commitment—not pregnancy, HIV/AIDS, substance abuse, sexual assault, or murder.
  - Agree on a plan to disclose bad news, including getting help making the disclosure, if necessary, rather than sitting on it.

After terror hits, there is much that youth workers and parents can do. That, of course, is what this book is mainly about.

- As the shock subsides, ask "Now what?" Give students a reason to think into the future about recovery, rebuilding, and prevention.
- Lead students in serving others in age-appropriate (and situationally-appropriate) ways. In general, think about starting near at hand and working outward, always looking for unmet needs you can responsibly address.
- Speak into the terror theologically.

- One of the most potent messages in the face of catastrophe is the declaration, "It's not supposed to be like this." If we're anywhere near right about the God they talk about in the Bible, our Creator takes no pleasure in the suffering and death of his creatures. The companion piece to the declaration, "It's not supposed to be like this," is the affirmation, "And someday it won't be." The hope of the gospel includes a new heaven and a new earth—the home of righteousness. We haven't seen it, but in faith we see it coming. In the meantime, life is grace *and* bad things happen; people are capable of breathtaking displays of love *and* staggering acts of oppression; the sun rises and the rain falls on the righteous *and* the unrighteous. Life is hard; God is good.

• Watch for signs of post-traumatic stress disorder. (For more on this, see section 5.13.)

PRE-FLIGHT INSTRUCTIONS

The nice people who look after our safety on airplanes give a little speech at the beginning of each flight, reminding us that in the unlikely event of a cabin depressurization, an oxygen mask will drop down from the overhead panel. We are to grasp the mask just so, put it over our noses and mouths, tighten the elastic straps, and breathe normally.

It seems safe to say we probably don't want to know what kind of force it takes to depressurize the cabin of a jetliner—enough to wreak quite a bit of havoc. So flight attendants end this part of their presentation with the admonition to secure our own mask before assisting children or others who may need help.

This is good advice, since it's no good passing out while helping someone else get oxygen. If there's a disaster, you're as likely to be terrorized as anyone else. Take a deep breath, and pull yourself together as well as you can. But don't take too many breaths before you start looking around to see if someone else is turning blue.

5.22 TROUBLE WITH THE **LAW**

There are several obstacles for youth workers responding to kids with legal problems:

- You can't help if you don't know. Many parents are reluctant to admit that a son or daughter is in trouble with the law.
- Fear keeps youth workers out of detention facilities. It's the fear of the unknown—easily overcome, but not until it's acknowledged.
- Misunderstanding keeps youth workers out of detention facilities—it's the misunderstanding that kids in trouble aren't still kids. The biggest difference between most kids in trouble with the law and most other kids is that some got caught. That's a bit of an exaggeration, but honestly, kids are kids. The truly evil are in a different class than most juvenile offenders.
- That's about it. Except for violent offenses, you're likely to find an open door from people in the legal system.

ACTION PLAN: GO INSIDE

- Find someone who will take you inside a juvenile detention facility so you can get acclimated.
- Find someone who will take you inside a juvenile court proceeding.

- Talk with law enforcement officers about good kids who get in trouble and bad kids everybody thought were good until they got caught.
- Convince parents through every available means that you are ready and eager to support them through the good and bad times. Let them know that you know good parents have good kids who make bad decisions and you'll be there if they ever find themselves in that position.
- Most parents have no idea how the courts handle kids. If they know you're familiar with the police and juvenile justice system, they'll be more inclined to seek your help in a time of need. Here are the basics:
  - Whether a teenager is apprehended for a relatively minor offense like shoplifting or is suspected of having committed a more serious offense like rape, the legal procedures used by most jurisdictions follow the same pattern.
  - Generally, when a suspected offender is arrested or brought in for questioning, an intake evaluation is completed. This includes gathering information from the arresting officer and the juvenile. If the offense is relatively minor and there are no prior offenses, a "lecture-release" may be deemed appropriate, in which case the young offender and his or her parent/guardian are given a warning and sent home.
  - Otherwise, a probable cause hearing is set to determine whether or not sufficient evidence exists to justify continuance of the complaint.
  - If probable cause is established, a trial date is set before a juvenile court judge, or in certain situations a judge and jury.
  - The young person may be remanded to the custody of his parent/guardian or to a juvenile detention facility to await trial.
  - During the entire process, some offenders will be detained in a juvenile facility because of prior offenses, severity of the crime, inability to post bond, unwillingness of custodial parents to receive the minor child back into their custody because the child is beyond their control, high flight risk, or any other factor the court believes

might prevent the juvenile from appearing for the next phase of the process.

- If the juvenile judge or judge and jury decide the evidence proves guilt beyond reasonable doubt, then a disposition hearing is set, during which time the judge weighs recommendations from the prosecution and defense, considers the statutory options, and renders a verdict spelling out what treatment or punitive measures are ordered by the court.

- Most short-term detention and long-term treatment facilities for juveniles welcome the involvement of clergy or church-related youth workers who desire to maintain a continuing relationship with young parishioners who've been institutionalized. Some facilities require strict adherence to regular visiting hour procedures, but most are flexible enough to accommodate a pastor or youth worker's schedule.

So, you're a youth worker. If you have a kid in jail, go do youth work. Yes, the culture is different—so what? The only way to overcome your uneasiness is to show up and figure out how to do what you do in a different culture.

• Take time to understand the institution's policies, procedures, and activities so you can better understand the young offender's situation. Incarceration is terribly difficult for most adolescents no matter how self-assured they may appear on the surface.

• Develop relationships with line staff, counselors, and chaplains within the institution. You'll enjoy greater freedom when those in charge see you as cooperative, trustworthy, and part of their team.

• Don't make assumptions about a facility because it's county or state operated. We're not talking public school here—you still have to be respectful, but you can talk plainly about faith.

RVP: *I was privileged to work for a decade in a thoroughly secular environment where I was afforded incredible freedom to do ministry with desperately needy adolescent guys and girls. The chaplain's office may already be offering outstanding programs and resources that you can support. Above all, recognize that you're not in competition with the institutional* *staff. Your support of their efforts and their support of yours can really benefit kids.*

- Be alert for manipulative behaviors. The well-meaning but naïve youth worker is a prime target for a developing con artist to practice on. In their desperate search for understanding, love, and acceptance, teenagers often manipulate adults for their own ends. They may take advantage of your relationship to earn favor with other staff members. The orientation and training sessions offered to volunteers by many institutions are helpful in learning how to discern and confront manipulative behaviors.
- Learn to be a deep listener. Institutionalized kids learn quickly that anything they say can and probably will be used against them! They become suspicious of everyone and tend to shy away from anything deeper than a surface connection. In *At Risk: Bringing Hope to Hurting Teenagers*, Dr. Scott Larson writes,

> Erick Erikson has pointed out that unless the issue of trust is resolved for a young person, that person will remain stunted in emotional (and spiritual) development. Honesty, consistency, and a stable presence through both good and bad times are what lay the critical foundation of trust. Our role is not to fix teenagers but to be there for them. And this, over time, will lay a foundation for God to bring into their lives others with whom they can build relationships of trust as well.[1]

- Keep promises you make, and don't make promises you may not be able to keep. If you say you're going to visit on a particular day, be there or have a note from your doctor. If you can't be there, call and let the youngster know you're sorry. Be consistent and dependable.
- Leave books, magazines, and CDs (if permissible) with the young person. Kids living in institutions generally have too much free time and may welcome reading and listening material.
- Be there when he gets out. Re-entry is tough. Give a brother a hand.

PRIVATE TREATMENT FACILITIES

Unless you've walked in the shoes of a parent living with a wildly out-of-control kid, it's hard to imagine the depth of their pain and heartbreak.

That said, whenever we're asked about placing a kid in a private residential treatment facility, we're quick to encourage parents to exhaust every other possible measure before entrusting an adolescent's emotional health and well-being to others in an institutional setting. The overwhelming majority of young people we've seen placed in residential treatment facilities have only become more adept in their acting-out behaviors as a result of being thrust into a community of like-minded peers. The behavior modification programs utilized in many of these facilities mainly teach kids how to play the game more effectively.

6.0 APPENDIXES

We've included several appendixes that we think you'll find helpful. When possible, we've also included updates on the Web at www.youthspecialties.com/store/crisis/

6.1 ACTION PLAN **WORKSHEET**

I. What is the identified problem (beyond the presenting problem)?

II. What are the possible outcomes (both negative and positive)?
A. Which is the most desirable outcome?
B. What general steps are required to move toward that outcome? (Return to more specific steps later.)

III. Who are the active participants, and what is their stake in the outcome?

IV. Who are the passive participants, and what is their stake? (And what can be expected from each stakeholder?)

V. What are the resources and roadblocks to reaching the goal?

VI. Who else should be involved in the solution?
A. Extended family?
B. Professional referral?
1. Medical doctor?
2. Psychiatrist, psychologist?
3. Social worker?
4. Law enforcement?
5. Lawyer?
6. Pastor?

7. School personnel?
8. Employer?
9. Friends?

VII. What specific steps must be taken?
    A. In what order?
    B. Who should take responsibility for each step?
    C. Who should provide support?

VIII. What is the timetable?

IX. What other resources are required?
    A. Money?
    B. Transportation?
    C. Temporary lodging?
    D. Food?
    E. Other?

X. Who will provide ongoing support and feedback?

6.2 CHILD ABUSE REPORTING **NUMBERS**

Each state designates specific agencies to receive and investigate reports of suspected child abuse and neglect. Typically, this responsibility is carried out by Child Protective Services (CPS) within a Department of Social Services, Department of Human Resources, or Division of Family and Children Services. In some states, police departments may also receive reports of child abuse or neglect.

For more information or assistance with reporting, call Childhelp USA®, 800-4-A-CHILD (800-422-4453), or your local CPS agency.

In most cases, the toll-free numbers listed below are only accessible from within the state listed. If calling from out-of-state, use the local (toll) number listed or call Childhelp USA® for assistance. Also listed below are links to state Web sites, which can provide additional information. Check www.youthspecialties.com/store/crisis/ for updates.

ALABAMA
Local (toll): (334) 242-9500
Web site: www.dhr.state.al.us/page.asp?pageid=304

ALASKA
Toll-free: (800) 478-4444
Web site: www.hss.state.ak.us/ocs/default.htm

ARIZONA
Toll-free: (888) SOS-CHILD (888-767-2445)
Web site: www.de.state.az.us/dcyf/cps/

ARKANSAS
Toll-free: (800) 482-5964
Web site: www.state.ar.us/dhs/chilnfam/child_protective_
services.htm

CALIFORNIA
Local (toll): (916) 445-2771
Web site: www.dss.cahwnet.gov/cdssweb/FindServic_716.htm

COLORADO
Web site: www.cdhs.state.co.us/cyf/cwelfare/cwweb.html
Contact local agency or Childhelp USA for assistance.

CONNECTICUT
TDD: (800) 624-5518
Toll-free: (800) 842-2288
Web site: www.state.ct.us/dcf/HOTLINE.htm

DELAWARE
Toll-free: (800) 292-9582
Local (toll): (302) 577-6550
Web site: www.state.de.us/kids/

DISTRICT OF COLUMBIA
Toll-free: (877) 671-SAFE (877-671-7233)
Local (toll): (202) 671-7233
Web site: http://cfsa.dc.gov/cfsa/cwp/view.asp?a=3&q=520663&
cfsaNav=%7C31319%7C

FLORIDA
Toll-free: (800) 96-ABUSE (800-962-2873)
Web site: http://www5.myflorida.com/cf_web/myflorida2/
healthhuman/childabuse/

GEORGIA
Web site: http://dfcs.dhr.georgia.gov/portal/site
Contact local agency or Childhelp USA for assistance.

HAWAII

Web site: http://www.state.hi.us/dhs/
Contact local agency or Childhelp USA for assistance.

IDAHO

Toll-free: (800) 926-2588
Web site: http://www.healthandwelfare.idaho.gov/portal/alias_
           Rainbow/land_en-US/tablD_3333/DesktopDefault.aspx

ILLINOIS

Toll-free: (800) 252-2873
Local (toll): (217) 785-4020
Web site: http://www.state.il.us/dcfs/child/index.shtml

INDIANA

Toll-free: (800) 800-5556
Web site: http://www.in.gov/fssa/families/protection/dfcchi.html

IOWA

Toll-free: (800) 362-2178
Local (toll): (515) 281-3240
Web site: http://www.dhs.state.ia.us/reportingchildabuse.asp

KANSAS

Toll-free: (800) 922-5330
Local (toll): (785) 296-0044
Web site: http://www.srskansas.org/services/child_protective_
           services.htm

KENTUCKY

Toll-free: (800) 752-6200
Local (toll): (502) 595-4550
Web site: http://cfc.state.ky.us/help/child_abuse.asp

LOUISIANA

Local (toll): (225) 342-6832
Web site: http://dss.state.la.us/departments/ocs/child_welfare_
           services.html

MAINE
Toll-free: (800) 452-1999
Local (toll): (207) 287-2983
Web site: http://www.maine.gov/dhhs/bcfs/abuse.htm

MARYLAND
Toll-free: (800) 332-6347
Web site: http://www.dhr.state.md.us/cps/

MASSACHUSETTS
Toll-free: (800) 792-5200
Local (toll): (617) 232-4882
Web site: http://www.mass.gov/portal/index.jsp?pageID=
        eohhs2subtopic&L=5&L0=Home&L1=Consumer&L2=
        Family+Services&L3=Violence%2c+Abuse+or+Neglect
        &L4=Child+Abuse+and+Neglect&sid=Eeohhs2

MICHIGAN
Toll-free: (800) 942-4357
Local (toll): (517) 373-3572
Web site: http://www.michigan.gov/fia/0,1607,7-124-5452_7119-
        21208--,00.html

MINNESOTA
Local (toll): (651) 291-0211
        Web   site: http://www.dhs.state.mn.us/CFS/Programs/
        ChildProtection/default.htm

MISSISSIPPI
Toll-free: (800) 222-8000
Local (toll): (601) 359-4991
Web site: http://www.mdhs.state.ms.us/fcs_prot.html

MISSOURI
Toll-free: (800) 392-3738
Local (toll): (573) 751-3448
Web site: http://www.dss.state.mo.us/dfs/csp.htm

MONTANA
Toll-free: (866) 820-KIDS (866-820-5437)
Local (toll): (406) 444-5900
Web site: http://www.dphhs.state.mt.us/about_us/divisions/
child_family_services/child_family_services.htm

NEBRASKA
Toll-free: (800) 652-1999
Local (toll): (402) 595-1324
Web site: http://www.hhs.state.ne.us/cha/chaindex.htm

NEVADA
Toll-free: (800) 992-5757
Local (toll): (775) 684-4400
Web site: http://dcfs.state.nv.us/page24.html

NEW HAMPSHIRE
Toll-free: (800) 894-5533
Local (toll): (603) 271-6556
Web site: http://www.dhhs.state.nh.us/DHHS/BCP/default.htm

NEW JERSEY
TDD: (800) 835-5510
Toll-free: (800) 792-8610
Web site: http://www.state.nj.us/humanservices/dyfs/index.html

NEW MEXICO
Toll-free: (800) 797-3260
Local (toll): (505) 841-6100
Web site: http://www.cyfd.org/index.htm

NEW YORK
TDD: (800) 369-2437
Toll-free: (800) 342-3720
Local (toll): (518) 474-8740
Web site: http://www.ocfs.state.ny.us/main/cps/

NORTH CAROLINA
Web site: http://www.dhhs.state.nc.us/dss/c_srv/cserv_protect.htm
Contact local agency or Childhelp USA for assistance.

NORTH DAKOTA
Local (toll): (701) 328-2316
Web site: http://www.state.nd.us/humanservices/services/
        childfamily/cps/

OHIO
Web site: http://jfs.ohio.gov/ocf/
Contact local agency or Childhelp USA for assistance.

OKLAHOMA
Toll-free: (800) 522-3511
Web site: http://www.okdhs.org/dcfs/

OREGON
TDD: (503) 378-5414
Toll-free: (800) 854-3508; Ext. 2402
Local (toll): (503) 378-6704
Web site: http://www.dhs.state.or.us/children/abuse/cps/
        cw_branches.htm

PENNSYLVANIA
Toll-free: (800) 932-0313
Local (toll): (717) 783-8744
Web site: http://www.dpw.state.pa.us/Child/ChildAbuseNeglect/

RHODE ISLAND
Toll-free: (800) RI-CHILD (800-742-4453)
Web site: http://www.dcyf.ri.gov/chldwelfare/reporting.htm

SOUTH CAROLINA
Local (toll): (803) 898-7318
Web site: http://www.state.sc.us/dss/

SOUTH DAKOTA
Local (toll): (605) 773-3227
Web site: http://www.state.sd.us/social/CPS/

TENNESSEE
Toll-free: (877) 237-0004
Web site: http://www.state.tn.us/youth/cps/index.htm

TEXAS
Toll-free: (800) 252-5400
After hours: (512) 832-2020
Local (toll): (512) 834-3784
Web site: http://www.tdprs.state.tx.us/

UTAH
Toll-free:(800) 678-9399
Web site: http://www.hsdcfs.utah.gov/

VERMONT
Toll-free: (800) 649-5285
After hours: (802) 863-7533
Web site: http://www.state.vt.us/srs/childcare/index.htm

VIRGINIA
Toll-free: (800) 552-7096
Local (toll): (804) 786-8536
Web site: http://www.dss.state.va.us/family/cps.html

WASHINGTON
Toll-free: (866) END-HARM (866-363-4276)
Web site: http://www1.dshs.wa.gov/ca/safety/prevAbuse.asp?1

WEST VIRGINIA
Toll-free: (800) 352-6513
Web site: http://www.wvdhhr.org/oss/children/cps.asp

WISCONSIN
Local (toll): (608) 266-3036
Web site: http://www.dhfs.state.wi.us/Children/CPS/index.HTM

WYOMING
Web site: http://dfsweb.state.wy.us/menu.htm
Contact local agency or Childhelp USA for assistance.

Information courtesy of the National Clearinghouse on Child Abuse and Neglect Information: http://nccanch.acf.hhs.gov/pubs/reslist/rl_dsp.cfm?rs_id=5&rate_chno=11-11172

6.3 EMOTIONAL **MAP**

HAPPY
Accepted
Appreciated
Approved Of
Blissful
Calm
Capable
Carefree
Cheerful
Comfortable
Confident
Content
Delighted
Ecstatic
Elated
Encouraged
Enthusiastic
Exhilarated
Exultant
Giddy

Glad
Gleeful
Grateful
High
Hilarious
Hopeful
Inspired
Jolly
Joyous
Knocked Out
Light
Lighthearted
Like a Contributor
Lively
Loved
Merry
Mirthful
Needed
Obnoxious
Optimistic

Overjoyed
Peaceful
Playful
Pleased
Rapturous
Satisfied
Secure
Serene
Significant
Spirited
Sunny
Thankful
Thrilled
Tranquil
Understood
Warm

UNHAPPY
Bored
Bothered

Cheerless

Choked Up

Cloudy

Dark

Dejected

Depressed

Despondent

Disappointed

Discontent

Discouraged

Disheartened

Distracted

Downcast

Downhearted

Dreadful

Dreary

Dull

Gloomy

Glum

Held Captive

Insignificant

Joyless

Melancholy

Moody

Mopey

Mournful

Oppressed

Out of Sorts

Quiet

Sad

Somber

Sorrowful

Spiritless

Sulky

Sullen

Upset

Vacant

Woeful

ANGRY

Annoyed

Belligerent

Bent Out of Shape

Bitter

Boiling

Bugged

Contemptuous

Defiant

Disgusted

Enraged

Exasperated

Fuming

Furious

Incensed

Indignant

Inflamed

Infuriated

Irate

Irritated

Mad

Peeved

Perturbed

Riled

Seething

Ticked Off

Touchy

Up in Arms

Worked Up

Wrathful

HURT

Abandoned

Accused

Aching

Afflicted

Agonized

Belittled

Betrayed

Defensive

Degraded

Deprived

Diminished

Discounted

Disrespected

Grieved

Hampered

Infuriated

Injured

In Pain

Knifed in the Back

Left Out

Let Down

Misused

Offended

Pathetic

Persecuted

Provoked

Put Down

Resentful

Taken Advantage Of

Tortured

Unappreciated

Unimportant

Unloved

Untrusted

Used

Victimized

Woeful

Worried

OVERWHELMED

Astounded

Beat

Bewildered

Blah

Blown Away

Broken

Burned Out

Cold

Confused

Crushed

Deflated

Demotivated

Disoriented

Dull

Dumbfounded

Empty

Exhausted

Flat

Floored

Fried

Grief-stricken

Heartbroken

Helpless

Hollow

Humble

Humiliated

In Despair

In Over My Head

Inconsolable

Insecure

Like Giving Up

Like I'm Drowning

Like Quitting

Like Running Away

Low

Lost

Miserable

Mortified

Mournful

Nauseated

Numb

Panicky

Paralyzed

Pessimistic

Plagued

Powerless

Reverent

Shook

Shut Down

Sick

Staggered

Stumped

Stunned

Tired

Weary

Worn Out

EXCITED

Fearless

Bold

Brave

Calm

Certain

Confident

Determined

Firm

Hungry

Impatient

Resolved

Seductive

Self-reliant

Sexy

Strong

ANXIOUS

Absorbed

Agitated

Alone

Apprehensive

Cautious

Concerned

Curious

Dependent

Distant

Distressed

Distrustful

Doubtful

Eager

Engrossed

Fascinated

Hesitant

Indecisive

Inquisitive

Intent

Interested

Intrigued

Itchy

Nosey

Perplexed

Questioning

Skeptical

Snoopy

Suspicious

Unbelieving

Uncertain

Uneasy

Uptight

Wavering

AFRAID

Aghast

Alarmed

Appalled

Apprehensive

Awed

Cautious

Chicken

Cowardly

Dismayed

Fainthearted

Fearful

Fidgety

Frightened

Hesitant

Horrified

Hysterical

Immobilized

Insecure

Lonely

Nervous

Panicky

Paralyzed

Petrified

Restless

Scared

Shaky

Sheepish

Suspicious

Terrified

Threatened

Timid

Trembly

GUILTY

Ashamed

Bad

Dumb

Embarrassed

Foolish

Incompetent

Infantile

Like a Failure

Like a Fool

Naïve

Remorseful

Repentant

Ridiculous

Self-conscious

Selfish

Silly

Slow

Stupid

Unfit

Useless

Weird

Worthless

Wrong

SYMPATHETIC

Compassionate

Concerned

Connected

Empathetic

Moved

Understanding

6.4   FIRST AID FOR AN **OVERDOSE**

Our concern for the safety of young people entrusted to our care and a sobering awareness of the litigious nature of our culture should motivate youth workers to be adequately prepared for emergencies. A working knowledge of first aid can mean the difference between life and death in critical circumstances.

- If the person is conscious, do not allow her to go to sleep. Keep her talking and as alert as possible. Find out what drug(s) were taken and in what quantity.
- If the person is unconscious or comatose, check breathing. Be certain that the throat is clear of foreign matter. Check the body for any necklace, bracelet, or emergency medical card identifying a medical condition that could cause the symptoms you are seeing. Otherwise, check for bottles, pill containers, or any other evidence of what might have been injested or injected. Ask friends who might know but are afraid to respond for fear that they might get in trouble.
- If you are able to identify what was ingested or injected and a phone is nearby, call either 911, the poison control center, or a local hospital and ask for instructions about what to do next. If you don't have access to a telephone and can get to help in a relatively short period of time, do not induce vomiting.
- If the person is conscious and has taken the overdose within a two-hour period, dilute the poison or drugs in the stomach with two or three cups of water, and induce vomiting. If

the overdose was injected, cleaning the stomach will be of little help.

- Get the person to the nearest hospital or emergency clinic as soon and as safely as possible. Bring any empty bottles or containers of the drugs you suspect were taken.
- Be sure another person rides along to the hospital with the driver and the overdosed person so he or she can monitor breathing and provide assistance if the teenager vomits.

6.5 STATE SEX OFFENDER **REGISTRIES**

ALABAMA
www.dps.state.al.us/public/abi/system/so

ALASKA
www.dps.state.ak.us/nSorcr/asp

ARIZONA
www.azsexoffender.org

ARKANSAS
www.acic.org/offender/index.htm

CALIFORNIA
http://caag.state.ca.us/megan

COLORADO
http://sor.state.co.us/default.asp

CONNECTICUT
www.state.ct.us/dps/Sex_Offender_Registry.htm

DELAWARE
www.state.de.us/dsp/sexoff/index.htm

DISTRICT OF COLUMBIA
http://mpdc.dc.gov/serv/sor/sor.shtm

FLORIDA
http://www3.fdle.state.fl.us/sexual_predators

GEORGIA
www.ganet.org/gbi/sorsch.cgi

HAWAII
http://pahoehoe.ehawaii.gov/sexoff

IDAHO
www.isp.state.id.us/identification/sex_offender/
public_access.htm

ILLINOIS
www.isp.state.il.us/sor/frames.htm

INDIANA
https://secure.in.gov/serv/cji_sor

IOWA
www.state.ia.us/government/dps/dci/isor

KANSAS
http://www.accesskansas.org/kbi/ro.shtml

Kentucky
http://kspsor.state.ky.us

LOUISIANA
www.lasocpr.lsp.org/socpr

MAINE
www.informe.org/sor

MARYLAND
www.dpscs.state.md.us/sor

MASSACHUSETTS
www.mass.gov/sorb

MICHIGAN
www.mipsor.state.mi.us

MINNESOTA
www.dps.state.mn.us/bca/Invest/Documents/Page-07.html

MISSISSIPPI
http://SOR.MDPS.STATE.MS.US

MISSOURI
www.mshp.dps.missouri.gov/MSHPWeb/PatrolDivisions/CRID/
SOR/SORPage.html

MONTANA
http://svor.doj.state.mt.us

NEBRASKA
www.nsp.state.ne.us/sor/

NEVADA
www.nvsexoffenders.gov/

NEW HAMPSHIRE
http://oit.nh.gov/nsor/

NEW JERSEY
www.njsp.org/info/reg_sexoffend.html

NEW MEXICO
www.nmsexoffender.dps.state.nm.us/servlet/hit_serv.class

NEW YORK
www.criminaljustice.state.ny.us/nsor

NORTH CAROLINA
http://sbi.jus.state.nc.us/DOJHAHT/SOR/Default.htm

NORTH DAKOTA
www.ndsexoffender.com

OHIO
www.esorn.ag.state.oh.us

OKLAHOMA
http://docapp8.doc.state.ok.us/servlet/page?_pageid=190&_
dad=portal30&_schema=PORTAL30

OREGON
www.oregonsatf.org/offender_registry.html

PENNSYLVANIA
www.psp2.state.pa.us/svp/pa_map.htm

RHODE ISLAND
http://courtconnect.courts.state.ri.us/pls/ri_adult/
ck_public_qry_main.cp_main_idx

SOUTH CAROLINA
www.sled.state.sc.us/SLED/default.asp?Category=
SCSO&Service=SCSO_01

SOUTH DAKOTA
http://dci.sd.gov/administration/id/sexoffender/index.asp

TENNESSEE
www.ticic.state.tn.us//SEX_ofndr/search_short.asp

TEXAS
http://records.txdps.state.tx.us

UTAH
www.udc.state.ut.us/asp-bin/sexoffendersearchform.asp

VERMONT
http://170.222.24.9/cjs/s_registry.htm

VIRGINIA
http://sex-offender.vsp.state.va.us/cool-ICE

WASHINGTON
http://ml.waspc.org/Accept.aspx?ReturnUrl=percent2fSearchAround.aspx

WEST VIRGINIA
www.wvstatepolice.com/sexoff

WISCONSIN
http://widocoffenders.org

WYOMING
http://attorneygeneral.state.wy.us/dci/so/so_registration.html

Individual FBI Field Offices serve as primary points of contact for persons requesting FBI assistance. For further information about FBI services or to request assistance, please contact a Crimes Against Children Coordinator at your local FBI Field Office. The above information was found at www.fbi.gov/hq/cid/cac/states.htm.

6.6 WHERE IN THE WORLD ARE **YOU?**

When it comes to our experience, our knowledge, and our awareness of sexuality, we're probably all over the map. Please read the following set of statements and circle the one that is most like you today.

I'll give you plenty of time to respond, so take your time. I'm more interested in honesty than anything else, so please don't put your name on this. I promise I won't use handwriting analysis or dust for fingerprints to figure out who wrote what. But if you want to talk with me about any of this, catch me when we're done, or give me a call at your convenience.

Instructions: Circle the percentage that describes the degree to which each statement applies to you. One hundred percent means it's completely true for you today. Fifty percent means it's half true today. Zero percent means it's not true at all today.

• I have very little interest in sex.	0%	50%	100%
• I think about sex, but I don't do anything about it.	0%	50%	100%
• I fool around a little.	0%	50%	100%
• I fool around a lot.	0%	50%	100%
• I've had sex.	0%	50%	100%
• I've been sexually molested.	0%	50%	100%

- I've been forced into sexual acts I didn't want to do.   0%   50%   100%
- I've been forced into sexual acts with someone in my extended family.   0%   50%   100%
- I've been forcibly raped.   0%   50%   100%
- I'm having sex in a current relationship, but I'm careful.   0%   50%   100%
- I'm having sex in a current relationship, and I'm not always careful.   0%   50%   100%
- I've been having sex for a while and with a number of partners, and I'm always very careful.   0%   50%   100%
- I've been having sex for a while and with a number of partners, but I'm not always careful.   0%   50%   100%
- I used to have more sex than I do now.   0%   50%   100%
- I'm not having sex right now, but that could change if the right person came along.   0%   50%   100%
- I haven't had sex yet, and I'm intentionally holding out for the right person, engagement, or marriage.   0%   50%   100%
- I've been tested for sexually transmitted diseases since the last time I had unprotected sex.   0%   50%   100%

- The last time I had sex was:
    _____ in the last week
    _____ in the last month
    _____ in the last three months
    _____ in the last six months
    _____ in the last year
    _____ in the last two years
    _____ in the last three years
    _____ more than three years ago
    _____ never

Circle the percentage that describes how you feel about talking about sexuality in our youth group.

• I have nothing to hide, nothing to fear, and nothing to lose.	0%	50%	100%
• I'll share most anything I think or feel pretty much anytime.	0%	50%	100%
• I'm glad for the chance to explore sexual issues in this group.	0%	50%	100%
• I really don't know very much, and I really don't have much to share.	0%	50%	100%
• I'll share some things about sexuality, as long as they're not too embarrassing or risky.	0%	50%	100%
• I don't want to look stupid or anything.	0%	50%	100%

If we were going to talk about sexual issues in the group, circle the percentage that describes your interest level.

• Reliable information about sexual biology.	0%	50%	100%
• An honest discussion of the issues surrounding abortion.	0%	50%	100%
• An honest discussion of the issues surrounding homosexuality.	0%	50%	100%
• An honest discussion of the issues surrounding bisexuality.	0%	50%	100%
• Clarifying the differences between males and females.	0%	50%	100%
• Clarifying the similarities between males and females.	0%	50%	100%
• What the Bible says about sexual behavior.	0%	50%	100%
• What the Bible doesn't say about sexual behavior.	0%	50%	100%
• How to start over.	0%	50%	100%
• Why people disagree so much about sexual behavior.	0%	50%	100%
• An honest discussion about sexual orientation.	0%	50%	100%

• An honest discussion about incest.	0%	50%	100%
• Dating.	0%	50%	100%
• Remaining single.	0%	50%	100%
• Abstinence.	0%	50%	100%
• An honest discussion about sexual molestation.	0%	50%	100%
• An honest discussion about rape.	0%	50%	100%
• An honest discussion about gender language.	0%	50%	100%
• How to help a friend who is in sexual danger.	0%	50%	100%
• How to help a friend who is pregnant.	0%	50%	100%
• How to help a friend who is sexually confused.	0%	50%	100%

If you're having trouble with the idea of talking about sex in our group, circle the percentage closest to your attitude.

• I'm willing, but I'm not entirely comfortable talking about sexuality in our group.	0%	50%	100%
• I'm willing, but I'm very uncomfortable talking about sexuality in our group.	0%	50%	100%
• I'm simply not comfortable talking about sexual issues in this group.	0%	50%	100%
• I'm not comfortable talking about sexual issues in this group because I think it will be judgmental.	0%	50%	100%
• I'm not comfortable talking about sexual issues in this group because I think it will be more liberal than I'm comfortable with.	0%	50%	100%
• I'm not comfortable talking about sexual issues in this group because I like what I'm doing and I don't want anybody to tell me to change.	0%	50%	100%
• I'm not comfortable talking about sexual issues anywhere.	0%	50%	100%

• I think sex is purely personal, and I'd rather not discuss it.	0%	50%	100%
• I'm sick of talking about this stuff. Let's just move on.	0%	50%	100%
• If you insist on talking about sex, let me know when you're done, and I'll consider coming back to the group at that point.	0%	50%	100%

This survey is adapted from *Good Sex: A Whole-Person Approach to Teenage Sexuality and God*, by Jim Hancock and Kara Eckmann Powell (Grand Rapids, Mich.: YS/Zondervan, 2001), page 29.

6.7 GLOSSARY OF CHILD PROTECTIVE
SERVICES TERMS

ACID: Common street name for LSD (Lysergic Acid Diethylamide).

ADDICTION: A chronic, relapsing disease characterized by compulsive drug seeking and abuse, and by long-lasting chemical changes in the brain.

ADJUDICATORY HEARINGS: Held by the juvenile and family court to determine whether a child has been maltreated or whether another legal basis exists for the state to intervene to protect the child.

ADOPTION AND SAFE FAMILIES ACT (ASFA): Designed to improve the safety of children, to promote adoption and other permanent homes for children who need them, and to support families. The law requires CPS agencies to provide more timely and focused assessment and intervention services to the children and families that are served within the CPS system.

ADOPTIVE PARENT: A person with the legal relation of parent to a child not related by birth, with the same mutual rights and obligations that exist between children and their birth parents. The legal relationship has been finalized.

AGE: Age calculated in years at the time of the report of abuse or neglect or as of December 31 of the reporting year.

ALLEGED PERPETRATOR: An individual who is alleged to have caused or knowingly allowed the maltreatment of a child as stated in an incident of child abuse or neglect.

ALLEGED VICTIM: Child about whom a report regarding maltreatment has been made to a CPS agency.

ALTERNATIVE RESPONSE SYSTEM: A maltreatment disposition system used in some states that provides for responses other than substantiated, indicated, and unsubstantiated. In such a system, children may or may not be determined to be maltreatment victims. Such a system may be known as a "diversified" system or an "in need of services" system.

AMPHETAMINES: Stimulant drugs whose effects are very similar to cocaine.

ANABOLIC STEROIDS: Synthetic substances related to the male sex hormone, which promote the growth of skeletal muscle and the development of male sexual characteristics.

ANALGESICS: A group of medications that reduce pain.

ANGEL DUST: Common street name for PCP (Phencyclidine).

ANONYMOUS or UNKNOWN REPORT SOURCE: An individual who notifies a CPS agency of suspected child maltreatment without identifying himself; or the type of report source is unknown.

ASSESSMENT: A process by which the CPS agency determines whether the child or other persons involved in the report of alleged maltreatment are in need of services.

BARBITURATE: A type of central nervous system (CNS) depressant often prescribed to promote sleep.

BENZODIAZEPINE: A type of CNS depressant prescribed to relieve anxiety; among the most widely prescribed medications, including Valium and Librium.

BIRTH COHORT: A birth cohort consists of all persons born within a given period of time, such as a calendar year.

BIOLOGICAL PARENT: The birth mother or father of the child.

BOY: A male child younger than 18 years old.

CANNABIS: The botanical name for the plant from which marijuana comes.

CAPTA: See Child Abuse Prevention and Treatment Act.

CAREGIVER: A person responsible for the care and supervision of the alleged child victim.

CASA: See Court-Appointed Special Advocate.

CASE-LEVEL DATA: Information submitted by the states in the child file containing individual child or report maltreatment characteristics.

CASEWORKER: A staff person assigned to a report of child maltreatment at the time of the report disposition.

CHILD: A person younger than 18 years old or considered to be a minor under state law.

CHILD ABUSE AND NEGLECT STATE GRANT: Funding to the states for programs serving abused and neglected children, awarded under the Child Abuse Prevention and Treatment Act (CAPTA). May be used to assist states in intake and assessment, screening and investigation of child abuse and neglect reports, improving risk and safety assessment protocols, training child protective service workers and mandated reporters, and improving services to disabled infants with life-threatening conditions.

CHILD ABUSE PREVENTION AND TREATMENT ACT
[42 U.S.C. 5101 ET SEQ.] (CAPTA): Law that provides the
foundation for federal involvement in child protection and child
welfare services. The 1996 Amendments provide for, among
other things, annual state data reports on child maltreatment to
the Secretary of Health and Human Services.

CHILD DAYCARE PROVIDER: A person with a temporary
caregiver responsibility, but who is not related to the child, such
as a daycare center staff member, a family daycare provider,
or a baby-sitter. Does not include persons with legal custody or
guardianship of the child.

CHILD DEATH REVIEW TEAM: A state team of professionals
who reviews all reports surrounding the death of a child.

CHILD MALTREATMENT: An act or failure to act by a parent,
caregiver, or other person as defined under state law that results
in physical abuse, neglect, medical neglect, sexual abuse,
emotional abuse, or an act or failure to act that presents an
imminent risk of serious harm to a child.

CHILD PROTECTIVE SERVICES (CPS): An official agency
of a state having the responsibility for child protective services
and activities. CPS receives reports, investigates, and provides
intervention and treatment services to children and families in
which child maltreatment has occurred. Frequently, this agency
is located within larger public social service agencies, such as
the Department of Social Services.

CHILD PROTECTIVE SERVICES (CPS) SUPERVISOR:
The manager of the caseworker assigned to a report of child
maltreatment at the time of the report disposition.

CHILD PROTECTIVE SERVICES (CPS) WORKER: The
person assigned to a report of child maltreatment at the time of
the report disposition.

CHILD PROTECTIVE SERVICES (CPS) WORKFORCE:
The CPS supervisors and workers assigned to handle a child

maltreatment report. May include other administrative staff, as defined by the state agency.

CHILD RECORD: A case-level record in the child file containing the data associated with one child in one report.

CHILD VICTIM: A child for whom an incident of abuse or neglect has been substantiated or indicated by an investigation or assessment. A state may include some children with alternative dispositions as victims.

CHILDREN'S BUREAU: Federal agency within the Administration on Children, Youth and Families, Administration for Children and Families, U.S. Department of Health & Human Services.

CHILD'S LIVING ARRANGEMENT: The home environment in which the child was residing at the time of the report (for example, family or substitute care).

CLOSED WITH NO FINDING: Disposition that does not conclude with a specific finding because the investigation could not be completed for such reasons as: The family moved out of the jurisdiction; the family could not be located; or necessary diagnostic or other reports were not received within required time limits.

CNS DEPRESSANTS: A class of drugs that slow CNS (Central Nervous System) functions, some of which are used to treat anxiety and sleeping disorders; includes barbiturates and benzodiazepines.

COCA: The plant, Erythroxylon, from which cocaine is derived. Also refers to the leaves of this plant.

COCAETHYLENE: Potent stimulant created when cocaine and alcohol are used together.

COCAINE: A highly addictive stimulant drug derived from the coca plant that produces profound feelings of pleasure.

COMMUNITY-BASED FAMILY RESOURCE AND SUPPORT GRANT: Grant provided under Section 210 of the Child Abuse Prevention and Treatment Act (CAPTA) that assists states in preventing child abuse and neglect and promoting positive development of parents and children by developing, operating, expanding, and enhancing a network of community-based, prevention-focused, family resource and support programs that coordinate resources among a broad range of human service organizations.

COURT ACTION: Legal action initiated by a representative of the Child Protective Services agency on behalf of the child. This includes authorization to place the child in foster care and filing for temporary custody, dependency, or termination of parental rights. It does not include criminal proceedings against a perpetrator.

COURT-APPOINTED REPRESENTATIVE: A person appointed by the court to represent a child in a neglect or abuse proceeding. May be an attorney or a Court-Appointed Special Advocate (or both) and is often referred to as a guardian ad litem. The representative makes recommendations to the court concerning the best interests of the child.

COURT-APPOINTED SPECIAL ADVOCATE (CASA): Adult volunteers trained to advocate for abused and neglected children who are involved in the juvenile court.

CRACK: Slang term for a smokable form of cocaine.

DEPRESSANTS: Drugs that relieve anxiety and produce sleep. Depressants include barbiturates, benzodiazepines, and alcohol.

DESIGNER DRUG: An analog of a restricted drug that has psychoactive properties.

DETOXIFICATION: A process of allowing the body to rid itself of a drug while managing the symptoms of withdrawal; often the first step in a drug treatment program.

DEXTROMETHORPHAN: A cough-suppressing ingredient in a variety of over-the-counter cold and cough medications abused for its intoxicating effects. Also called DXM and Robo.

DIFFERENTIAL RESPONSE: An area of Child Protective Services reform that offers greater flexibility in responding to allegations of abuse and neglect. Also referred to as "dual track" or "multi-track" response, it permits CPS agencies to respond differentially to children's needs for safety, the degree of risk present, and the family's needs for services and support. (See Dual Track.)

DISPOSITION: See Investigation Disposition.

DRUG: A chemical compound or substance that can alter the structure and function of the body. Psychoactive drugs affect the function of the brain, and some of these may be illegal to use and possess.

DRUG ABUSE: The use of illegal drugs or the inappropriate use of legal drugs. The repeated use of drugs to produce pleasure, to alleviate stress, or to alter or avoid reality (or all three).

DUAL TRACK: Term reflecting Child Protective Services response systems that typically combine a non-adversarial, service-based assessment track for cases where children are not at immediate risk with a traditional CPS investigative track for cases where children are unsafe or at greater risk for maltreatment. (See Differential Response.)

DXM: Common street name for dextromethorphan.

ECSTASY (MDMA): A chemically modified amphetamine that has hallucinogenic as well as stimulant properties.

EDUCATIONAL PERSONNEL: Employees of a public or private educational institution or program; includes teachers, teacher assistants, administrators, and others directly associated with the delivery of educational services.

FAMILY ASSESSMENT: The stage of the child protection process when the Child Protective Services caseworker, community treatment provider, and the family reach a mutual understanding regarding the behaviors and conditions that must change to reduce or eliminate the risk of maltreatment, the most critical treatment needs that must be addressed, and the strengths on which to build.

FAMILY GROUP CONFERENCING MODEL: A family meeting model used by Child Protective Services agencies to optimize family strengths in the planning process. This model brings together the family, extended family, and others important in the family's life (for example, friends, clergy, or neighbors) to make decisions regarding how best to ensure safety of the family members.

FAMILY PRESERVATION SERVICES: Activities designed to help families alleviate crises that might lead to out-of-home placement of children, maintain the safety of children in their own homes, support families preparing to reunify or adopt, and assist families in obtaining services and other supports necessary to address their multiple needs in a culturally sensitive manner.

FAMILY SUPPORT SERVICES: Community-based preventive activities designed to alleviate stress and promote parental competencies and behaviors that will increase the ability of families to nurture their children successfully, enable families to use other resources and opportunities available in the community, and create supportive networks to enhance childrearing abilities of parents.

FAMILY UNITY MODEL: A family meeting model used by Child Protective Services agencies to optimize family strengths in the planning process. This model is similar to the Family Group Conferencing model.

FATALITY: Death of a child as a result of abuse or neglect; because either an injury resulting from the abuse or neglect was the cause of death, or abuse or neglect were contributing factors to the cause of death.

FOSTER CARE: Twenty-four-hour substitute care for children placed away from their parents or guardians and for whom the state agency has placement and care responsibility. This includes family foster homes, foster homes of relatives, group homes, emergency shelters, residential facilities, child-care institutions, and pre-adoptive homes, regardless of whether the facility is licensed and whether payments are made by the state or local agency for the care of the child, or whether there is federal matching of any payments made. Foster care may be provided by those related or not related to the child. All children in care for more than 24 hours are counted.

FOSTER PARENT: An individual licensed to provide a home for orphaned, abused, neglected, delinquent, or disabled children, usually with the approval of the government or a social service agency. May be a relative or non-relative acquainted with the child, the parent, or caregiver, including landlords, clergy, or youth group workers (for example, Scout leaders or Little League coaches).

FULL DISCLOSURE: Child Protective Services information given to the family regarding the steps in the intervention process, the requirements of CPS, the expectations of the family, the consequences if the family does not fulfill the expectations, and the rights of the parents to ensure that the family completely understands the process.

GIRL: A female child younger than 18 years old.

GROUP HOME OR RESIDENTIAL CARE: A non-familial 24-hour care facility that may be supervised by the state agency or governed privately.

GUARDIAN AD LITEM: A lawyer or layperson representing a child in juvenile or family court. Usually this person considers the "best interest" of the child and may perform a variety of roles, including those of independent investigator, advocate, advisor, and guardian for the child. A layperson who serves in this role is sometimes known as a Court-Appointed Special Advocate (CASA). (See Court-Appointed Representative.)

HALLUCINOGENS: A diverse group of drugs that alter perceptions, thoughts, and feelings. Hallucinogenic drugs include LSD, mescaline, MDMA (ecstasy), PCP, and psilocybin (magic mushrooms).

HEROIN: The potent, widely abused opiate that produces addiction. It consists of two morphine molecules linked together chemically.

HOME VISITATION PROGRAMS: Prevention programs that offer a variety of family-focused services to pregnant mothers and families with new babies. Activities frequently encompass structured visits to the family's home and may address positive parenting practices, nonviolent discipline techniques, child development, maternal and child health, available services, and advocacy.

IMMUNITY: Established in all child abuse laws to protect reporters from civil law suits and criminal prosecution resulting from filing a report of child abuse and neglect.

INDICATED OR REASON TO SUSPECT: An investigation disposition that concludes that maltreatment cannot be substantiated under state law or policy, but there is reason to suspect the child may have been maltreated or was at risk of maltreatment. This is applicable only to states that distinguish between substantiated and indicated dispositions.

INHALANT: Any drug administered by breathing in its vapors. Inhalants commonly are organic solvents, such as glue and paint thinner, or anesthetic gases, such as ether and nitrous oxide.

INITIAL ASSESSMENT OR INVESTIGATION: The stage of the Child Protective Services case process where the CPS caseworker determines the validity of the child maltreatment report; assesses the risk of maltreatment; determines if the child is safe; develops a safety plan, if needed, to assure the child's protection; and determines services needed. If face-to-face contact with the alleged victim isn't possible, initial investigation would be when CPS first contacted any party who could provide information essential to the investigation or assessment.

INTAKE: The activities associated with the receipt of a referral, the assessment or screening, the decision to accept, and the enrollment of individuals or families into services.

INTENTIONALLY FALSE: The unsubstantiated investigation disposition that indicates a conclusion that the person who made the allegation of maltreatment knew the allegation was not true.

INTERVIEW PROTOCOL: A structured format to ensure that all family members are seen in a planned strategy, that community providers collaborate, and that information gathering is thorough.

INVESTIGATION: The gathering and assessment of objective information to determine if a child has been or is at risk of being maltreated. Generally includes face-to-face contact with the victim and results in a disposition as to whether or not the alleged report is substantiated.

INVESTIGATION DISPOSITION: A determination made by a social service agency that evidence is or is not sufficient under state law to conclude that maltreatment occurred.

INVESTIGATION DISPOSITION DATE: The point in time at the end of the investigation or assessment when a Child Protective Services worker declares a disposition to the child maltreatment report.

INVESTIGATION START DATE: The date when Child Protective Services initially contacted or attempted to have face-to-face contact with the alleged victim. If this face-to-face contact is not possible, the date would be when CPS initially contacted any party who could provide information essential to the investigation or assessment.

JUVENILE AND FAMILY COURTS: Established in most states to resolve conflict and to intervene otherwise in the lives of families in a manner that promotes the best interest of children. These courts specialize in areas such as child maltreatment, domestic violence, juvenile delinquency, divorce, child custody, and child support.

KINSHIP CARE: Formal child placement by the juvenile court and child welfare agency in the home of a child's relative.

LEGAL GUARDIAN: Adult person who has been given legal custody and guardianship of a minor.

LEGAL, LAW ENFORCEMENT, OR CRIMINAL JUSTICE PERSONNEL: People employed by a local, state, tribal, or federal justice agency including law enforcement, courts, district attorney's office, probation or other community corrections agencies, and correctional facilities.

LIAISON: The designation of a person within an organization who has responsibility for facilitating communication, collaboration, and coordination between agencies involved in the child protection system.

LIVING ARRANGEMENT: See Child's Living Arrangement.

LSD (Lysergic Acid Diethylamide): A hallucinogenic drug that acts on the serotonin receptor.

MALTREATMENT TYPE: A particular form of child maltreatment determined by investigation to be substantiated or indicated under state law. Types include physical abuse, neglect or deprivation of necessities, medical neglect, sexual abuse, psychological or emotional maltreatment, and other forms included in state law.

MANDATED REPORTER: Individuals required by state statutes to report suspected child abuse and neglect to the proper authorities (usually Child Protective Services or law enforcement agencies). Mandated reporters typically include professionals such as educators and other school personnel, health care and mental health professionals, social workers, childcare providers, and law enforcement officers. Some states identify all citizens as mandated reporters.

MARIJUANA: A drug, usually smoked but can be eaten, that is made from the leaves of the cannabis plant. The main psychoactive ingredient is THC.

MDMA (ECSTASY): Common chemical name for 3,4-methlyen edioxymethamphetamine.

MEDICAL NEGLECT: A type of maltreatment caused by failure of the caregiver to provide for the appropriate health care of the child although financially able to do so or offered financial or other means to do so.

MEDICAL PERSONNEL: People employed by a medical facility or practice, including physicians, physician assistants, nurses, emergency medical technicians, dentists, chiropractors, coroners, and dental assistants and technicians.

MEDICATION: A drug that is used to treat an illness or disease according to established medical guidelines.

MENTAL HEALTH ORGANIZATION: An administratively distinct public or private agency or institution whose primary concern is the provision of direct mental health services to the mentally ill or emotionally disturbed.

- Freestanding psychiatric outpatient clinics provide only out-patient services on either a regular or emergency basis. The medical responsibility for services is generally assumed by a psychiatrist.
- General hospitals providing separate psychiatric services are non-federal general hospitals that provide psychiatric services in either a separate psychiatric inpatient, outpatient, or partial hospitalization service with assigned staff and space.
- Multiservice mental health organizations directly provide two or more of the program elements defined under Mental Health Service Type and are not classifiable as a psychiatric hospital, general hospital, or a residential treatment center for emotionally disturbed children.
- Partial care organizations provide a program of ambulatory mental health services.
- Private mental hospitals are operated by a sole proprietor, partnership, limited partnership, corporation, or nonprofit organization primarily for the care of persons with mental disorders.
- Psychiatric hospitals are hospitals primarily concerned with providing inpatient care and treatment for the mentally ill.
- Residential treatment centers for emotionally disturbed children must meet all of the following criteria:
  (a) not licensed as a psychiatric hospital and its primary purpose is to provide individually planned mental health treatment services in conjunction with residential care;
  (b) includes a clinical program that is directed by a psychiatrist, psychologist, social worker, or psychiatric nurse with a graduate degree;
  (c) serves children and youth primarily under the age of 18; and
  (d) the primary diagnosis for the majority of admissions is mental illness, classified as other than mental retardation, developmental disability, and substance-related disorders.
- State and county mental hospitals are under the auspices of a state or county government or operated jointly by a state and county government.

MENTAL HEALTH PERSONNEL: People employed by a mental health facility or practice, including psychologists, psychiatrists, and therapists.

MENTAL HEALTH SERVICE TYPE: Refers to the following kinds of mental health services—

- Inpatient care is the provision of 24-hour mental health care in a mental health hospital setting.
- Outpatient care is the provision of ambulatory mental health services for less than three hours at a single visit on an individual, group, or family basis, usually in a clinic or similar organization. Emergency care provided on a walk-in basis, as well as care provided by mobile teams who visit patients outside these organizations are included.
- Partial care treatment is a planned program of mental health treatment services generally provided in visits of three or more hours to groups of patients. Included are treatment programs that emphasize intensive short-term therapy and rehabilitation; programs that focus on recreation or occupational program activities, including sheltered workshops; and education and training programs, including special education classes, therapeutic nursery schools, and vocational training.
- Residential treatment care is the provision of overnight mental health care in conjunction with an intensive treatment program in a setting other than a hospital. Facilities may offer care to emotionally disturbed children or mentally ill adults.

METHADONE: A long-acting synthetic medication that is effective in treating opioid (opiate) addiction.

METHAMPHETAMINE: A commonly abused, potent stimulant drug that is part of a larger family of amphetamines.

MULTIDISCIPLINARY TEAM: Established between agencies and professionals within the child protection system to discuss cases of child abuse and neglect and to aid in decisions at various stages of the Child Protective Services case process. These teams may also be designated by different names, including child protection teams, interdisciplinary teams, or case consultation teams.

NCANDS: The National Child Abuse and Neglect Data System.

NEGLECT OR DEPRIVATION OF NECESSITIES: A type of maltreatment that refers to the failure by the caregiver to provide needed, age-appropriate care although financially able to do so or offered financial or other means to do so.
- Physical neglect can include not providing adequate food, clothing, appropriate medical care, supervision, or proper weather protection (heat or coats).
- Educational neglect includes failure to provide appropriate schooling or special educational needs, or allowing excessive truancies.
- Psychological neglect includes the lack of any emotional support and love, chronic inattention to the child, exposure to spouse abuse, or drug and alcohol abuse.

NEIGHBOR: A person living in close geographical proximity to the child or family.

NONCAREGIVER: A person who is not responsible for the care and supervision of the child, including school personnel, friends, and neighbors.

NONPARENT: Includes other relatives, foster parents, residential facility staff, child daycare provider, foster care provider, unmarried partner of parent, legal guardian, and "other."

NOTIFIABLE DISEASE: A notifiable disease is one that, when diagnosed, health providers are required, usually by law, to report to state or local public health officials. Notifiable diseases are those of public interest by reason of their contagiousness, severity, or frequency.

OPIOIDS: Controlled drugs or narcotics most often prescribed for the management of pain; natural or synthetic chemicals based on opium's active component, morphine, that work by mimicking the actions of pain-relieving chemicals produced in the body.

OUT-OF-COURT CONTACT: A meeting, which is not part of the actual judicial hearing, between the court-appointed representative and the child victim. Such contacts enable the court-appointed representative to obtain a firsthand understanding of the situation and needs of the child victim, and to make recommendations to the court concerning the best interests of the child.

OUT-OF-HOME CARE: Child care, foster care, or residential care provided by persons, organizations, and institutions to children who are placed outside their families, usually under the jurisdiction of juvenile or family court

PARENS PATRIAE DOCTRINE: Originating in feudal England, a doctrine that vests in the state a right of guardianship of minors. This concept has gradually evolved into the principle that the community, in addition to the parent, has a strong interest in the care and nurturing of children. Schools, juvenile courts, and social service agencies all derive their authority from the state's power to ensure the protection and rights of children as a unique class.

PARENT: The birth mother or father, adoptive mother or father, or stepmother or father of the child victim.

PCP: Phencyclidine, a dissociative anesthetic abused for its mind-altering effects.

PERPETRATOR: The person who has been determined to have caused or knowingly allowed the maltreatment of a child.

PERPETRATOR AGE: Age of an individual determined to have caused or knowingly allowed the maltreatment of a child. Age is calculated in years at the time of the report of child maltreatment.

PERPETRATOR RELATIONSHIP: Primary role of the perpetrator to a child victim.

PHYSICAL ABUSE: Type of maltreatment that refers to non-accidental physical acts that caused or could have caused physical injury to a child. This may include burning, hitting, punching, shaking, kicking, beating, or otherwise harming a child. It also may have been the result of over-discipline or physical punishment inappropriate to the child's age.

PHYSICAL DEPENDENCE: An adaptive physiological state that occurs with regular drug use and results in a withdrawal syndrome when drug use is stopped; usually occurs with tolerance.

PLACEBO: An inactive substance used in experiments to distinguish between actual drug effects and effects that are expected by the volunteers in the experiments.

POLYDRUG USER: An individual who uses more than one drug.

POST-INVESTIGATION SERVICES: Activities provided or arranged by the Child Protective Services agency, social services agency, or the child welfare agency for the child or family as a result of needs discovered during the course of an investigation. Includes such services as family preservation, family support, and foster care. Post-investigation services are delivered within the first 90 days after the disposition of the report.

PRESCRIPTION DRUG ABUSE: The intentional misuse of a medication outside of the normally accepted standards of its use.

PRESCRIPTION DRUG MISUSE: Taking a medication in a manner other than that prescribed or for a different condition than that for which the medication is prescribed.

PREVENTIVE SERVICES: Activities aimed at preventing child abuse and neglect. Such activities may be directed at specific populations identified as being at increased risk of becoming abusive and may be designed to increase the strength and stability of families, to increase parents' confidence and competence in their parenting abilities, and to afford children a stable and supportive environment. They include child abuse and neglect preventive services provided through such federal funds as the Child Abuse and Neglect Basic State Grant, Community-based Family Resource and Support Grant, the Promoting Safe and Stable Families Program (title IV-B, subpart 2), Maternal and Child Health Block Grant, Social Services Block Grant (title XX),and state and local funds. Such activities do not include public awareness campaigns.

PRIMARY PREVENTION: Activities geared to a sample of the general population to prevent child abuse and neglect from occurring. Also referred to as "universal prevention."

PRIOR CHILD VICTIM: A child victim with previous substantiated, indicated, or alternative response reports of maltreatment.

PROMOTING SAFE AND STABLE FAMILIES PROGRAM: Program that provides grants to the states under Section 430, title IV–B, subpart 2 of the Social Security Act, as amended, to develop and expand four types of services—community-based family support services; innovative child welfare services, including family preservation services; time-limited reunification services; and adoption promotion and support services.

PROTECTIVE FACTORS: Strengths and resources that appear to mediate or serve as a "buffer" against risk factors, which contribute to vulnerability to maltreatment or against the negative effects of maltreatment experiences.

PROTOCOL: An interagency agreement that delineates joint roles and responsibilities by establishing criteria and procedures for working together on cases of child abuse and neglect.

PSYCHEDELIC DRUG: A drug that distorts perception, thought, and feeling. This term is typically used to refer to drugs with actions like those of LSD.

PSYCHOACTIVE: Having a specific effect on the mind.

PSYCHOACTIVE DRUG: A drug that changes the way the brain works.

PSYCHOLOGICAL OR EMOTIONAL MALTREATMENT: Type of maltreatment that refers to acts or omissions, other than physical abuse or sexual abuse, that caused, or could have caused, conduct, cognitive, affective, or other mental disorders. Includes emotional neglect, psychological abuse, and mental injury. Frequently occurs as a pattern of verbal abuse or excessive demands on a child's performance that convey to children that they are worthless, flawed, unloved, unwanted, endangered, or only of value to meeting another's needs. This can include parents or caretakers using extreme or bizarre forms of punishment or threatening or terrorizing a child. The term "psychological maltreatment" is also known as emotional abuse or neglect, verbal abuse, or mental abuse.

PSYCHOTHERAPEUTICS: Drugs that have an effect on the function of the brain and that often are used to treat psychiatric disorders can include opioids, CNS depressants, and stimulants.

RACE: The primary taxonomic category of which the individual identifies himself or herself as a member, or of which the parent identifies the child as a member (namely: American Indian or Alaska Native, Asian, Black or African-American, Hispanic or Latino, Native Hawaiian or Other Pacific Islander, White, or Unable to Determine).

RECEIPT OF REPORT: The log-in of a referral to the agency alleging child maltreatment.

REFERRAL: Notification to the Child Protective Services agency of suspected child maltreatment. This can include one or more children.

RELAPSE: In drug abuse, relapse is the resumption of drug use after trying to stop taking drugs. Relapse is a common occurrence in many chronic disorders, including addiction, that require behavioral adjustments to treat effectively.

RELATIVE: A person connected to the child by blood, such as parents, siblings, or grandparents.

REPORT: A referral of child abuse or neglect that was accepted for an investigation or assessment by a Child Protective Services agency.

REPORT DATE: The month, day, and year that the responsible agency was notified of the suspected child maltreatment.

REPORT DISPOSITION: The conclusion reached by the responsible agency regarding the report of maltreatment pertaining to the child.

REPORT SOURCE: The category or role of the person who notifies a Child Protective Services agency of alleged child maltreatment.

RESIDENTIAL FACILITY STAFF: Employees of a public or private group residential facility, including emergency shelters, group homes, and institutions.

RESPONSE TIME WITH RESPECT TO THE INITIAL INVESTIGATION: A determination made by Child Protective Services and law enforcement regarding the immediacy of the response needed to a report of child abuse or neglect. Also the time between the log-in of a call to the state agency alleging child maltreatment and the face-to-face contact with the alleged victim where appropriate (or to contact with another person who can provide information when direct contact with the alleged victim would be inappropriate).

RESPONSE TIME WITH RESPECT TO THE PROVISION OF SERVICES: The time from the log-in of a call to the agency alleging child maltreatment to the provision of post-investigation services, often requiring the opening of a case for ongoing services.

REVIEW HEARINGS: Held by the juvenile and family court to review dispositions (usually every six months) and to determine the need to maintain placement in out-of-home care or court jurisdiction of a child.

RISK: The likelihood that a child will be maltreated in the future.

RISK ASSESSMENT: To assess and measure the likelihood that a child will be maltreated in the future, frequently through the use of checklists, matrices, scales, and other methods of measurement.

RISK FACTORS: Behaviors and conditions present in the child, parent, or family that will likely contribute to child maltreatment occurring in the future.

ROBO: Common street name for dextromethorphan.

SAFETY: Absence of an imminent or immediate threat of moderate-to-serious harm to the child.

SAFETY ASSESSMENT: A part of the Child Protective Services case process in which available information is analyzed to identify whether a child is in immediate danger of moderate or serious harm.

SAFETY PLAN: A casework document developed when it is determined that the child is in imminent or potential risk of serious harm. In the safety plan, the caseworker targets the factors causing or contributing to the risk of imminent serious harm to the child and identifies, along with the family, the interventions that will control the safety factors and assure the child's protection.

SCREENED-IN REPORTS: Referrals of child maltreatment that met the state's standards for acceptance.

SCREENED-OUT REFERRAL: Allegations of child maltreatment that did not meet the state's standards for acceptance.

SCREENING: The process of making a decision about whe‌n or not to accept a referral of child maltreatment.

SECONDARY PREVENTION: Activities targeted to prevent breakdowns and dysfunctions among families who have been identified as at-risk for abuse and neglect.

SERVICE AGREEMENT: The casework document developed between the Child Protective Services caseworker and the family that outlines the tasks necessary to achieve goals and outcomes necessary for risk reduction.

SERVICE DATE: The date activities began as a result of needs discovered during the Child Protective Services response.

SERVICE PROVISION: The stage of the Child Protective Services casework process when CPS and other service providers provide specific services geared toward the reduction of risk of maltreatment.

SERVICES: Non-investigative public or private nonprofit activities provided or continued as a result of an investigation or assessment.

SEXUAL ABUSE: A type of maltreatment that refers to the involvement of the child in sexual activity to provide sexual gratification or financial benefit to the adolescent or adult perpetrator, including contacts for sexual purposes by fondling a child's genitals, making the child fondle the adult's genitals, intercourse, molestation, statutory rape, prostitution, pornography, exposure, exhibitionism, incest, sodomy, exposure to pornography or other sexually exploitative activities. To be considered child abuse, these acts have to be committed by a person responsible for the care of a child (for example a baby-sitter, a parent, or a daycare provider) or related to the child. If a stranger commits these acts, it would be considered sexual assault and handled solely by the police and criminal courts.

SOCIAL SERVICES BLOCK GRANT: Funds provided by title XX of the Social Security Act that are used for services to the states, which may include child care, child protection, child and foster care services, and daycare.

SOCIAL SERVICES PERSONNEL: Employees of a public or private social services or social welfare agency, or other social worker or counselor who provides similar services.

STATE AGENCY: The agency in a state that is responsible for child protection and child welfare.

STEPPARENT: The husband or wife, by a subsequent marriage, of the child's mother or father.

STIMULANTS: A class of drugs that elevates mood, increases feelings of well-being, and increases energy and alertness. These drugs produce euphoria and are powerfully rewarding. Stimulants include cocaine, methamphetamine, and methylphenidate (Ritalin).

SUBSTANTIATED: A type of investigation disposition that concludes that the allegation of maltreatment or risk of maltreatment was supported or founded by state law or state policy. A Child Protective Services determination means that credible evidence exists that child abuse or neglect has occurred. This is the highest level of finding by a state agency.

SYSTEM OF CARE: A system of care is a process of partnering an array of service agencies and families, working together to provide individualized care and supports designed to help children and families achieve safety, stability, and permanency in their home and community.

TERTIARY PREVENTION: Treatment efforts geared toward addressing situations where child maltreatment has already occurred and with the goals of preventing child maltreatment from occurring in the future and of avoiding the harmful effects of child maltreatment.

THC: Delta-9-tetrahydrocannabinol; the main active ingredient in marijuana, which acts on the brain to produce its effects.

TOLERANCE: A condition in which higher doses of a drug are required to produce the same effect as during initial use; often leads to physical dependence.

TOXIC: Temporary or permanent drug effects that are detrimental to the functioning of an organ or group of organs.

TRANQUILIZERS: Drugs prescribed to promote sleep or reduce anxiety; this National Household Survey on Drug Abuse classification includes benzodiazepines, barbiturates, and other types of CNS depressants.

TREATMENT: The stage of the child protection case process when specific services are provided by Child Protective Services and other providers to reduce the risk of maltreatment, to support families in meeting case goals, and to address the effects of maltreatment.

UNIVERSAL PREVENTION: Activities and services directed at the general public with the goal of stopping the occurrence of maltreatment before it starts. Also referred to as primary prevention.

UNMARRIED PARTNER OF PARENT: Someone who has a relationship with the parent and lives in the household with the parent and maltreated child.

UNSUBSTANTIATED (NOT SUBSTANTIATED): An investigation disposition that determines there is not sufficient evidence under state law or policy to conclude that the child has been maltreated or is at risk of maltreatment. A Child Protective Services determination means that credible evidence does not exist that child abuse or neglect has occurred.

VICTIM: A child having a maltreatment disposition of substantiated, indicated, or alternative response victim.

WITHDRAWAL: Symptoms that occur after chronic use of a drug is reduced or stopped.

This information was compiled from the following sources—

Administration for Children and Families, U.S. Department of Health & Human Services, "Appendix B: Glossary—Child Maltreatment 2002", Children's Bureau. Available online at http://www.acf.hhs.gov/programs/cb/publications/cm02/appendb.htm.

Center for Disease Control and Prevention, National Center for Health Statistics, Health United States, 2004, "NCHS Definitions." Available online at http://www.cdc.gov/nchs/hus.htm.

National Institute on Drug Abuse, http://www.drugabuse.gov/NIDAHome.html.

U.S. Department of Health & Human Services, Administration for Children & Families, National Clearinghouse on Child Abuse and Neglect Information. Available online at http://nccanch.acf.hhs.gov/admin/glossary.cfm.

6.8 INTAKE INTERVIEW **FORM**

Date _____ Name _____

Date of Birth _____ Age _____

Address _____ Phone _____

Mother's Name _____

Address _____ Phone _____

Father's Name _____

Address _____ Phone _____

Source of Referral:

Nature of Problem:

Family Situation:

Action Taken or Recommended:

Referral to:

7.0 ENDNOTES

1.1 | UNDERSTANDING CRISIS

1. Gary Collins, *How to Be a People Helper* (Santa Ana, Calif.: Vision House, 1976), 71.

2. Luke 13:4.

3. Matthew 5:45.

1.2 | DANGEROUS OPPORTUNITY

1. Madeleine L'Engle, as quoted in Tim Hansel's, *Holy Sweat* (Waco, Tex.: Word Publishing, 1987), 53.

2. Doug Stevens, *Called To Care: Youth Ministry and the Church* (Grand Rapids, Mich.: Zondervan, 1985), 27.

2.1 | TRIAGE

1. Henri Nouwen, *Reaching Out* (New York: Doubleday, 1975), 94.

3. Psalm 34:18.

2.2 | MAKING CONNECTIONS

1. Robert Veninga, *A Gift of Hope, How We Survive Our Tragedies* (New York: Ballantine Books, 1996), 60.

2. Michael Craig Miller, "How Important Is the Therapeutic Alliance?" Questions & Answers, *Harvard Mental Health Letter* (September 2004). *www.health.harvard.edu/*

3. Ann Kaiser Stearns, *Living Through Personal Crisis* (Chicago: Thomas More Press, 1983), 93.

4. Veninga, *A Gift of Hope*, 60 (emphasis added).

5. "You get bigger as you go" is a fragment of poetry from the singer Bruce Cockburn—it's pronounced Coe-burn; he's Canadian.

> one small step for freedom
> from foregone conclusion
>
> you get bigger as you go
> no one told me—I just know
> bales of memory like boats in tow
> you get bigger as you go
>
> (*You Get Bigger As You Go,* Humans, 1980, Columbia)

We're in this struggle for the wellbeing of kids because we don't believe in the inevitable. When Frederick Beuchner—it's pronounced Beek-ner; his ancestors were German—when Frederick Beuchner says the comedy of grace is that it's what doesn't have to happen and can't possibly happen but happens anyway "in the dark that only just barely fails to swallow it up," we say, "We're with him" (*Telling The Truth: The Gospel As Tragedy,* Comedy & Fairy Tale, Harper & Row, 1977, p. 58).

That said, learning to believe and act on behalf of what's bound to not happen takes time and practice and faith; but somehow in God's goodness, we get bigger as we go.

2.3 | DEEP LISTENING

1. M. Scott Peck, M.D., *The Road Less Traveled* (New York: Simon and Schuster, 1978), 121.

2. Jim Petersen and Mike Shamy, *The Insider: Bringing the Kingdom of God into Your Everyday World* (Colorado Springs, Colo.: NavPress, 2003), 148.

3. Peck, *The Road Less Traveled*, 121.

4. Barbara Varenhorst, *Real Friends: Becoming the Friend You'd Like to Have* (San Francisco: Harper and Row, 1983),107.

5. Paul W. Swets, *The Art of Talking with Your Teenager* (Holbrook, Mass.: Adams Media Corporation, 1995), 86.

2.4 | ACTION PLAN

1. Lee Ann Hoff, *People in Crisis: Understanding and Helping* (Menlo Park, Calif.: Addison-Wesley, 1978), 56-60.

2. Ann Landers, *The Denver Post*, April 8, 1985.

3. John 5:6.

3.1 | REFERRAL

1. M. Scott Peck, *People of the Lie* (New York: Touchstone, 1983), 47ff.

3.2 | LEGAL AND ETHICAL CONSIDERATIONS

1. A mandated reporter is someone who is required by law to report suspicion or knowledge of child abuse of any kind (physical, emotional, or sexual) to the appropriate authorities. See section 3.2 for more information about who should make a report and section 6.2 for more information about where to report child abuse in your state.

2. David Elkind, *All Grown Up and No Place To Go* (Reading, Mass.: Addison-Wesley Publishing Company, 1984), 36.

3. Carl Lansing, *Legal Defense Handbook* (Colorado Springs, Colo.: NavPress, 1992), 11.

4. John 17.

5. Matthew 10:16-17 (TNIV).

6. Jack Crabtree, *Better Safe Than Sued* (Loveland, Colo.: Group Publishing, 1998), 237.

7. Lansing, *Legal Defense Handbook*, 253.

4.0 | PREVENTIVE PARTNERSHIPS

1. Job 5.

2. Ernest Hemingway, *A Farewell to Arms* (New York: Scribner's and Sons, 1957), 249.

3. *www.clarkefoundation.org/projects*

4.1 | YOUTH GROUPS

1. Jesus said, "If you love those who love you, what credit is that to you? Even 'sinners' love those who love them. And if you do good to those who are good to you, what credit

is that to you? Even 'sinners' do that" (Luke 6:32-33). Paul picks up the other end of the thread: "So in Christ Jesus you are all children of God through faith, for all of you who were baptized into Christ have clothed yourselves with Christ. There is neither Jew nor Greek, neither slave nor free, neither male nor female, for you are all one in Christ Jesus" (Galatians 3:26-28, TNIV). James joins the chorus, zeroing in on socioeconomic factors. His argument comes to a fine point in James 2:8-9: "If you really keep the royal law found in Scripture, 'Love your neighbor as yourself,' you are doing right. But if you show favoritism, you sin and are convicted by the law as lawbreakers."

We bring this up only to say that openness to others springs from openness to the God who invites all and sundry into the kingdom of heaven. We have great reason to create open, inviting, accepting faith communities. The Acts of the Apostles spends a lot of ink recording the disruption caused by people who preferred closed communities because their taste in friends was more refined than God's.

2. Romans 3:23.

3. Romans 5:19.

4. Romans 3:10.

4.2 | PARENTS

1. Not to beat a dead horse, but this is really important: If you pursue this option, take special care to do no harm to the student you're trying to help.

2. See, for example, Centers for Disease Control and Prevention, "Guidelines for Investigating Clusters of Health Events," Recommendations and Reports, *Morbidity and Mortality Weekly Report* 39(RR-11): 1-16. July 27, 1990. www.cdc.gov/mmwr/preview/mmwrhtml/00001797.htm

3. *http://youthspecialties.com/free/email/student_newsletter/*

4. We're not endorsing this organization for its theology—the last time we looked at their Web site (*www. capabilitiesinc.com/*) they didn't have a corporate theology. But what they offer can easily be adapted to your theology. Depending on where you go, the training of trainers can be expensive; but beyond that the costs are minimal and the benefits maximal.

4.4 | LAW ENFORCEMENT

1. The U.S. Department of Education in cooperation with the U.S. Department of Justice, "The Problem of Truancy in America's Communities," Manual to Combat Truancy. July 1996. www.ed.gov/pubs/Truancy/index.html

2. U.S. Department of Education, "Departments of Justice and Education Host National Truancy Prevention Conference", Press Releases. December 6, 2004. www.ed.gov/news/pressreleases/2004/12/12062004.html

3. U.S. Department of Health & Human Services, National Clearinghouse on Child Abuse and Neglect Information, Glossary – N. Updated October 15, 2003. http://nccanch. acf.hhs.gov/admin/glossaryn.cfm

5.6 | DEATH

1. Elisabeth Kübler-Ross, *On Death and Dying* (New York: Touchstone, 1969).

5.7 | DIVORCE

1. Mary Giffin, M.D., *A Cry for Help* (Garden City, N.Y.: Doubleday, 1983), 153.

2. Elkind, *All Grown Up*, 110.

3. Warner Troyer, *Divorced Kids* (New York: Harcourt, Brace, Jovanovich, 1979), 166.

5.8 | DROPPING OUT

1. Federal Interagency Forum on Child and Family Statistics, *America's Children in Brief: Key National Indicators of Well-Being, 2004.* www.childstats.gov/ac2004/ed5.asp

2. Compare the information found at www.childstats.gov/ac2004/ed6.asp with the information in the above note.

3. U.S. Department of Education, Press Releases. December 6, 2004. www.ed.gov/news/pressreleases/2004/12/12062004.html

5.9 | EATING DISORDERS

1. All puns in this section are intentional, more or less. Hancock, a recovering food addict, reserves the right to make a little jest here and there. The alternative finds him sitting alone in his car with a one-pound bag of KC Masterpiece BBQ Potato Chips and pint of Ben & Jerry's Chunky Monkey. And, it goes without saying, a Bladder Buster sized Diet Coke.

2. Pam W. Vredevelt and Joyce R. Whitman, *Walking a Thin Line: Anorexia and Bulimia, The Battle Can Be Won* (Portland, Ore.: Multnomah, 1985), 29-31.

5.10 | HAZING

1. Nadine C. Hoover and Norman J. Pollard, *Initiation Rites in American High Schools: A National Survey* (Alfred, N.Y.: Alfred University, August 2000). Also available online at www.alfred.edu/hs_hazing/

5.11 | INCEST

1. Diana E. H. Russell, Introduction to *The Secret Trauma: Incest in the Lives of Girls and Women* (New York: BasicBooks/Perseus Press, 1999), xvii.

2. M. Glasser, I. Kolvin, D. Campbell, A. Glasser, I. Leitch, and S. Farrelly, "Cycle of Child Sexual Abuse: Links between Being a Victim and Becoming a Perpetrator," *The British Journal of Psychiatry* 179 (2001): 482-494.

3. New York City Alliance Against Sexual Assault, *Alliance: Factsheets: Incest.* Copyright 1997. Available online at www.nycagainstrape.org/printable/printable_survivors_ factsheet_37.html

4. Ruth S. Kempe and C. Henry Kempe, *The Common Secret* (New York: W.H. Freeman, 1984), 86.

5. Donna Pence and Charles Wilson, *The Role of Law Enforcement in the Response to Child Abuse and Neglect* (U.S. Department of Health & Human Services, National Center on Child Abuse and Neglect, 1992), 18.

5.12 | *INTERVENTIONS*

1. Alan I. Leshner, "The Essence of Drug Addiction," *National Institute of Drug Abuse, National Institutes of Health:* www.drugabuse.gov/Published_Articles/Essence.html

2. From a conversation with Jim Hancock.

5.13 | POST-TRAUMATIC STRESS DISORDER (PTSD)

1. National Institute of Mental Health Fact Sheet, Publication No. OM-99 4157 (2002 Revised); and *Disaster Mental Health Response Handbook*, State Health Publication No: (CMH) 00145, Centre for Mental Health and the New

South Wales Institute of Psychiatry, North Sydney, NSW, Australia, 2000.

2. National Institute of Mental Health, "Facts About Post-Traumatic Stress Disorder," Publication No. OM-99 4157 (Revised) 2002, 2. Available online at http://www.nimh.nih.gov/publicat/ptsdfacts.cfm (Posted April 9, 2004).

5.16 | SEXUAL ABUSE

1. Administration for Children and Families, U.S. Department of Health & Human Services, "Appendix B: Glossary—Child Maltreatment 2002", *Children's Bureau*. Updated on March 12, 2004. http://www.acf.hhs.gov/programs/cb/publications/cm02/appendb.htm

2. U.S. Department of Health & Human Services, National Clearinghouse on Child Abuse and Neglect Information, Glossary – S. Updated December 17, 2003. http://nccanch.acf.hhs.gov/admin/glossaryn.cfm

3. U.S. Department of Health & Human Services, Glossary – S. http://nccanch.acf.hhs.gov/admin/glossarys.cfm

4. Legal Information Institute, "§ 2256 Definitions for Chapter," *U.S. Code Collection*. Release date: August 6, 2004. http://assembler.law.cornell.edu/uscode/html/uscode18/usc_sec_18_00002256----000-.html

5. W. Predergast in *The Merry-Go-Round of Sexual Abuse: Identifying and Treating Suvivors* (New York: Haworth Press, 1993), as cited in M. Glasser, et al., "Cycle of Child Sexual Abuse," *The British Journal of Psychiatry* 179 (2001): 491.

6. Howard N. Snyder, Ph.D., "Sexual Assault of Young Children as Reported to Law Enforcement: Victim, Incident, and Offender Characteristics," *Bureau of Justice Statistics* (U.S. Department of Justice and Office of Justice Programs, NCJ 182990, July 2000), 4. Also available online at: http://www.ojp.usdoj.gov/bjs/pub/pdf/saycrle.pdf

7. Ibid.

8. U.S. Department of Justice, Bureau of Justice Statistics, "Summary Findings," *Crime Characteristics*. Available online at: www.ojp.usdoj.gov/bjs/cvict_c.htm#relate

5.17| SEXUAL IDENTITY CONFUSION

1. John Colapinto, *As Nature Made Him* (New York: HarperCollins, 2000). ·

2. Mass communication may make sexual ambiguity seem more common than it really is. It's become the subject of daytime television and popular magazines. The effect of this exposure leads to a sensitivity that is not unlike the misapprehension many elder adults have that violent crime is increasing when, statistically, the opposite is true. It's just that television reports crimes of violence from around the world—often while they're in progress. This is not to say every act of violence and each incidence of sexual ambiguity isn't real and significant and tragic to those involved. But we're not seeing increased incidence; we're seeing increased access.

3. *Autoerotic* is a compound word; break it down. (Hint: It has nothing to do with cars.)

4. Barbara L. Frankowski, M.D., M.P.H., and American Academy of Pediatrics Committee on Adolescence, "Sexual Orientation and Adolescents," *Pediatrics* 113, No. 6 (June 2004): 1827-1832. Online version at www.pediatrics.org/cgi/content/full/113/6/1827

5.18 | SEXUALLY TRANSMITTED DISEASES (STDs)

1. Alan Guttmacher Institute, Facts in Brief, "Teen Sex and Pregnancy," Revised September 1999. Available online at www.agi-usa.org/pubs/fb_teen_sex.html#tp

1. Centers for Disease Control and Prevention, *Surveillance Summaries*, May 21, 2004. MMWR 2004: 53 (No. SS-2). Every two years the survey is conducted during the spring semester in a representative sample of ninth through twelfth graders in public and private schools. The most current reports are available at www.cdc.gov/HealthyYouth/yrbs/index.htm

2. T. Santibanez, L. Barker, J. Santoli, C. Bridges, G. Euler, and M. McCauley, "Alcohol-Attributable Deaths and Years of Potential Life Lost—United States, 2001," *Morbidity and Mortality Weekly Report* 53, no. 37 (September 24, 2004): 866. Available online at http://www.findarticles.com/p/articles/mi_m0906/is_37_53/ai_n6256683

3. *Tenth Special Report to Congress on Alcohol and Health from the Secretary of Human Services* (June 2000), DHHS Publication No. 00-1583, www.niaaa.nih.gov/databases/cost8.txt

4. A. Hyland, C. Vena, J. Bauer, Q. Li, G.A. Giovino, J. Yang, K.M. Cummings, P. Mowery, J. Fellows, T. Pechacek, and L. Pederson, "Cigarette Smoking-Attributable Morbidity—United States, 2000" *Morbidity and Mortality Weekly Report* 52, no. 35 (September 5, 2003): 842. Available online at http://www.findarticles.com/p/articles/mi_m0906/is_35_52/ai_109443279

5. Elkind, *All Grown Up*, 110.

6. Dr. Gary G. Forrest, *How to Cope with a Teenage Drinker* (New York: Scribner, 1983), 1.

7. See Mary E. Larimer and Jessica M. Cronce, *Journal of Studies on Alcohol*, Supplement no. 14 (2002): 152.

8. Alan I. Leshner, Ph.DT., National Institute on Drug Abuse, *The Science of Drug Abuse and Addiction*, "The

Essence of Drug Addiction," www.drugabuse.gov/
Published_Articles/Essence.html

5.20 | SUICIDE

1. Salman Rushdie, *The Ground Beneath Her Feet*, (New York: Picador, 2000), 206.

2. National Institute of Mental Health, "In Harms Way: Suicide in America", NIH Publication No. 03-4594, Printed January 2001; Revised April 2003. Available online at www.nimh.nih.gov/publicat/harmaway.cfm (Posted: April 9, 2004).

Also, American Association of Suicidology, "United States Suicide Statistics", summarized and prepared by Dr. John L. McIntosh. www.suicidology.org/displaycommon.cfm?an=1&subarticlenbr=21

3. 2 Timothy 2:13.

5.22 | TROUBLE WITH THE LAW

1. Dr. Scott Larson, *At Risk: Bringing Hope to Hurting Teenagers* (Loveland, Colo.: Group, 1999), 49.

Help! My Kids Are Hurting! outlines a wide range of appropriate inter-ventions and fundamental helping skills ,as well as ways that youth workers can recognize their limitations and learn the principles of effective referral. This practical and informative book is essential for volunteers and will prove a vital tool for youth workers to share with their staffs.

Help! My Kids Are Hurting!
A Survival Guide to Working with Students in Pain
Marv Penner
RETAIL $9.99
ISBN 978-0-310-26708-9

youth
specialties

In *Teenager Guys*, author Steve Gerali breaks down the stages of development that adolescent guys go through, providing stories from his own experiences in ministry and counseling, as well as practical research findings to equip youth workers (both male and female) to more effectively minister to teenage guys. Each chapter includes advice from counselors and veteran youth workers, as well as discussion questions.

Teenage Guys
Exploring Issues Adolescent Guys Face and Strategies to Help Them
Steve Gerali
RETAIL $17.99
ISBN 978-0-310-26985-4

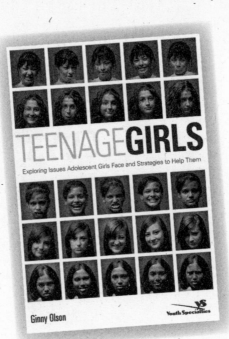

In *Teenager Girls*, you'll find advice from counselors and veteran youth workers, along with helpful suggestions on how to minister to teenage girls. In addition to the traditional issues people commonly associate with girls (eating disorders, self-image issues, depression, etc.), author Ginny Olson will guide you through some of the new issues on the rise in girls' lives.

Teenage Girls
Exploring Issues Adolescent Girls Face and Strategies to Help Them
Ginny Olson
RETAIL $17.99
ISBN 978-0-310-26632-7

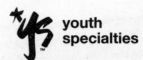

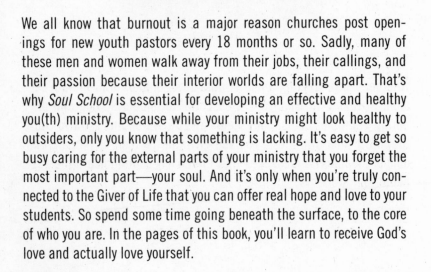

We all know that burnout is a major reason churches post openings for new youth pastors every 18 months or so. Sadly, many of these men and women walk away from their jobs, their callings, and their passion because their interior worlds are falling apart. That's why *Soul School* is essential for developing an effective and healthy you(th) ministry. Because while your ministry might look healthy to outsiders, only you know that something is lacking. It's easy to get so busy caring for the external parts of your ministry that you forget the most important part—your soul. And it's only when you're truly connected to the Giver of Life that you can offer real hope and love to your students. So spend some time going beneath the surface, to the core of who you are. In the pages of this book, you'll learn to receive God's love and actually love yourself.

Soul School
Enrolling in a Soulful Lifestyle for Youth Ministry
Jeanne Stevens
RETAIL $15.99
ISBN 978-0-310-27496-4

Whether you're struggling to make anything work in your youth ministry or finding that most things are clicking along, this book will help you develop a practical theology—to ask what is happening, what should be happening, and how you can make it happen. Each chapter is followed by discussion questions to help you process in a group or on your own.

Deep Ministry in a Shallow World
Not So Secret Findings About Youth Ministry
Kara Powell and Chap Clark
RETAIL $18.99
ISBN 978-0-310-26707-2

Contemplative Youth Ministry is a more organic approach to youth ministry, allowing you to create meaningful silence, foster covenant communities, engage students in contemplatice activities, and maximize spontaneity—and to help your students recognize the presence of Jesus in their everyday lives.

Contemplatice Youth Ministry
Practicing the Presence of Jesus
Mark Yaconelli
RETAIL $12.99
ISBN 978-0-310-26777-5

Grounded in experience with real churches, this book chronicles the journey of more than a dozen youth ministries working to move Christian spirituality out of the retreat center and into the youth room. Youth pastors are growing tired of simply providing a ministry to distract and entertain teenagers. There is a growing desire for deeper, more authentic forms of adolescent discipleship.

Growing Souls
Experiments in Contemplatice Youth Ministry
Mark Yaconelli
RETAIL $21.99
ISBN 978-0-310-27328-8

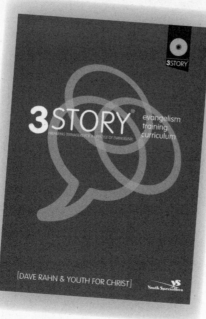

This curriculum course (based on Youth for Christ's 3Story training) offeres an interactive learning experience that equips students to live and practice the 3Story way of life—a biblically based, culturally relevant form of discipleship-evangelism. With eight 50-minute training sessions, this curriculum kit is an ideal resource for teaching students how to build deep, authentic relationships with Jesus and genuine, transparent relationships with their friends.

3Story® Evangelism Training DVD Curriculum Kit
Preparing Teenagers for a Lifestyle of Evanglism
Youth for Christ
RETAIL $99.99
ISBN 978-0-310-27370-7